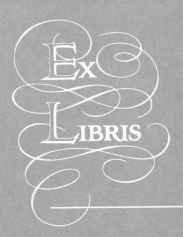

INTRODUCTION

"Some of my most treasured books have come from Guideposts," a woman on the West Coast wrote us recently. "I have never yet been disappointed with one of your selections. How do you do it?"

Of course, we always are encouraged to hear that Guideposts book selections are helping people. As to how we go about making our choices, perhaps a word of purpose is in order.

Over the years, the staff of Guideposts has reviewed many hundreds of books which we thought to be of special significance. Out of these, we have chosen what we consider inspirational classics and many possible classics-to-be. The criterion we use is a simple one: will *this* book help the reader in his spiritual growth and understanding?

For nearly 20 years we have never strayed from that formula, never offered anything but books we felt sure would inspire, nurture, instruct or guide.

This year, we are proud to add *God's Psychiatry* by Charles L. Allen and *. . . But God Can* by Robert V. Ozment. They are two more selections in the Guideposts tradition of outstanding spiritual writing.

In the first book of this 2-in-1 volume, Charles Allen brings into sharp focus the healing power of God upon the total man — body, mind and soul. For structure, he turns to four of the greatest passages in the Bible, — The Twenty-Third Psalm, The Ten Commandments, the Lord's Prayer and the Beatitudes.

Robert Ozment, like Charles Allen a pastor with real sensitivity to the needs of people, takes a penetrating look at some of man's eternal problems and answers each frustration, each intolerable situation, each doubt with positive insight and the rejoinder . . . *But God Can.* Practical, uncomplicated, concise . . . Robert Ozment's solutions are as old as the Gospel, as new as tomorrow's paper.

Together, we believe these two books will be helpful to every reader — no matter how far along the pathway he or she may be.

— The Editors

GOD'S PSYCHIATRY

CHARLES L. ALLEN

...BUT GOD CAN

ROBERT V. OZMENT

GUIDEPOSTS ASSOCIATES, INC.
Carmel, New York

GOD'S PSYCHIATRY

The Twenty-third Psalm
The Ten Commandments
The Lord's Prayer
The Beatitudes

CHARLES L. ALLEN

GUIDEPOSTS ASSOCIATES, INC.
Carmel, New York

To my father
THE LATE REVEREND J. R. ALLEN
and to my mother
LULU FRANKLIN ALLEN

*Guideposts edition published by arrangement with
Fleming H. Revell Company*

Printed in the United States of America

CONTENTS

The Healing of Mind and Soul ... ix

PART III: HOW TO TALK TO GOD

THE LORD'S PRAYER

PART IV: THE KEYS TO THE KINGDOM

THE BEATITUDES

THE HEALING OF MIND AND SOUL

OUR MODERN word "psychiatry" comes from the two Greek words Ψυχή (*psyche*) and ιατρεία (*iatreia*): *psycheiatreia*. The word "psyche" really means the person, and is variously translated as "breath," "soul," "mind," "reason," and the like.

The word *iatreia* means "treatment," "healing," "restoring," and the like.

So, put the two words together and we have "the healing of the mind," or, as David might have said, "the restoring of the soul."

The word can mean medical treatment, or the treatment by a physician, but that is only one of its meanings, and I feel that the science of psychiatry is not to be limited to the medical profession. Often the minister is a psychiatrist, because he deals not only with the minds of people but also with their souls.

In fact, the very essence of religion is to adjust the mind and soul of man, and we have long ago learned, as in this book I quote Augustine as saying, "My soul is restless until it finds its rest in Thee, O God." Healing means bringing the person into a right relationship with the physical, mental and spiritual laws of God.

The physician is a minister of God. All true scientific research is merely an organized effort to learn the laws of God and how they operate.

The teacher is also a minister of God. The teacher seeks to train the mind, to seek truth and know truth when it is found. A mind which thinks error is a sick mind. So a teacher is practicing part of the great science of psychiatry.

Beyond our bodies and minds are our souls. The minister is concerned with man's soul; he believes that if his soul is sick the man is sick, indeed. And only God can heal the soul.

So, the first and most important psychiatry must be God's psychiatry, the essence of which I find contained in the four best known passages of The Bible: The Twenty-Third Psalm, The Ten Commandments, The Lord's Prayer, and The Beatitudes.

As the pastor of a church located on a main thoroughfare in Atlanta, it has been my privilege to counsel with many people who needed help. As a result of writing a daily column for *The Atlanta Constitution* and speaking regularly for some years over WSB radio and WSB-TV, my mail has brought me many letters from people telling me of their problems. I have not yet found one in need of the healing of his or her mind or situation where I have not also found that somewhere back down the line in that life one of the basic principles that I write about in this book was violated. So I say that most of all we need God's Psychiatry.

In this small volume I have not concerned myself so much with cases or techniques as I did in two earlier books—*Roads to Radiant Living* and *In Quest of God's Power*. Instead, I have sought here to explain the great principles that God has ordained to govern the life of man, believing, as I do, that if man lives according to these principles, his life will be whole and healthy. If he violates them, he will be sick. As someone has put it:

> He who formed our frame,
> Made man a perfect whole;
> And made the body's health
> Depend upon the soul.

There are many to whom I would like to express deep appreciation. To the members of the Grace Methodist Church in Atlanta, whose love and loyal support are far greater than I deserve; to my secretary, Mrs. Charles T. Moss, who not only is efficient but also is kind and understanding and loyal; to my assistant, Miss Mary Hogan, who daily does much work that I should be doing and thereby allows me more time for my study and speaking engagements; to my lovely wife, Leila, who continues to love me, though I give so much of my time to my work and to other people.

C. L. A.

Grace Methodist Church
458 Ponce de Leon Avenue, N.E.
Atlanta, Ga.

PUBLISHER'S NOTE

Dr. Allen is now minister of the First Methodist Church, Houston, Texas.

PART I

HOW TO THINK OF GOD

THE TWENTY-THIRD PSALM

*The Lord is my shepherd; I shall
not want.*

*He maketh me to lie down in green
pastures; he leadeth me beside the still
waters.*

*He restoreth my soul: he leadeth me
in the paths of righteousness for his
name's sake.*

*Yea, though I walk through the valley
of the shadow of death, I will fear no
evil: for thou art with me; thy rod and
staff they comfort me.*

*Thou preparest a table before me in
the presence of mine enemies: thou
anointest my head with oil; my cup runneth
over.*

*Surely goodness and mercy shall follow
me all the days of my life: and I will
dwell in the house of the Lord for ever.*

CHAPTER I

A Pattern of Thinking

A MAN I admire very much came in to see me. Many years ago he started with his company at the bottom but with determination to get to the top. He has unusual abilities and energy and he used all he had. Today he is president of his company and he has all the things that go with his position.

Yet, along the way, he left out something, and one of the things he did not achieve is happiness. He was a nervous, tense, worried, and sick man. Finally, one of his physicians suggested that he talk with a minister.

We talked of how his physicians had given him prescriptions and he had taken them. Then I took a sheet of paper and wrote out my prescription for him. I prescribed the Twenty-third Psalm, five times a day for seven days.

I insisted that he take it just as I prescribed. He was to read it the first thing when he awakened in the morning. Read it carefully, meditatively, and prayerfully. Immediately after breakfast, he was to do exactly the same thing. Also immediately after lunch, again after dinner, and, finally, the last thing before he went to bed.

It was not to be a quick, hurried reading. He was to think about each phrase, giving his mind time to soak up as much

1

of the meaning as possible. At the end of just one week, I promised, things would be different for him.

That prescription sounds simple, but really it isn't. The Twenty-third Psalm is one of the most powerful pieces of writing in existence, and it can do marvelous things for any person. I have suggested this to many people and in every instance which I know of it being tried it has produced results. It can change your life in seven days.

One man told me that he did not have time to be bothered with reading it during the day, so he just read it five times in the morning. However, when a physician prescribed a medicine after each meal, or every certain number of hours, no right thinking person would take the full day's dose at one time.

Some have told me that after two or three days they felt they knew it sufficiently, and thus, instead of taking time to read it thoughtfully, they would just think about it through the day. That won't work. To be most effective, it must be taken exactly as prescribed.

Ralph Waldo Emerson said, "A man is what he thinks about all day long." Marcus Aurelius said, "A man's life is what his thoughts make it." Norman Vincent Peale says, "Change your thoughts and you change your world." The Bible says, "For as he thinketh in his heart, so is he" (Proverbs 23-7).

The Twenty-third Psalm is a pattern of thinking, and when a mind becomes saturated with it, a new way of thinking and a new life are the result. It contains only 118 words. One could memorize it in a short time. In fact, most of us already know it. But its power is not in memorizing the words, but rather in thinking the thoughts.

The power of this Psalm lies in the fact that it represents a positive, hopeful, faith approach to life. We assume it was written by David, the same David who had a black chapter of sin and failure in his life. But he spends no time in useless regret and morbid looking back.

David possesses the same spirit that St. Paul expresses:

"Forgetting those things which are behind, and reaching forth unto those things which are before, I press toward the mark" (Philippians 3:13), or the spirit of our Lord when He said, "Neither do I condemn thee; go and sin no more" (John 8:11).

Take it as I prescribe, and in seven days a powerful new way of thinking will be deeply and firmly implanted within your mind that will bring marvelous changes in your thinking and give you a new life.

CHAPTER II

The Lord is My Shepherd; I Shall Not Want

IMMEDIATELY after World War II the allied armies gathered up many hungry, homeless children and placed them in large camps. There the children were abundantly fed and cared for. However, at night they did not sleep well. They seemed restless and afraid.

Finally, a psychologist hit on a solution. After the children were put to bed, they each received a slice of bread to hold. If they wanted more to eat, more was provided, but this particular slice was not to be eaten—it was just to hold.

The slice of bread produced marvelous results. The child would go to sleep, subconsciously feeling it would have something to eat tomorrow. That assurance gave the child a calm and peaceful rest.

In the Twenty-third Psalm, David points out something of the same feeling in the sheep when he says, "The Lord is my shepherd; I shall not want." Instinctively, the sheep knows the shepherd has made plans for its grazing tomorrow. He knows the shepherd made ample provision for it today, so will he tomorrow, so the sheep lies down in its fold with, figuratively speaking, the piece of bread in its hand.

So this Psalm does not begin with a petition asking God

for something, rather it is a calm statement of fact—"The Lord *is* my shepherd." We do not have to beg God for things.

As Roy L. Smith and others have pointed out, God made provision for our needs long before we even had a need. Before we ever felt cold, God began storing up oil, coal, and gas to keep us warm. He knew we would be hungry, so, even before He put man on the earth, God put fertility into the soil and life into the seeds. "Your father knoweth what things ye have need of, before ye ask him," said Jesus (Matthew 6:8).

The greatest source of human worry is about tomorrow, as it was with the women going to the tomb of Jesus Easter morning. They missed the beauty of the early morning sun and the glory of the flowers along the way. They were worrying about who would roll away the stone. And when they got there it was already rolled away.

In another place (Psalm 37:25) David says, "I have been young, and now am old: yet have I not seen the righteous forsaken, nor his seed begging bread." Come to think about it, neither have I. Have you?

All life came from God. That includes my life. God keeps faith with fowls of the air and the grass of the field. And Jesus asks us to think that if God will do so much for a simple bird or a wild flower, how much more will He do for us (Matthew 6:25,34).

St. Paul says, "My God shall supply all your needs" (Philippians 4:19). David puts it, "The Lord is my shepherd, I shall not want." With that faith we can work today without worrying about tomorrow.

CHAPTER III

He Maketh Me to Lie Down in Green Pastures

ONE MORNING as I was hurriedly dressing to begin a full and thrilling day I felt a pain in my back. I mentioned it to my wife but was sure it would soon pass away. However, she insisted I see a physician, and he put me in a hospital.

In the hospital I was very unhappy. I had no time to be wasting there in bed. My calendar was full of good activities and the doctor had told me to cancel all my appointments for at least a month. A dear minister friend of mine came to see me. He sat down and very firmly said, "Charles, I have only one thing to say to you—'He *maketh* me to lie down.'"

I lay thinking about those words in the Twenty-third Psalm long after my friend had gone. I thought about how the shepherd starts the sheep grazing about 4 o'clock in the morning. The sheep walk steadily as they graze; they are never still.

By 10 o'clock, the sun is beaming down and the sheep are hot, tired, and thirsty. The wise shepherd knows that the sheep must not drink when it is hot, neither when its stomach is filled with undigested grass.

So the shepherd makes the sheep lie down in green pastures, in a cool, soft spot. The sheep will not eat lying down, so he chews his cud, which is nature's way of digestion.

6

Study the lives of great people, and you will find every one of them drew apart from the hurry of life for rest and reflection. Great poems are not written on crowded streets, lovely songs are not written in the midst of clamoring multitudes; our visions of God come when we stop. The Psalmist said, "Be still, and know that I am God" (Psalm 46:10).

Elijah found God, not in the earthquake or the fire, but in "a still small voice." Moses saw the burning bush as he was out on the hillside. Saul of Tarsus was on the lonely, quiet road to Damascus when he saw the heavenly vision. Jesus took time to be alone and to pray.

This is perhaps the most difficult thing for us to do. We will work for the Lord, we will sing, preach, teach. We will even suffer and sacrifice. Lustily we sing, "Work, for the night is coming," "Onward, Christian soldiers," "Stand up, stand up for Jesus."

We sometimes forget that before Jesus sent out His disciples to conquer the world, He told them to tarry for prayer and the power of God.

Sometimes God puts us on our backs in order to give us a chance to look up: "He maketh me to lie down." Many times we are forced, not by God, but by circumstances of one sort or another to lie down. That can always be a blessed experience. Even the bed of an invalid may be a blessing if he takes advantage of it!

> *Take from our souls the strain and stress,*
> *And let our ordered lives confess—*
> *The beauty of Thy peace.*

> —WHITTIER

CHAPTER IV

He Leadeth Me Beside the Still Waters

THE SHEEP is a very timid creature. Especially is it afraid of
swiftly moving water, which it has good reason to fear.

The sheep is a very poor swimmer because of its heavy coat
of wool. It would be like a man trying to swim with his over-
coat on. The water soaks into the sheep's coat and pulls it
down.

Instinctively, the sheep knows it cannot swim in swift cur-
rent. The sheep will not drink from a moving stream. The
sheep will drink only from still waters.

The shepherd does not laugh at the sheep's fears. He does
not try to force the sheep. Instead, as he leads his sheep across
the mountains and valleys, he is constantly on the watch for
still waters, where the thirst of the sheep may be quenched.

If there are no still waters available, while the sheep are
resting, the shepherd will gather up stones to fashion a dam
across a small stream to form a pool from which even the
tiniest lamb may drink without fear.

This petition of the Twenty-third Psalm has wonderful
meaning for us. God knows our limitations, and He does not
condemn us because we have weaknesses. He does not force
us where we cannot safely and happily go. God never demands
of us work which is beyond our strength and abilities.

8

Instead, God is constantly ministering to our needs. He understands the loads upon our shoulders. He also knows where the places of nourishment and refreshment are located.

It gives one confidence to know that even while he is sleeping, the Shepherd is working to prepare for his needs tomorrow.

We are told, "He will not suffer thy foot to be moved: he that keepeth thee will not slumber. Behold, he that keepeth Israel shall neither slumber nor sleep" (Psalm 121:3,4).

One of the finest ways to relieve a tension in your life is to picture still water clearly in your mind. Maybe a little lake nestling among some pines. Maybe a tiny, cool spring on some hillside. Maybe a calm sea with gentle, rippling waves.

After the picture becomes clear, then start repeating and believing, "He leadeth me beside the still waters." Such an experience produces a marvelous surrender and trust that enables one to face the heat of the day confidently, knowing there is refreshing and relaxed power awaiting under the leadership of one wiser than we.

The great Martin Luther used to sing:

> *A mighty fortress is our God,*
> *A bulwark never failing:*
> *Our helper He, amidst the flood*
> *Of mortal ills prevailing.*

That is the feeling David had when he wrote the Twenty-third Psalm.

As this Psalm saturates your mind it gives you that same assurance, too.

CHAPTER V

He Restoreth My Soul

A LETTER to me concludes with: "Life ended for me some-where during these years . . . through a slow process. It took years to stifle my faith; but now it is entirely gone. . . . I am only a shell. Perhaps the shell . . . [is] gone."

I would like to talk with the writer of that letter about the meaning of David's words in the Twenty-third Psalm, "He restoreth my soul." David remembered that as the sheep start out in the morning to graze, each takes a definite place in line and holds that same position all during the day.

However, some time during the day each sheep leaves its place in line and trots over to the shepherd. The shepherd gently rubs the nose and ears, lightly scratches the ears, and whispers in an ear of the sheep. Reassured and encouraged, the sheep takes its place in line again.

David remembered how close he once was to God, how God protected him as he went out to meet the giant Goliath, how God guided him along the way to success. Then David got busy. He was able to look after himself. He felt no need of God.

David lost his nearness to God. He did wrong. He became

unhappy. His burden of guilt became too heavy to bear. Then he repented. God heard, forgave, and restored. He became a new man.

The human mind is like the human body. It can be wounded. Sorrow is a wound. It cuts deeply, but sorrow is a clean wound, and will heal unless something gets into the wound, such as bitterness, self-pity, or resentment.

Wrong is also a wound.

When I violate my standards I wound my mind, and it is an unclean wound. Time will not heal that wound. Gradually, a sense of guilt can destroy a life and make it "only a shell." There is only one physician who can heal. The Fifty-first Psalm is the prayer David prayed.

"He restoreth my soul" can have another meaning. Moffatt translates it to read, "He revives life in me." Like a watch, the human spirit can just run down. We love our drive and push. We become less willing to attempt the difficult. We are crusaders no longer.

Like squeezing the juice from an orange and leaving just the pulp, life has a way of squeezing the spirit out of a person. A person can become "only a shell." We feel the thrill of no new enthusiasm, the dawn of a new day leaves us cold and hopeless.

The Bible tells that God made the first man "and breathed into his nostrils the breath of life; and man became a living soul" (Genesis 2:7). And God has the power and the willingness to breathe a new breath of life into one who has lost.

Only God has the power. Speaking to a large number of physicians in Atlanta, Dr. R. B. Robins declared, "The psychiatrist's couch cannot take the place of the church in solving the problems of a frustrated society."

"He restoreth my soul"—"He revives life in me."

CHAPTER VI

He Leadeth Me in the Paths of Righteousness for His Name's Sake

ON A PLAQUE at Florida's Singing Tower you can read these words; "I come here to find myself. It is so easy to get lost in the world." That is true.

We come to the forks of life's road and cannot decide which way to turn. There are decisions to be made and yet it is so hard to decide. We do get lost. We need guidance, and confidently David in the Twenty-third Psalm declares, "He leadeth me in the paths of righteousness" (in the right paths).

Doubtless David remembers his own experiences as a shepherd. He knew that the sheep has no sense of direction. A dog, a cat, or a horse, if lost, can find its way back. They seem to have a compass within themselves. Not so with a sheep.

The sheep has very poor eyes. It cannot see ten or fifteen yards ahead. Palestinian fields were covered with narrow paths over which the shepherds led their sheep to pasture. Some of these paths led to a precipice over which the stupid sheep might fall to its death.

Other paths lead up a blind alley. But some paths lead to green pastures and still waters. The sheep followed the shepherd, knowing it was walking in the right path. Sometimes the shepherd led over steep and difficult places, but the paths he followed always ended up somewhere.

The sheep was willing to trust that "somewhere" to the shepherd's judgment. Even as we sing,

> Lord, I would place my hand in Thine,
> Nor ever murmur nor repine;
> Content, whatever lot I see,
> Since 'tis my God that leadeth me.

Perhaps David remembered his forefathers as they made their way across a trackless wilderness from Egypt to the Promised Land. God sent a pillar of fire by night and a pillar of cloud by day. Following it, the Israelites did come to the land they longed for.

For some the paths of righteousness means hard going at times. Dr. Ralph W. Sockman tells about an English lad who decided to join the army for service in India. When asked the reason for his choice, he said: "I hear that in the Indian army they pay you a lot for doing a little. When you get on further, they pay you more for doing less. When you retire, they pay you quite a lot for doing nothing."

Though God does not put a bed of roses on the battlefield or a carpet on the race track; though He does not promise us an easy, effortless life, He does promise us strength and He does promise to go with us.

Notice that the Psalm says, "He *leadeth* me." God doesn't drive. He is climbing the same hill that we climb—man is not alone. As we take life one step at a time, we can walk with Him the right paths.

The wise man says, "In all thy ways acknowledge him and he shall direct thy paths" (Proverbs 3:6). That is true. The person who sincerely seeks to do God's will, whatever His will may be, will know the leadership of Eternal Wisdom.

He will lead you to your Promised Land.

CHAPTER VII

Yea, Though I Walk Through the Valley of the
Shadow of Death, I Will Fear No Evil: For
Thou Art With Me

LET ME draw an illustration from the story of a mother who
collapsed when news came that her son had been killed. She
went into her room, closed the door, and would see no one.

Her minister came and sat down by her bedside, but she
would not speak to him. For a little while all was quiet and
then slowly he began saying, "The Lord is my shepherd, I
shall not want." Phrase by phrase, he gently spoke the words
of the Psalm, and she listened.

When he came to that great phrase of comfort, she joined
in and together they said, "Yea, though I walk through the
valley of the shadow of death, I will fear no evil; for thou
art with me."

A smile flickered on her lips, and she said, "I see it dif-
ferently now."

Henry Ward Beecher says the Twenty-third Psalm is the
nightingale of the Psalms. The nightingale sings its sweetest
when the night is darkest. And for most of us death is the
most terrifying fact of life.

After a funeral, someone said to me. "You conduct a lot

of funerals; doesn't it become routine for you?" The answer is no. You never become accustomed to death. Each one is a new and fresh experience.

We bring our flowers and we have lovely music, but not even flowers and music can make a tomb a place of cheer. And death makes us afraid. We feel so helpless and alone.

Of course, "the valley of the shadow of death" refers to more than the actual experiences of physical death. It has been translated, "the glen of gloom." It might refer to every hard and terrifying experience of life.

The Basque Sheepherder describes an actual Valley of the Shadow of Death in Palestine. It leads from Jerusalem to the Dead Sea and is a very narrow and dangerous pathway through the mountain range. The path is rough, and there is danger that a sheep may fall at any moment to its death.

It is a forbidding journey that one dreads to take. But the sheep is not afraid. Why? Because the shepherd is with it.

And so come those dark places in life through which we are compelled to pass. Death is one. Disappointment is another. Loneliness is another. There are many more.

I have said to many people in "the valley of the shadow" to get off by themselves in a quiet place. Quit struggling for a little while. Forget the many details. Stop your mind for a little while from hurrying on to the morrow and to next year and beyond.

Just stop, become still and quiet, and in the midst of your "glen of gloom" you will feel a strange and marvelous presence more powerfully than you have ever felt it before. Many have told me of feeling that presence—of hearing the nightingale sing in the darkness.

Wherever my pathway leads, I will not be afraid, said David, and countless multitudes also have rid themselves of fear. Why? "For thou art with me." There is power in His presence.

CHAPTER VIII

Thy Rod and Thy Staff They Comfort Me

I ONCE knew a man who was hurt badly in a cyclone. From then on much of the joy of life was gone for him. Not because of his injury, but rather because he was afraid that another cyclone might come. There was nothing he could do.

He worried because there was still nothing he would be able to do if he saw another cyclone coming—until one day his children decided to build a cyclone cellar. They completed it and the man looked at it with relaxed joy. Now, no matter how hard a cyclone blew, he had protection. It was a great comfort to him.

In the Twenty-third Psalm we read, "Thy rod and thy staff they comfort me." The sheep is a helpless animal. It has no weapon with which to fight. It is easy prey to any wild beast of the field. It is afraid.

But the shepherd carries a rod, which is a heavy, hard club two to three feet long. When David wrote this Psalm he probably remembered his own need for such a rod. In I Samuel 17, David tells Saul how he slew a lion and a bear in protecting his sheep.

Also, the shepherd carried a staff, which was about eight feet long. The end of the staff was turned into a crook. Many paths in Palestine were along the steep sides of mountains. The sheep would lose its footing and slip down, hanging helplessly on some ledge below.

With his staff the shepherd could reach down, place the crook over the small chest of the sheep and lift it back onto the pathway. The sheep instinctively is comforted by the shepherd's rod and staff.

It is the comfort of knowing that the shepherd will be able to meet an emergency.

I have insurance on my automobile. I hope I will never need it, but I am comforted by the fact that I do have it.

I regret that my country finds it necessary to spend so much money on military preparedness. Yet, when I think of the condition of the world, my country's strength comforts me.

There are needs of my life that I cannot meet, and, like St. Paul it comforts me to say, "Now unto him that is able to do exceeding abundantly above all that we ask or think" (Ephesians 3:20).

Seemingly there is overwhelming evil in the world. We are a scared people. Many times we feel helpless; then we find comfort in realizing the power of God.

Certainly I do not think of God as just a cyclone cellar or an insurance policy. Yet I can say with James Montgomery:

God is my salvation: what foe have I to fear?
In darkness and temptation, my light, my help is near:
Though hosts encamp around me, firm in the fight I stand,
What terror can confound me, with God at my right hand?

"Thy rod and thy staff"—that takes a lot of the dread and fear of the future out of my heart.

CHAPTER IX

Thou Preparest a Table Before Me in the Presence of Mine Enemies

IN ONE town where we lived there arose an issue over whether or not a poolroom should be permitted to open. My father vigorously crusaded against it, and I remember someone rather jokingly asked him if he thought he would be tempted to play pool.

He said no, but that he had some boys and he did not want his boys in a poolroom. He might have kept his boys away, but he felt it would be safer to keep the poolroom away. My father's feeling in the matter serves to illustrate what David meant in the Twenty-third Psalm when he said: "Thou preparest a table before me in the presence of mine enemies."

In the pastures of the Holy Land grew poisonous plants which were fatal to the sheep if eaten. Also, there were plants whose sharp thorns would penetrate the soft noses of the sheep and cause ugly sores.

Each spring the shepherd would take his mattock and dig out these enemies of the sheep, pile them up and burn them. Thus the pastures were safe for the sheep to graze. The pasture became, as it were, a table prepared. The present enemies were destroyed.

We constantly must do this for our children. When my children go and come from school, a police woman stands on the corner. She is there to protect my children.

Happily, in Atlanta our school children have not yet been faced with a serious dope situation. But I want my city to keep it that way, exercising all possible vigilance. I feel the same way about obscene literature and many other things that harm and destroy life. We must constantly crusade against the enemies of life.

It is not enough for the farmer to plant his seed. He must go through his crop again and again to destroy the weeds. So must the spirit of God in man militantly crusade. It is not enough just to preach the Gospel. We must destroy the enemies.

Recently my children were vaccinated against some disease. I thank medical science for going before to prevent or destroy the cause of the disease. Parents, scientists, government, society as a whole, must prepare a table, destroying the enemies, so that all good life may be safely nourished.

After a sermon on race prejudice, a good man took me to task for not preaching the Gospel. But I have seen prejudice and false ideas of racial superiority destroy the opportunities for children of God. I feel my sermon was a compulsory part of the Gospel.

It is not enough just piously to sit around being good. There are times when "the Son of God goes forth to war."

One other thought—Jesus expresses the petition of David when He prays, "Lead us not into temptation." As we move along through life, we know there will be enemies seeking to destroy. Many worry because of a fear they will not be able to hold out—the fear of failure and of falling.

But the Shepherd of men is out ahead, and we can be assured of the protection of His strength. There is "the victory that overcometh the world, even our faith" (I John 5:4).

CHAPTER X

Thou Anointest My Head with Oil; My Cup Runneth Over

I WILL never forget what the coach said to us the first day I went out for football practice. He told us that football is a rough game and that if we expected to play it, we must also expect sometimes to get hurt.

So with life. It you expect to live it, you must also expect some bruises and hurt. That is just the way it is. And David, thinking of that fact, said in the Twenty-third Psalm, "Thou anointest my head with oil; my cup runneth over."

Sometimes, as the sheep grazed, its head would be cut by the sharp edge of a stone buried in the grass. There were briars to scratch and thorns to stick.

Then, some days the sheep had to walk steep paths under a hot, merciless sun. At the end of the day it would be tired and spent.

So the shepherd would stand at the door of the fold and examine each sheep as it came in. If there were hurt places the shepherd would apply soothing and healing oil. Instead of becoming infected, the hurt would soon heal.

Also, the shepherd had a large earthen jug of water, the kind of a jar which kept the water refreshingly cool through evaporation. As the sheep came in, the shepherd would dip down into the water with his big cup and bring it up brimful. The tired sheep drank deeply of the life-quickening draught.

Remember how, as little children, we would bruise a finger or stump a toe. We would come running to mama, who would kiss the hurt away. There was mystic healing in her loving concern.

As older children we still get hurt. A heart can be broken, a conscience can ache like an infected tooth, feelings can be hurt, the world can deal cruelly and harshly. One can become discouraged and tired. Sometimes the burden of life can be unbearable.

But also there is the tender Shepherd who understands the hurt of His children and is ever ready and able to minister to that hurt. Harry Lauder, the famous Scotch comedian, was grief-stricken at the loss of his son. But he found the Shepherd.

Later he was giving a concert in Chicago before an overflow crowd. He responded to repeated encores, and finally he quieted the audience and said very quietly, "Don't thank me. Thank the good God who put the songs in my heart."

Notice David said, "Thou anointest *my* head with oil, *my* cup . . ." He didn't say "our" heads. It is the singular, personal pronoun. All day long the shepherd has been concerned with the flock. But as they go into the fold he takes them one by one.

I had a professor in college one year who never did learn my name. Somehow, I never liked him very much. I read that Jesus said, "He calleth his own sheep by name" (John 10:3). I like that. It makes me feel important.

The Psalmist said, "He healeth the broken in heart. . . . He telleth the number of the stars" (Psalm 147:3,4). The power of the universe is power at *my* disposal.

CHAPTER XI

---

*Surely Goodness and Mercy Shall Follow Me
all the Days of My Life*

IN THE play "South Pacific," Mary Martin sang a song that I
think is wonderful. In that song she sang: "I'm stuck like a
dope, with a thing called hope, I can't get it out of my heart."

David says the same thing in different words: "Surely goodness and mercy shall follow me all the days of my life." He is
not wistfully thinking. He says *surely . . . surely . . . surely.*

David was an old man when he wrote the Twenty-third
Psalm. He had seen tragedies and disappointments, but he
also had come to know God—a God who knows the needs of
His children and who abundantly provided for those needs,
a God who can restore life and take away fear. In spite of
dark clouds on the horizon, with a God like Him whom David
knew, David was sure the sun would shine tomorrow.

We hear a lot about the wickedness of men and the destruction of the world. We know of bombs which can destroy cities
with one awful blast. We tremble at the sound of dire predic-
tions of the vengeful judgment of God.

But, somehow, as our minds are filled with the picture of
the loving Shepherd leading his sheep we feel confident that
He will lead us through the dark valleys.

22

One of the greatest teachers America has ever produced was Professor Endicott Peabody, headmaster of Groton for many years. One day at chapel he told his boys, "Remember, things in life will not always run smoothly. . . . The great fact to remember is that the trend of civilization is forever upward."

Those words stuck in the mind of one of his students, and about forty years later that student gave new heart to the nation when he said, "The only thing we have to fear is fear itself." Franklin D. Roosevelt will always be remembered for the hope he gave to a hopeless nation.

Many people think themselves into disaster. They feel a little bad and they fill their minds with the thought of being sick. They start out the day with dread of something bad happening. They look to tomorrow with fear and trembling.

There is a very successful teacher I have read about who teaches people to sit quietly and conceive of their minds as being absolutely blank. Think of the mind as being a motion-picture screen.

Then flash on the screen of the mind a picture of something good you want to happen. Then take the picture off. Flash it on again. Take it off. Repeat that process until the picture becomes clear and sharp.

Through that process the picture becomes firmly established in one's conscious and subconscious minds. Then the professor tells the student to go to work to make that picture a reality, to maintain a spirit of prayer and faith.

It is amazing how completely and how quickly that picture in the mind will be developed in life.

Quit predicting disaster for your world and yourself. Say with the Psalmist, "This is the day which the Lord hath made; we will rejoice and be glad in it" (Psalm 118:24).

Begin the morning with hope. Plant this firmly in your mind, "Surely goodness and mercy shall follow me," and they will.

CHAPTER XII

And I Will Dwell in the House of the Lord for Ever

It is always a thrilling experience to me to be downtown in Atlanta about 5 o'clock in the afternoon. The streets are filled with people and cars. Extra buses are running, and every one is packed with people standing.

It is thrilling because the people are going home.

John Howard Payne had been away from home for nine years. One afternoon he stood at the window watching the throngs of people, happy, hurrying, going home. Suddenly he felt lonely, there in a Paris boardinghouse room.

Impatiently he turned from the window. He had work to do. It was perhaps an important play he was writing. He had no time for sentimental dreaming. But the mood and the memories of a little town on Long Island would not leave him.

He picked up a pencil and began writing:

> 'Mid pleasures and palaces though we may roam,
> Be it ever so humble, there's no place like home.

And now for more than a hundred years that song has had a special place in the hearts of the people. There really is "no place like home."

24

But I also feel sadness as I watch the crowds going home. I know some who have no home to which to go. Some wander around seeking a cheap bed for the night, others can afford the nicest hotel suite in the city—still it isn't home.

I have dealt with a lot of alcoholics. Especially have a number of women told me how they started. They would go to an empty cheerless room or small apartment, be alone. There is not much fun in living alone. So many started drinking that way.

Much much more pathetic than seeing a homeless person at the end of the day is to find a person who is not sure of God and has no hope of the eternal home, who, at the close of life's day, can look forward only to some dark grave and oblivion.

David closes the Twenty-third Psalm with a mighty crescendo of faith when he declares, "I will dwell in the house of the Lord for ever."

One of the heart-stirring passages in Bunyan's *Pilgrim's Progress* is that in which "Mr. Feeble Mind" speaks of his hope of home. He says:

But this I am resolved on: to run when I can, to go when I cannot run, and to creep when I cannot go. . . . My mind is beyond the river that hath no bridge, though I am, as you see, but of a feeble mind.

Sometimes the greatest inspiration for living comes when your "mind is beyond that river that hath no bridge." Were it not for that assurance, many experiences of life would be unbearable.

David did not have the insights that we have. He never heard the words: "I am the resurrection, and the life: he that believeth in me, though he were dead, yet shall he live: and whosoever liveth and believeth in me shall never die" (John 11:25,26).

Just knowing intimately a God like he describes in the Twenty-third Psalm gave David assurance that at the close of life's day he would go home.

CHAPTER XIII

"He Knows the Shepherd"

THERE IS a story—I do not know its source—of an old man and a young man on the same platform before a vast audience of people.

A special program was being presented. As a part of the program each was to repeat from memory the words of the Twenty-third Psalm. The young man, trained in the best speech technique and drama, gave, in the language of the ancient silver-tongued orator, the words of the Psalm.

"The Lord is my shepherd . . ." When he had finished, the audience clapped their hands and cheered, asking him for an encore so that they might hear again his wonderful voice.

Then the old gentleman, leaning heavily on his cane, stepped to the front of the same platform, and in feeble, shaking voice, repeated the same words—"The Lord is my shepherd . . ."

But when he was seated no sound came from the listeners. Folks seemed to pray. In the silence the young man stood to make the following statement:

"Friends," he said, "I wish to make an explanation. You asked me to come back and repeat the Psalm, but you remained silent when my friend here was seated. The differ-

26

ence? I shall tell you. I know the Psalm, but he knows the Shepherd!"

Perhaps the figure of the shepherd and the flock may mean little to the modern city dweller. Yet, if ever a people of this earth resembled a flock of frightened sheep it is now. Governments are afraid of each other. People are afraid of their governments, of other people, and of themselves.

This Psalm of David has sung its way across the barriers of time, race, and language. For twenty-five centuries it has been treasured in the hearts of people. Today it is more beloved than ever before.

The reason it lives? Not just because it is great literature. Because it tells that above all the strife and fears, the hungers and weaknesses of mankind, there is a Shepherd.

A shepherd who knows his sheep one by one, who is abundantly able to provide, who guides and protects and at the close of the day opens the door to the sheepfold—the house not made with hands.

In the quietness of the South Pole Admiral Byrd suddenly realized he was "not alone." That assurance caused faith to well up within him, and even though he stood in "the coldest cold on the face of the earth," he felt a comforting warmth.

The Twenty-third Psalm gives men that same assurance. That is why it lives in the hearts of men, regardless of race or creed.

PART II

GOD'S RULES FOR LIVING

The Ten Commandments

And God spake all these words, saying,

I am the Lord Thy God, which have brought thee out of the land of Egypt, out of the house of bondage.

Thou shalt have no other gods before me.

Thou shalt not make unto thee any graven image, or any likeness of any thing that is in heaven above, or that is in the earth beneath, or that is in the water under the earth:

Thou shalt not bow down thyself to them, nor serve them: for I the Lord thy God am a jealous God, visiting the iniquity of the fathers upon the children unto the third and fourth generation of them that hate me;

And shewing mercy unto thousands of them that love me, and keep my commandments.

Thou shalt not take the name of the Lord thy God in vain; for the Lord will not hold him guiltless that taketh his name in vain.

Remember the sabbath day, to keep it holy.

Six days shalt thou labour, and do all thy work:

But the seventh day is the sabbath of the Lord thy God: in it thou shalt not do any work, thou, nor thy son, nor thy daughter, thy man-servant, nor thy maidservant, nor thy cattle, nor thy stranger that is within thy gates:

*For in six days the Lord made heaven and
    earth, the sea, and all that in them is,
    and rested the seventh day: wherefore the
    Lord blessed the sabbath day, and hallowed it.*

*Honour thy father and thy mother: that thy
    days may be long upon the land which the
    Lord thy God giveth thee.*

Thou shalt not kill.

Thou shalt not commit adultery.

Thou shalt not steal.

*Thou shalt not bear false witness against
    thy neighbour.*

*Thou shalt not covet thy neighbour's house,
    thou shalt not covet thy neighbour's wife,
    nor his manservant, nor his maidservant, nor
    his ox, nor his ass, nor any thing that is
    thy neighbour's.   Exodus 20:1-17*

CHAPTER I

Thou Shalt Have No Other Gods Before Me

SHORTLY AFTER Moses led the children of Israel away from the bondage of Egypt on their journey to the promised land, God called Moses up on Mt. Sinai. He must have said something like this: "Moses, your people are now headed toward prosperity. The land I have promised to them is rich and productive and will supply not only their needs, but much more. In fact, the land flows with milk and honey. But, Moses, people cannot be made happy and successful merely by the possession of things. The way they live is more important than what they have. So, I am going to give you ten rules for living. I want you to teach the people these rules. If they live by them, I promise they will be blessed. But I warn you, if they break these rules they will be severely penalized. And one other thing, Moses, these are to be the rules of living for all peoples of all times. They will never go out of date, they will never be repealed or changed."

We have those rules, known as The Ten Commandments, recorded in Exodus 20. They are not only the basis of conduct, both moral and spiritual, but also the basis of peace and prosperity for the individual and for the world. The Bible says, "The fool hath said in his heart, There is no God"

(Psalm 14:1), and it is only a fool who thinks he is big enough or smart enough to violate the unchangeable laws of the eternal God and get by with it. No man can break God's law, he breaks only himself.

Very important is the order in which God stated His laws. The first four deal with man's relationship with God, the last six with man's relationship with man. Before man can live rightly with each other, he must first get right with God. Someone has said, "The golden rule is my religion," but the golden rule is nobody's religion, because it is not a religion. It is merely the expression of religion.

As H. G. Wells put it, "Until a man has found God he begins at no beginning; he works to no end."

The first commandment is somewhat surprising. We would think that it would be, "Thou shalt believe in a God," a law against atheism. There is no such law. God took care of that in our creation. We do not teach a baby to hunger or to thirst, nature does that. However, we must train our children to satisfy their hungers and thirsts with the right things.

Man instinctively believes and worships. Nowhere does the Bible attempt to prove the existence of God. Man is created incomplete, and he cannot be at rest until there is a satisfaction of his deepest hunger, the yearning of his soul. The danger lies in that fact that man can pervert his worship instinct and make for himself a false god.

St. Augustine said, "My soul is restless until it finds it can rest in Thee, O God." No false god satisfies the longing of the soul, but we can, and many do, squander their lives seeking satisfaction from false objects of worship. So the first of God's rules for life is: "Thou shalt have no other gods before me."

At Vicksburg, Miss., an engineer showed me an almost dry channel. He explained that once the great Mississippi river flowed there but now it had been changed into another channel, which had been dug. The flow of the river could not be stopped, but it could be diverted. So with our worship of God. Man is incomplete without an object of worship; the yearning of his soul demands attention. But man can turn from the one true God and make for himself another god. There have been people who worshiped the sun, or a star, or a mountain. In some countries people worship a cow, or a river, or something else. We think of those people as being primitive. They are, but no more primitive than multitudes of people in this enlightened land we call America. God said, "Thou shalt have no other gods before me," and that law of life we are guilty of breaking.

There are five objects of worship which multitudes today have put before God: wealth, fame, pleasure, power, and knowledge. While most of us have no idea of ever being really rich, we never become satisfied with what we can reasonably possess. Maybe that is good, except when that dissatisfaction obscures our feelings for God and diverts us in our search for God. I can become so interested in what I have that I forget the needs of my soul.

Most of us never expect to be famous, yet the little child says, "See how high I can jump or watch me run." We are born with the desire to be noticed. That is not wrong. God made us separate identities, and we do want to be known. Yet, as a minister, I counsel with many people who have wrecked their lives and destroyed their happiness simply because they have not received the attention they desired. Many get their feelings hurt at the smallest slight. We spend in America more money on cosmetics, for example, than we spend on the entire program of the kingdom of God. It isn't wrong to want to look our best. But it is wrong when putting ourselves forward becomes our first desire, thus our god.

All men want to be happy but we make a mistake when we think pleasure is the way to get happiness. There is forgetfulness of life's routines in pleasures, but they do not satisfy the soul. Pleasure is like dope; gradually we must increase the dose with more excitement, more thrill, more sensation, until, eventually, we find ourselves groping among the tombstones of our dead passions. It is like making our meals out of pickles and pepper. One of our greatest temptations is to put pleasure before God.

Power is not wrong, neither is knowledge. The electric power in America is the equal of one hundred and fifty slaves for each of us and is a great blessing to us. But power worshiped turns us into little Hitlers. Knowledge is good, but the worship of knowledge destroys obedience, just as the worship of power destroys character.

To worship God leads us to be like God and to obey His will. Thus we become good and walk in the paths of right living when we have no other gods before God.

CHAPTER II

Thou Shalt Not Make Unto Thee Any Graven Image

THE SECOND rule of God is, "Thou shalt not make unto thee any graven image." This is the one rule that most people feel less guilty of breaking, yet more is said about this one in the Bible than any other. Primitive man found it hard to realize a God he could not see, so he made aids to assist his imagination, to bring reality into his worship. That is not wrong. Frank Boreham tells of a man who prayed with a vacant chair before him. He imagined God sitting in that chair, and it made his prayers more real.

On my desk are several copies of the Bible. I use them in my studying and devotional reading, yet they would be of value to me, even if I never opened them. Their very presence serves to remind me of God. Of course, one can worship anywhere, but worship is easier in the church building. Not only the building, but the ritual, the music and the sermon also are aids to worship.

The danger lies in the fact that it is so easy to worship the means instead of the goal. The Bible, churches, music, and ministers, and all our symbols and aids to worship are sacred only because they lead us to God. For example, denominationalism can be a violation of this rule. I am a Methodist, but

I could be just as good a Christian as a Baptist or as a Presbyterian or in any denomination which says with Peter, "Thou are Christ, the son of the living God" (Matthew 16: 16).

Even more dangerous than our aids to worship are some other images we make. We are told that "God created man in his own image" (Genesis 1:27). But to live a life in conformity with our creation is difficult. In fact, it is so difficult that all of us fall far short. Thus, instead of being like God, we seek to create Him in our own image. It is so much easier to make God like ourselves than for us to be like Him.

God tells us not to do wrong, but there are some things we want to do, right or wrong. So we create a God who doesn't care what we do. We think of the God of the blue skies, majestic mountains and lovely flowers, but turn our backs on the God who said, "Ye have robbed me in tithes and offerings" (Malachi 3:8), or the God who said, "Whatsoever a man soweth, that shall he also reap" (Galatians 6:7). It has been well pointed out that Christ was not crucified because He said, "Consider the lilies, how they grow," but rather because He said, "Consider the thieves, how they steal."

It is so much easier to whittle God down to our size instead of repenting, changing our way of living, and being Godly ourselves. When Horace Bushnell was a college student he felt he was an atheist. One day a voice seemed to say to him, "If you do not believe in God, what do you believe?" He answered back, "I believe there is a difference between right and wrong." "Are you living up to the highest you believe?" the voice seemed to ask. "No," he said, "but I will." That day he dedicated his life to his highest belief. Years later, after he had been pastor of one church forty-seven years, he said, "Better than I know any person in my church, I know Jesus Christ." When he began conforming his life to his beliefs, instead of making his beliefs fit his life, he was led to a realization of God.

The very process of thinking requires mental pictures or images. Think of an apple and you see one in your imagination. Think of Abraham Lincoln and his face is flashed on the screen of your mind. And when one thinks of God he sees some picture of God. The danger lies in the fact that it can be the wrong picture, which can be tragic. One becomes like his image of God, and if it is the wrong image the man becomes wrong. So the Bible contains more warning in regard to God's second rule for life, "Thou shalt not make unto thee any graven image (Exodus 20:4), than in regard to any of the other ten.

Man sees a little of God in many forms, majesty in His mountains, greatness in His seas, loveliness in His flowers, righteousness in His saints. But all of these are insufficient. With Philip, the heart of each of us says, "Lord, show us the Father." Jesus replied, "He that hath seen me hath seen the Father" (John 14:8,9). The only perfect image of God we have is Christ, and that is sufficient.

As you see Him through the words of the Gospels—Matthew, Mark, Luke, and John, you are impressed with His eyes. Those who were with Him in the flesh neglected to tell us much about His physical appearance, but they could not forget His eyes. "And the Lord turned, and looked upon Peter" (Luke 22:61), and Peter broke down. Sometimes Jesus' eyes flashed with merriment, sometimes they melted in tenderness, and other times they were filled with stern rebuke. When I read, "The ways of man are before the eyes of the Lord" (Proverbs 5:21), I stop still in my tracks and think on my ways.

When we look at Jesus' face we know it was a happy face. Little children ran to get in His lap and clasp Him around His neck. People invited Him to their parties. Seeing God in Christ, we are not afraid of Him; instead we want to be closer to Him. We listen as He says, "Neither do I condemn thee; go and sin no more" (John 8:11), and we are ashamed of our sins, we want forgiveness, and we come to Him repenting and asking for His cleansing.

We look as "he steadfastly set his face to go to Jerusalem" (Luke 9:51). Though it meant death, He would not go back on the high purposes of His life. Seeing Him puts the steel in our own backbones to make the right decision. We watch as He walked seven miles to Emmaus to give hope to the down-hearted (Luke 24:13-32), or as He gave a new chance to His friends who failed Him (John 20:19-31), and we take new heart and new hope.

How wonderful it is to see God. To encourage the early Christians who were bearing almost the unbearable John says to them that those who are faithful "shall see his face" (Rev. 22:4). The promise of seeing Him compensated for any sacrifice.

One thing more. After Thorwaldsen had completed his famous statue of Christ, he brought a friend to see it. Christ's arms were outstretched, His head bowed between them. The friend said, "But I cannot see His face." The sculptor replied, "If you would see the face of Christ you must get on your knees." He is the perfect image of God; let us have no other.

CHAPTER III

Thou Shalt Not Take the Name of the Lord Thy God in Vain

GOD's THIRD rule for living is, "Thou shalt not take the name of the Lord thy God in vain" (Exodus 20:7). The first rule is, put God first; the second is, get the right picture of God; the third is, think about God in the right way. What a person thinks about determines what he is. Hawthorne tells about the boy Ernest who would look longingly at the great stone face on the side of the mountain. It was a strong, kind, honorable face that thrilled the heart of this boy. There was a legend that some day a man would appear who would look like the Great Stone Face. Through all his childhood, and even after he became a man, Ernest kept looking at the great face and for the man who was like it. One day, when the people were discussing the legend, someone suddenly cried out, "Behold, behold, Ernest is himself the likeness of the Great Stone Face." Indeed he was; he had become like his thoughts.

The secret desires of our hearts eventually show up in our very appearance. Once someone wanted Lincoln to meet a certain man. "I do not want to see him," Lincoln said. But his friend protested, "You do not even know him." Lincoln replied, "I do not like his face." "A man cannot be held responsible for his face," the friend said. "Any grown man is responsible for the look on his face," the president insisted. And Lincoln was right. His own face was an example. Though homely and rough, in Lincoln's face one sees the very principles of sympathy and honesty which made him the greatest of all Americans.

Some psychologists have made extensive studies which show that a person's thoughts show up in his features. I have noticed that married couples who have lived together happily and harmoniously over a number of years come to look more like brother and sister than like husband and wife. As they live together, enjoy common experiences, think alike, they tend to look alike.

Ralph Waldo Emerson, one of the wisest of Americans, said, "A man is what he thinks about all day long." But that was not original with him. Marcus Aurelius, the wisest man of ancient Rome, said, "Our life is what our thoughts make of it." But before Aurelius siad it, the wise men of the Bible said, "For as he thinketh in his heart, so is he" (Proverbs 23:7).

Once a football coach was worried because one of his boys who was capable of being a really great player was not showing up well. The coach decided to go the the boy's room one night and have a talk with him. There on the walls he saw a number of lewd and immoral pictures and then he understood. No boy could fill his mind with filth and trash and give his best performance on the field of play.

God's third rule is that we put something high and holy in our thinking to reverence, to be inspired by. St. Paul tells us: "Whatsoever things are true . . . honest . . . just . . . pure . . . lovely . . . of good report . . . think on these things" (Philippians 4:8). Those are qualities of God. As we think of Him it lifts and inspires our lives and makes us Godly.

There are at least three ways we profane God's name. First, by our language. We have all kinds of maniacs but one of the most common types we have in America is "swearomaniacs."

It is alarming how our language is being filled with profanity. Many of our modern novels I would enjoy reading, but they contain such vile language that I will not read them because I do not want those words in my mind. The word "hell" has become one of our most common words. We say, "It is cold as hell," "It is hot as hell," "It is raining like hell," etc., etc. One man came in to see me recently who I thought used the word correctly. He said, "Preacher, I am in a helluva shape," and he was. Hell is down, not up, and to fill my mind with hell and the language of hell degrades my very soul. The word "profane" comes from two Latin words—"pro" meaning in front of and "fane" meaning temple. A profane word is one you would not use in church, and that is a mighty good way to judge the language we use.

Second, we take God's name in vain by not taking Him seriously. We admit there is a God, but our belief is merely lip service. Jesus said, "Whosoever heareth these sayings of mine, *and doeth them* . . ." (Matthew 7:24). To talk about God and not to live like God is profanity worse than vile language. Belief that does not make a radical difference in life is mere sham and hypocrisy. As Elton Trueblood put it, "An empty, meaningless faith may be worse than none."

A third way we take God's name in vain is by refusing His fellowship and His help. If I say a man is my friend, yet never want to be with him and do not call on him when I need his help, then I am lying when I use the word "friend." If I believe in a mechanic, then I will go to him when my car needs attention. If I believe in a physician I will call him when I become sick. Yet, when Adam and Eve sinned, they ran and hid from God. Their descendants have been doing likewise ever since.

On our lives is the stain of sin. There is only one who can forgive sin, and to refuse to pray, to close our Bibles, to turn our backs on the altar of His church is profanity of the worst sort. Once, when I was a little boy, I saw a soft drink truck which seemed unattended. I slipped one of the bottles in a pocket, and when I got around the bend of the road opened it. The driver stepped up just then and demanded payment, but I had no nickel. He sternly said, "Get the money for me in thirty minutes or I will put you in jail."

I ran home to my father and told him what I had done. He neither condemned nor humiliated me. My own wrong had done that. Instead, he gave me a nickel and quietly said, "Go, pay the man." That is a picture of God. We do wrong and our very conscience condemns us to a hell from which we cannot escape. Then we remember, "If we confess our sins, he is faithful and just to forgive us our sins, and to cleanse us from all unrighteousness" (I John 1:9). Humbly we bow before Him and receive His forgiveness. Then we live for Him and according to His ways. That is belief that is not in vain.

CHAPTER IV

Remember the Sabbath Day, to Keep it Holy

EACH ONE of God's ten rules for living is vital, but in giving them to Moses, God said more about the fourth than any other. God needed only four words in regard to killing, but He used ninety-four words to tell us to "remember the sabbath day, to keep it holy." In the first place, God tells us to remember. In a scientific sense, one never forgets anything. Every thought we have is registered forever on our minds, but, practically, we can forget almost everything. We forget dates and names, we forget duties and even God. Some things we forget on purpose because the remembrance of them is not pleasant. Other things we forget because our minds are preoccupied with other matters. We forget to keep God's day. But God says man needs to set aside a day each week to keep it holy, and to fail to keep that day holy is to suffer.

In the first place, God gave to man the Sabbath as a reward for his labor. The man who labors deserves to rest, and to forget God's gift is only to cheat ourselves.

In his book, *East River*, Sholem Asch quotes the words of an old Jew, Moshe Wolf, in regard to the Lord's day. It is about the best statement on keeping the Sabbath I know. He said: "When a man labors not for a livelihood, but to accumulate wealth, then he is a slave. Therefore it is that God granted the Sabbath. For it is by the Sabbath that we know that we are not working animals, born to eat and to labor. We are men. It is the Sabbath which is man's goal; not labor, but the rest which he earns from his labor. It was because the Jews made the Sabbath holy to God that they were redeemed from slavery in Egypt. It was by the Sabbath that they proclaimed that they were not slaves, but free men."

Second, God gave us Sunday because every man needs to be re-created. Just as a battery can run down and need to be recharged, so can a person. Gerald Kennedy tells of two parties who started out across the plains in the pioneer days, going west to California. One was led by a religious man and one was led by an irreligious man. One group stopped all of each Lord's day for worship and rest. The other party was so anxious to reach the gold of California that it would not take time to stop. The men drove every day. The amazing thing is that the party which observed the Sabbath arrived first. We have now well established the fact in our own nation that one can do more work in six days, even in five, than in seven. A run-down person is an unproductive person.

Also, we need to re-create our souls. A group of American explorers went to Africa. They employed some native guides. The first day they rushed, as they did also on the second, third, and every day. On the seventh day they noticed the guides sitting under a tree. "Come on," they shouted. One of the guides replied, "We no go today. We rest today to let our souls catch up with our bodies." For that purpose, God says, "Remember the Sabbath."

We have spent so much time arguing about what we should not do on Sunday that we sometimes forget what we should do. God gave us the day, not as a time of prohibitions but rather to give us opportunity for the finest and most important things of life. An old miner once explained to a visitor, "I let my mules spend one day a week outside the mines to keep them from going blind." And the person who does not spend time away from the daily grind of life goes blind in his soul. The philosopher Santayana tells us, "A fanatic is one who, having lost sight of his aim, redoubles his effort." And much of the feverish haste we see today is by aimless, purposeless people. God says we need a day a week to keep our aim. Or, as Carlyle put it, "The man who does not habitually worship is but a pair of spectacles behind which there is no eye."

As a pastoral counselor, I have seen many people who had lost their nerve control. Life for many had become a miserable experience. But it is rare, very rare, to find an uncontrolled person who regularly worships God and keeps His day holy. We have a slang expression, "That got my goat." That phrase has an interesting beginning. Owners of sensitive, high-strung race horses used to keep a goat in the stalls with the horses. The very presence of the calm, relaxed goat helped the horses to relax. On the day before an important race rival owners would sometimes steal another owner's goats. Thus the horse would not run its best the next day.

Well, we get sensitive and high-strung, and thus we falter in the race of life. Man needs relaxed re-creation and spiritual inspiration. Oliver Wendell Holmes said: "I have in my heart a small, shy plant called reverence; I cultivate that on Sundays." And well it will be if we all cultivate the plant of reverence within our hearts, because, as Dostoevski reminds us, "A man who bows down to nothing can never bear the burden of himself." Many of our fears, worries, and nervous tensions would be saved if we kept this fourth rule of God.

We are in too big a hurry, and we run by far more than we catch up with. The Bible tells us to "be still, and know that I am God" (Psalm 46:10). Beauty doesn't shout. Loveliness is quiet. Our finest moods are not clamorous. The familiar appeals of the Divine are always in calm tones, a still, small voice. Here is the New Testament picture of Jesus: "Behold, I stand at the door, and knock: if any man hear my voice, and open the door, I will come in to him, and will sup with him, and he with me" (Revelation 3:20). The Divine is not obtrusive. He bursts in no one's life unbidden. He is reserved and courteous. "We need a day when we can hear such a voice as His. A day when we give the Highest a hearing," as Dr. Fosdick so well said.

Just as men build telescopes to gain a clearer view of the stars, so almost since the dawn of civilization, have men built churches and set aside a day to worship, in order to gain a clearer view of God and the high purposes of life. "Remember the sabbath day, to keep it holy," said God.

_____

CHAPTER V

Honor Thy Father and Thy Mother

GOD GAVE us ten rules to live by. The first four deal with our relationship to Him, the last five deal with our relationship with other people. The fifth rule has been called the centerpiece of God's law. "Honor thy father and thy mother" involves both our relationship with God and with our fellow men. When God made man He also set up the pattern by which men must live together. First, a man and a woman come together in marriage, and out of the union come children. The parents provide love, care, and control for the child, and, in reality, the parent is to the child its first god. As the child learns to love and respect its parents, so later does it love and respect God.

Also, the parents are the greatest social influence on the life of the child. It is in the home that a child first learns to respect the personalities of others, to have regard for the rights of others, to learn obedience to the laws for the welfare of all people. A child's respect for both authority and democracy usually must begin, if it begins at all, in the home. So, upon the parent and child relationship in the home rests almost our entire civilization.

Of course, the relationship of the parent and child is an

ever changing one. At first, the baby must be carried. Later, it learns to walk, holding its mother's hands; still later, it learns to walk alone. Up to about ten the child thinks its parents know everything. At about sixteen the child is not so sure about its parents. At nineteen the child feels it has surpassed the parents in knowledge and at twenty-two he completely outgrows the parent. But at thirty we remember that our parents were right about a lot of things, and at forty we decide they were just about perfect. That is usually about the normal process.

As I study this rule of God to honor our parents, to me it means three things: (1) It means that the parents must be honorable.

Once a mother carried her little boy to the zoo. He was asking about each of the animals, and when he saw some little ones in a cage, he asked, "What are those?" The mother told him they were little wildcats. He then asked, "Why are they wild cats?" We know the answer. Their mamas and papas were wildcats. Usually, children are the reflection of their parents, because it is the most natural thing for a child so to reverence its parents that it will live according to the principles it sees in them.

When Quentin Roosevelt was on the Western Front during World War I, an observer said, "I come here especially to tell you how millions of Americans appreciate the splendid way in which the sons of Theodore Roosevelt are acquitting themselves in this conflict." "Well, you see," Quentin replied, "it's up to us to practice what father preaches. I'm Roosevelt's son. It's up to me to live like a Roosevelt."

General Douglas MacArthur expressed the thought I have when he said: "By profession I am a soldier and take pride in that fact. But I am prouder to be a father. My hope is that my son, when I am gone, will remember me not from battle, but in the home, repeating with him one simple prayer, 'Our Father which art in heaven.'"

That is the first meaning of this rule which God gave us.

(2) To "honor thy father and thy mother" means not only that parents should be honorable, it means also that children should recognize, respect, and love their parents. It seems to me that just common decency would cause us to honor our parents. Once, when I was pastor of a little country church, I was out visiting and saw a woman picking cotton. I stopped and went down in the field to speak to her. She told me her son had been offered a job in the near-by furniture factory, which would pay good wages, and that she had said to him, "Son, since your father died, I have been working this field to support you in school. You lack just one more year now, and I can keep on so you can finish."

Her hands were rough and calloused, her face was weather-beaten and her back was stooped, but as that boy looks at her, if he does not feel she is the most beautiful woman in all the world, then he is utterly unworthy of her. Maybe our parents made some mistakes, but they gave us life, they nurtured us as babies, and they loved us, which is more, far more, than any one else has done or ever can do.

(3) But this rule of life includes more than our immediate parents. It means that we must recognize our debt to the past and be thankful for it. As I stand in my pulpit each Sunday I am proud to be there. But as I look at the congregation I see men and women who have been there for forty, fifty, and even sixty years. For nearly a hundred years consecrated people have worked to build the church in which I preach. Back of that is upwards of two thousand years of Christian history, "in spite of dungeon, fire and sword." And still beyond are the prophets of old of Abraham's faith. All the chance and opportunity I have come from the contributions of others better than I. So nothing I could ever do would be equal to what has been done for me.

So many things came crowding in on me the night my father died. I thought of the struggle of his youth to get what little education he could and the even greater struggle to give his children a better chance than he had. I thought of how as a little boy I went with him to his country churches and how proud of him I was as he preached. Of how that after I became a preacher I would preach for him and he for me. And now his voice was still. My first feeling of loneliness was overcome by the realization that now I had not only my work to do, but also his to carry on. Sometimes people tell me I attempt to do too much, but I am caught up by the conviction that I must do the work of two men.

So it is with all of us. What we have and what we are is because of what we have received. We must not only be vessels in which our heritage is carried to the next generations, we must increase that wealth. Each of us is an investment. Our responsibilities differ in that to some have been given five talents, to others two, and to others one. But to take what we have received, be it little or much, and to fail to increase it, is to become a "wicked and slothful servant."

> *Faith of our fathers, we will love*
> *Both friend and foe in all our strife;*
> *And preach thee, too, as love knows how,*
> *By kindly words and virtuous life:*
> *Faith of our fathers, holy faith,*
> *We will be true to thee till death.*
>
> —FREDERICK W. FABER

CHAPTER VI

Thou Shalt Not Kill

GOD MADE us to live with each other, and the very process of living requires certain rules. Without rules to go by the process of living together would be impossible. Here is a highway over which many cars can travel safely if they obey such rules as driving on the right side, not passing except with proper clearance, maintaining a reasonable speed, etc. To break the rules makes the highway unsafe for all who use it, and, instead of an instrument of service, the highway becomes an instrument of death and destruction. Now, life can be good or bad—it depends on how well we keep the rules as we go along. God laid down five rules to govern our relationships with each other. The first one is: "Thou shalt not kill" (Exodus 20:13).

First, this applies to our own selves. We did not create our lives, and we do not have the authority to destroy our lives. The very fact of life carries with it an inescapable obligation to live. Frequently the question of suicide comes up. Clearly, it is a violation of God's law. Now as to what God does about one who so breaks His law I gladly leave to Him, and I do not know what the eternal result is. God reserves the judgment for Himself, and surely He takes into account all the circumstances and one's mental responsibility.

53

Not only suicide, murder, too, is prohibited. All sensible and sane people agree we should not take a gun and shoot either ourselves or another person. But involved in this rule are the laws of health, which to violate is to kill, even though it may be by degrees. This commandment forbids exposing ourselves or others to needless physical risks, such as excessive speed on the highways, unsafe working conditions, improper housing, harmful pleasures, and the like.

Also forbidden is exposing ourselves or others to needless moral or spiritual risks. We can kill by killing faith or ideals. In talking about a man who had leaped from the window of a high building, an old negro janitor who knew the man's life very wisely said, "When a man has lost God, there ain't nothing to do but jump." Jotham was a king who did not go to church. Being a strong man, he still remained morally upright. But others, seeing his example, did not go either. The result was, "And the people did yet corruptly" (II Chronicles 27:2). Also, such things as ingratitude, neglect, cruelty, indifference can be slow but sure instruments of death.

Also forbidden are the destructive emotions of men: fear, hate, jealousy, anger, envy, anxiety, excessive grief, and the others. To counteract them requires developing within our lives the healing and life-giving emotions, such as, faith, hope, laughter, creativeness, and love. Love, for example, is a process of giving; giving through love destroys selfishness which in turn, results in the destruction of wrong desire, which, in turn, results in the destruction of jealousy, which, in turn, results in the end of hate which, in turn, will eliminate the hate murders.

It is a very involved process, not nearly as simple as I state it here. But take excessive grief, for another example. That is a form of self-pity, which grows out of selfishness, which is the lack of outgoing love. "Thou shalt not kill" involves the entire realm of living and the reasons for life. To reverence the life of all men is God's law for us.

To live and let live is only half the meaning of "Thou shalt not kill." Positively, it means to live and help live. Jesus did not find it necessary to warn us against becoming gangsters and murderers, but very clearly does He condemn those who pass by on the other side of a wounded brother. The very foundation of this commandment is the fact that God values every man as He values me. One God who hath made of one blood all nations. One God who is the Father and all men who are brothers. The rule of living means that we look at all men in the proper light.

Lorado Taft, in setting up a statue of a boy by Donatello, put some lights around it. First, he had them down on the floor shining up on the boy's face. As he stepped back and looked at it he was shocked—the boy looked like a moron. He changed the lights. He tried every arrangement. Finally, he put them up above, until they came down on the boy's face. Then he stood back and smiled, for the boy looked like an angel.

That is a wonderful story. When you look at men from merely the earthly level some do look like morons. Others look inferior, and it is so easy to feel, "Those people do not matter." But when we look at man, any man, through the eyes of the Christian faith, with the light streaming down on him from God, then you see the divinity in him. All life becomes sacred, and you say, "I must not kill—I must help to live."

One of the high moments of *Quo Vadis* was in the arena at night. Queen Lygia had been captured in the early days of Christianity and brought to Rome. Also, her servant Ursus, a giant. Both were Christians and were to be fed to the lions. Their hour came, thousands were in the arena, and the giant Ursus was led to the center. He kneels in prayer and intends to stay on his knees, offering no resistance. Then dashes in a wild bull, with Lygia the object of his fury.

Seeing the danger of his queen, Ursus seizes the horns of the bull. It was a tremendous struggle, brute strength is pitted against the strength and heart of the giant. Slowly the feet of each sinks into the sand and then slowly the head of the bull begins to go down. In the quietness the people hear the cracking of the bones in the bull's neck as Ursus breaks it. Gently Ursus frees his queen and carries her to safety.

That is the positive side of living. Such beasts as hate, greed, prejudice, war, ignorance, poverty, disease, leave us unmoved until they endanger someone we love. It is then we exert all our strength against them. And as we come to love all men, so we enter the war against all enemies of men.

One thing more. I know a man who, though well past seventy years, is spending the major portion of his energy in helping to build a school. He told me that he would never be able to see many of the children who would be blessed by his school, but he knew they would be coming and he wanted to prepare for them. That same man is concerned about the conservation of natural resources, about every matter which will make life fuller for the next generation. So much concerned that he gives himself for—

> *The day in whose clear-shining light,*
> *All wrong shall stand revealed,*
> *When justice shall be clothed with might,*
> *And every hurt be healed.*
> —Frederick L. Hosmer

CHAPTER VII

Thou Shalt Not Commit Adultery

FOR A MINISTER to speak on the Seventh Commandment
—"Thou shalt not commit adultery"—requires unusual tact
and reverence, lest even his rebukes should be like the lights
of the Pharos, which sometimes helped to wreck the vessels
they were meant to save. It is a sin which should be discussed
as little as possible, but, since God lists it in seriousness next
to murder, and since a large area of our modern society tends
to consider it more a harmless moral breach than a breaking
of God's eternal law, we need to be reminded that God says,
"Thou shalt not . . ."

Morris Wee tells that one day his theological professor said
to the class, "About fifty per cent of all human misery is
caused by the violation of this commandment." That seems
an extreme statement—"About fifty per cent . . ." The students
did not believe it, but after a score of years in the ministry,
Dr. Wee says he now knows it is so. Sit with me in my study in
a church on a main thoroughfare of a great city. Listen to my
telephone, read my mail, talk with many who come in person.
You, too, will begin to believe the professor was right.

Let me ask three questions which I shall try to answer:
What is adultery? Why is it wrong? What can one who has
violated the law do about it?

Adultery is violation of the marriage vow of faithfulness to each other. Any sex experience outside the marriage bond is adultery. Jesus goes even further and says lust in our hearts, even though unexpressed, is adultery (Matthew 5:27, 28). We know that sometimes wrong thoughts slip into the mind and we cannot help it, but to turn that thought into lust means to keep it in the mind, secretly to enjoy it, to make friends with it.

It is wrong because God said it is wrong. He said it is wrong because it hurts people. Any person who has any conscience at all feels a deep sense of guilt over the violation of this law. People have told me of stealing and justifying it to the point where they feel they have done no wrong. A man can even commit murder under certain circumstances and not feel he has done wrong. But I have never had one person to name the sin of adultery and seek to justify it. We know it is wrong, and there is no circumstance under which it can be justified. Thus, having broken the law, our mind becomes wounded. David's reaction to the transgression of this law is universal: "My sin is ever before me" (Psalm 51:3).

It is wrong because it brings further wrong. A wound in the mind is like a wound in the body. Cut a finger and it won't hurt much, but if the cut becomes infected, the infection will get into the blood stream, course through the body and eventually kill one. Sorrow is a wound. It cuts deeply and hurts terribly, but it is a clean wound, and, unless bitterness, resentment or self-pity gets into the wound, it will heal. But when I do wrong the result is an unclean wound, which will not heal. It robs me of my peace of mind, it makes my conscience hurt, it distorts my thinking, it sets up conflicts within me, it weakens my will power, it destroys my soul.

Phillips Brooks said, "Keep clear of concealment, keep clear of the need of concealment. It is an awful hour when the first necessity of hiding anything comes. When there are eyes to be avoided and subjects which must not be touched, then the whole bloom of life is gone."

The main reason adultery is wrong is that it destroys marriage. You remember the lovely scene in the story, "Mrs. Miniver." They had just acquired a new car and she also had a new hat. When they go to bed that night they are not sleepy but are thinking of their good fortune. Mrs. Miniver says, "We are the luckiest people." Her husband asks, "Why, because of the new car or the new hat?" "No dear, it is because we have each other." For a happy marriage, a lot of things are not necessary. Money and the things that money can buy are good to have but can be done without. But in marriage there are two things which must exist. First, a solid affection, a love for each other entirely different from the love for anyone else. Second, complete trust in each other. Adultery destroys both.

Beautiful was the custom of the Cherokee Indians. In the marriage ceremony the couple would join hands across a running stream to signify that forever their lives would flow together.

Suppose one is guilty of adultery, can anything be done about it? Turn to the eighth chapter of St. John's Gospel and read there how a guilty one was brought before Jesus. The crowd had no solution but to stone her. They asked Jesus' opinion. His solution to any wrong never was stoning. He hated the sin but He never ceased to love the sinner.

When I was a little boy living in Tate, Georgia, I once was deeply impressed with a story I heard Mr. Sam Tate tell. There was an habitual drunkard in the community, and one morning he said, "Sam, the boys rocked me last night." "Maybe they were trying to make a better man out of you," replied Mr. Tate. "Well," the poor fellow said, "I never heard of Jesus throwing rocks at a man to make him better."

In the midst of the crowd with the guilty woman before Him Jesus said nothing. Instead, He stooped down and began writing on the ground. I wonder what He wrote. After a while, He spoke softly, yet so all could hear, "He that is without sin among you, let him cast the first stone." Again He stooped down and wrote on the ground. Perhaps He knew the crowd of self-righteous people who were always ready to push some-body further down. My guess is He wrote such words as "liar," "thief," "hypocrite." One by one, the men who were so ready to condemn dropped their rocks and shame-facedly slipped away.

Now comes one of the grandest scenes in the entire Bible. The matchless Saviour is alone with the woman. Not one harsh word comes from His lips. Not even a look of rebuke. Instead, gently and tenderly He says, "Neither do I condemn thee: go, and sin no more." In my mind I see her as she stands. She rises to her full height, her chin goes up and her shoulders back as the burden of her soul is lifted. She is caught up in the power of new self-respect and another chance.

Tradition has it that it was she who stood by Mary, the virgin mother, at the foot of the cross that day. Also, that it was she who first received the message of His resurrection and was given the blessed privilege of telling others. To announce His birth, God sent His angels from heaven. That privilege was not given to mortal man. But to tell of His living again, this fallen one was selected. Whatever my sin, Christ, and Christ alone, can take away the guilt and let me live again.

CHAPTER VIII

Thou Shalt Not Steal

Goᴅ's ᴇɪɢʜᴛʜ rule for life, "Thou shalt not steal," is the foundation of our entire economic system, because it recognizes the fact that one has a right, a God-given right, to work, earn, save, and own. To take away from one that which is rightfully his is wrong in the sight of God. In the creation story we are told how God made the earth, the sea and everything on the earth and in the sea. Then He made man and gave to man dominion over His creation (Genesis 1:26). Actually no person owns anything. All belongs to God, but while man is on earth he has the God-given right of possession. To deny any man that right violates the very basis of God's creation.

Since the beginning of time various economic systems have been tried, but only one will really work and that is free enterprise by Godly people. It has been pointed out that the first Christians tried a form of collective ownership, but it also needs to be remembered that their experiment failed and they soon abandoned it. St. Paul writes, "If any would not work, neither should he eat" (II Thessalonians 3:10).

Once Jesus told a story of a man who was taking a journey from Jerusalem down to Jericho. He fell among thieves, who robbed and beat him and left him wounded by the roadside.

61

A priest and a Levite came along, saw the man, but passed by on the other side. A Samaritan came along, helped the man, and made financial provision for his keep while he could not care for himself (Luke 10:30, 37). In that simple story we have clearly demonstrated the three possible philosophies of wealth. The interpretation is not original with me.

First, the philosophy of the thieves is: "What belongs to my neighbor belongs to me and I will take it." There is aggressive stealing—by the robber, the embezzler, and all the others. Included also is such a thing as living beyond one's means. To go in debt without a reasonable probability of being able to pay back is stealing. To fail to give an honest day's work is also stealing. Once a servant girl applied for membership in a church, but could give no evidence of her conversion and was about to be sent away. The pastor asked, "Is there no evidence which would indicate a change of heart?" She replied, "Now I don't sweep under the rugs in the house where I am employed." "It is enough," he said, "we will receive her into our fellowship."

Also, we can steal from another his inner supports. One does not live by bread alone. When Mark Twain married Olivia Langdon she was a very devout Christian. He was so unsympathetic with her faith that gradually she gave up her religious practices. Later, there came into her life a very deep sorrow. He urged, "Livy, lean on your faith." Sadly she told him, "I can't. I haven't any left." To his dying day he was haunted by the fact that he had taken from her that which had meant so much.

Shakespeare put his finger on the worst form of stealing when he told us: "He that filches from me my good name robs me of that which not enriches him and makes me poor indeed." Before repeating something bad about another person, ask yourself these three questions: Is it true? Is it necessary for me to tell it? Is it kind to tell it?

There are many ways of aggressive stealing.

Second, not only can we steal by taking from another, we

also steal by withholding from our fellows. The philosophy of
the priest and Levite in the story of the Good Samaritan was:
"What belongs to me is mine and I will keep it." Some people's
measure of success is how much they can grab hold of and
hold on to. As I go about I see a lot of "coffin" men. They have
room for themselves and nobody else. They live in the spirit of
the little girl who said;

> *I gave a little party this afternoon at three;*
> *'Twas very small, three guests in all, just I, myself and me.*
> *Myself ate up all the sandwiches, while I drank up the tea,*
> *And it was I who ate the pie, and passed the cake to me.*

Jesus told us of such a man. He was very successful and
accumulated more than he needed. What did he do? "I will
pull down my barns, and build greater; and there will I bestow all my fruits and my goods." Saving is a virtue, but a
very dangerous virtue. Every dollar I possess carries with it
a corresponding obligation. This man was so blinded by his
greed that he failed to see his opportunities and his obligations. The result was he lost his soul" (Luke 12:16-21).

The prophet Malachi asked the sobering question, "Will a
man rob God?" He answers by saying we have robbed God
"in tithes and offerings" (Malachi 3:8). It is a clear law of
God that we return unto Him ten per cent of all He permits
us to possess, and it is a fearful thing to come before Him in
judgment with His money that we had kept or used for ourselves.

Third, the Good Samaritan saw his brother's need and his
philosophy was, what belongs to me belongs to others, and I
will share it. Let us never forget that the right of private enterprise and ownership is not something we have earned. Rather
is it our God-given privilege. God expresses His faith in us,
but He also demands an accounting. Ability, talents, opportunity, material resources are really not ours. They are God's
investments in us. And like any wise investor, God expects
dividends. Suppose I put my money into a company and the

officers of the company use all the profits for themselves. I would be cheated. Likewise can we cheat God.

But how can I give to God what is rightfully His? There is only one way; that is in service to others. So, the positive meaning of "Thou shalt not steal" is consecrated service, both of my material resources and of my life. Bernard Shaw once said, "A gentleman is one who puts more into life than he takes out."

One thing more. Once Jesus went home with a man named Zacchaeus. Later on, we hear Zacchaeus saying, "Lord, the half of my goods I give to the poor; and if I have taken any thing from any man I restore him fourfold." Jesus replied, "This day is salvation come to this house" (Luke 19:1,9). Stealing demands restitution. No man has room for both Christ and dishonest gains. He must decide between the two. It is often not an easy decision to make. But it may help to decide by asking ourselves, "For what shall it profit a man, if he shall gain the whole world, and lose his own soul?" (Mark 8:36.)

CHAPTER IX

Thou Shalt Not Bear False Witness Against Thy Neighbor

OF THE Ten Commandments, the one we break the most is the ninth—"Thou shalt not bear false witness against they neighbor." One reason for this is that we talk most about people. Those of great minds discuss ideas, people of mediocre minds discuss events, and those of small minds discuss other people. Most of us have never made much mental development. Another reason we break this commandment is because it ministers to our own pride. It takes some of the sting out of our own failures if we can rub off the glitter of someone else's crown. It is a sure sign of an inferiority complex when a person tells of the faults of another. Back of much gossip is jealousy.

However, hardly anybody feels guilty of violating this law. I have had people confess to me the breaking of every one of the Ten Commandments except this one. I have never heard a person admit gossiping. We say, "I don't mean to talk about him, but . . ." and off we go. We assume a self-righteous attitude which we feel gives us license to condemn sin. But all the time we enjoy talking about the sin, and, in a back-handed way, brag of ourselves because we have not done exactly what the person we are telling about has done.

Sometimes our gossip takes the form of a false sympathy. "Isn't it too bad how Mr. Blank beats his wife? I am so sorry for her." Or maybe we just ask a question. "Is it true that Mr. and Mrs. Blank are on the verge of divorce?" That is the method of the devil. He would not accuse Job of any wrong-doing. Instead, he merely asked, "Doth Job fear God for nought?" (Job 1:9). The mere question raises a suspicion as to Job's sincerity.

Then we gossip just by listening. There cannot be a noise unless there is an ear to hear it. A noise is caused by the vibrations of the ear drums. And neither can there be a bit of gossip without an ear to hear. The law holds the receiver of stolen goods as guilty as the thief. It is really an insult to you for someone to tell you of the vices of another man, because in so doing he is passing judgment, not only on the subject of his gossip, but also on you. If someone tells you a dirty joke his very action is saying that he thinks of you as one interested in dirty jokes. For one to tell you of another's sins means that the gossiper's opinion of you is that you would be glad to know such things. It is really an insult to you.

Usually we do not mean to hurt others whom we talk about. We think of talebearing as a bit of harmless pastime. But let us remember the words of our Lord, "Judge not, that ye be not judged. For with what judgment ye judge, ye shall be judged: and with what measure ye mete, it shall be measured to you again" (Matthew 7:1,2). That statement scares me. It drives me to my knees. I want God to be kinder toward me than I have been toward others. Don't you?

"So live," advised Will Rogers, "that you would not be ashamed to sell the family parrot to the town gossip." That is good advice, but I am afraid not many of us have lived up to it. Therefore, we should remind ourselves of the old saying:

There is so much good in the worst of us,
And so much bad in the best of us,

That it ill behooves the best of us,
To talk about the rest of us.

A modern translation of Jesus' words in Matthew 7:5 is: "Thou hypocrite, first cast out the two by four out of thine own eye; and then shalt thou see clearly to cast out the splinter out of thy brother's eye."

Whenever I think of the ninth commandment, "Thou shalt not bear false witness," I am haunted by a story which Pierre Van Paassen tells in his book, *The Days of Our Years.* I have seen the story quoted in many places, but would like to tell it briefly again. There was a hunchback by the name of Ugolin who fell sick. He never knew his father, and his mother was a drunken outcast. He had a lovely sister named Solange. Because she loved Ugolin so much and because she could get the money to buy his medicine in no other way, she sold her body on the streets.

People talked so harshly that Ugolin drowned himself in the river, and Solange shot herself. For their funeral the little village church was crowded. The minister mounted the pulpit and began his sermon:

"Christians" [the word was like a whip-lash], "Christians, when the Lord of life and death shall ask me on the Day of Judgment, 'Where are thy sheep?' I shall not answer Him. When the Lord asks me the second time, 'Where are thy sheep?' I will yet not answer Him. But when the Lord shall ask me a third time, 'Where are thy sheep?' I shall hang my head in shame and I will answer Him, 'They were not sheep, Lord, they were a pack of wolves.' "

In a recent sermon I said the person who talks about one who sins is worse than the one who actually commits the sin. That is a rather extreme statement which I made extemporaneously in an off-guarded moment. I am not sure it is true. Yet I am not sure it isn't true. What do you think? Before you answer turn over and read the story about Noah getting drunk (Genesis 9:20,27).

Noah was a preacher. Now, it is shameful for any person to

get drunk, but for one who wears the royal purple of the prophet it is a double shame. Noah lay in his tent disgracefully naked. After a while his son Ham came and saw his father and he went out and told it. Noah's two other sons, Shem and Japheth, refused to look upon their father. Instead, they backed into the tent and covered their father with a garment.

Many generations later, when the author of Hebrews writes of the great men of faith, he tells of Noah's mighty work and does not remember his fall against him (Hebrews 11:7). Undoubtedly God forgot it also. Japheth and Shem were blessed of God and they prospered. But Ham, the son who told of his father's nakedness, was cursed and was condemned to the life of a servant. Maybe, after all, he who actually commits the sin comes out better than he who tells about it.

Jim was considered the bad boy of the community. He was blamed for everything. He took his whippings at school without complaint and with no tears. But one year a new schoolteacher came, and when something happened, naturally everyone blamed that boy. He expected the usual beating. Instead, the teacher said, "Now, let Jim tell his side." To the surprise of everyone, Jim began to cry. When the teacher asked, "What is the matter?" Jim replied, "This is the first time anybody ever said I had a side."

One of my favorite verses of Scripture is: "Brethren if a man be overtaken in a fault, ye which are spiritual, restore such a one in the spirit of meekness; considering thyself, lest thou also be tempted" (Galatians 6:1).

CHAPTER X

Thou Shalt Not Covet

GOD'S FINAL rule for life is, "Thou shalt not covet." Of course, that does not mean that all desire is wrong. Without desires, no one would have any ambition, we would not work, we would not make progress. To covet means that I think of myself and of what I can get. God would have us forget ourselves and think of what we can give. This same commandment is stated by Jesus in a positive way. St. Paul quotes Him as saying, "It is more blessed to give than to receive" (Acts 20:35).

The word "covet" comes from a Greek word which means, "grasping for more." No matter how much one gets, he is always discontented, and, eventually, after covetousness drives him unmercifully through life, it kills him and leaves him with nothing. Tolstoy told a story which illustrates the activity of covetousness. A peasant was offered all the land he could walk around in a day. So the man started, hurrying to get around as much as possible. But the exertion he put forth was so great that he fell dead just as he got back to where he had begun. He ended up with nothing.

God gave these ten laws for our good. He wants us to be our very best and to get the most that is possible out of life. His last rule brings us to the very climax of living, which is contentment. That is what we all want. Contentment gives peace and joy in our minds and hearts, which is the reward of living God's way. But this must be the last of the ten rules. Without the other nine, it is impossible to observe. How does one root out of his life wrong desire? It is by filling his life with right desires.

The best summary of the Ten Commandments is the one Jesus gave: "Thou shalt love the Lord they God with all thy heart, and with all thy soul, and with all thy mind. . . . Thou shalt love thy neighbor as thyself" (Matthew 22:37,39). Put God and others first, get something into your mind greater than yourself. In so doing you lose yourself, selfishness is blotted out; instead of making ourselves miserable by what we do not have, we begin to gain the blessed thrill of giving what we can give.

There is a good story of four men who climbed a mountain. The first complained that his feet hurt. The second had a greedy eye and kept wishing for each house and farm he could see. The third saw clouds and was worried for fear that it might rain. But the fourth fixed his eyes on the marvelous view. In looking away from himself and from the valley below, the little worries which made the others so unhappy were unnoticed.

And when in our view appears the vision of God and of opportunities of service to our fellow men, we experience, not misery-giving selfishness, but the fruits of the spirit. In losing our selfish desires, we gain love, joy, peace, long-suffering, gentleness, goodness, faith, meekness, and temperance. Those are the fruits of the spirit, the results of living God's way (Galatians 5:22,23).

As we study the Ten Commandments we become almost overwhelmed by a sense of guilt and of shame. We have not lived up to God's rules; in so many places have we failed.

I do not know what the final Judgment Day of God is like. We have a mental picture of Him sitting as the judge with a big book before Him in which are listed all our transgressions.

Maybe it will not be that way at all. However, one thing we know, there will be a judgment. How will you plead? Did you worship idols in the place of God?—Guilty! Did you fail to live up to your highest belief, profane God's name, pay no respect to His day?—Guilty! Were you untrue to the best of the past, did you fail to support life as you might have done, were you dishonest and unclean?—Guilty! Did you bear false witness, have evil desire?—Guilty!

As we think of tomorrow we are painfully conscious of our inadequacy and our inability to live as we should. We almost give up to hopelessness and despair. Then we think of something else—the greatest something which can occupy a human mind. Let me give here a story of which Morris Wee reminds us.

As a young man, Dr. A. J. Cronin was in charge of a small hospital. One evening he performed an emergency operation on a little boy. It was a very delicate operation, and the doctor felt great relief when the little fellow breathed freely after it was over. He gave orders to the young nurse and went home filled with gratitude for the success. Late that night came a frantic call for the doctor. Everything had gone wrong, and the child was in desperate condition. When Dr. Cronin got to the bedside the boy was dead.

The nurse had become frightened and had neglected her duty. Dr. Cronin decided she should not be trusted again, and he wrote a letter to the board of health which would end her career as a nurse. He called her in and read the letter to her. She listened in shame and misery, saying nothing. Finally, Dr. Cronin asked, "Have you nothing to say?" She shook her head. She had no excuse to offer. Then she did speak, and this is what she said, "Give me another chance."

God gave us these ten rules to live by. Surely His heart has been grieved as again and again we violated them. We stand before Him in shame and misery, condemned without excuse. Not because we deserve it, but because of His infinite mercy, God gives us another chance. "For God so loved the world, that He gave His only begotten Son, that whosoever believeth in Him should not perish, but have everlasting life" (John 3:16).

If you have not broken one of God's commandments, I suppose you do not need the Saviour. But is there one among us who is innocent? We can only sing: "Just as I am, without one plea, but that Thy blood was shed for me." And as we look to the future we triumphantly say with the Apostle, I can do all things through Christ which strengtheneth me" (Philippians 4:13). Through faith in Christ and obedience to His will our sins are forgiven and we have strength for victory tomorrow.

PART III

HOW TO TALK TO GOD

THE LORD'S PRAYER

After this manner therefore pray ye:
Our Father which art in heaven,
Hallowed be thy name.

Thy kingdom come. Thy will be done
in earth, as it is in heaven.

Give us this day our daily bread.

And forgive us our debts, as we forgive
our debtors.

And lead us not into temptation, but
deliver us from evil: For thine is
the kingdom, and the power, and the
glory, for ever. Amen. (Matthew 6:9-13)

CHAPTER I

Not Saying But Praying

THEY STOOD one day on the deck of a ship in the midst of a raging sea. They heard Him say quietly but with authority, "Peace, be still," and they were amazed as the winds and the waves obeyed His voice. He would speak to one paralyzed for many years, and they watched the man get up and walk.

They picked up twelve baskets full of left-overs after a crowd of 5,000 had eaten, yet all He had to begin with was a boy's lunch of five loaves and two fishes. They saw blind people, epileptics, lepers, even mentally deranged, healed with just a word from His lips. They saw the haunting burden of guilt drain out of human faces as He forgave. They heard Him speak as no man ever spoke. They felt the magnetism of His own life.

But their amazing wonder was changed into fearful responsibility when they heard Him say, "As my Father hath sent me, even so send I you." Surely they could not be expected to work His miracles. It was too much to ask of them. But they were filled with an awe-inspiring sense of possibility as He said to them: "Verily, verily, I say unto you, He that believeth on me, the works that I do shall he do also; and greater works than these shall he do; because I go unto my Father."

Could it be true that such power could be theirs? He said so, thus it was so. But how? Would He teach them His secrets? One day the answer burst upon them. There was one golden key to the power-house of God. Eagerly they said, "Lord, teach us to pray" (Luke 11:1). Learning to pray was the one, the only, secret they needed to know.

In response, Jesus gave them a prayer (Matthew 6:9-13). It can be said in one quarter of a minute, just fifteen seconds. Even for a large congregation of people to repeat it slowly takes only half a minute. Yet Jesus would spend half the night praying that same prayer. Today there are 500 million people who can say that prayer, but very few ever learn to pray it. The power comes, not in the saying, but in the praying of the prayer.

Praying is not saying words. Words merely form the frame on which the temple of thought is built. The power of the Lord's Prayer is not in the words, but rather in the pattern of thinking in which our minds are formed. The Bible tells us, "Be ye transformed by the renewing of your mind" (Romans 12:2). When our thoughts begin to flow in the channels of the Lord's Prayer our minds do become new, and we are transformed.

To the extent that we think the thoughts of Christ, to that same extent do we have the power of Christ. We remember how the king in Shakespeare's "Hamlet" miserably fails in prayer. In explanation, he says:

> *"My words fly up, my thoughts remain below;*
> *Words without thoughts never to heaven go."*

That's it! We, too, fail because our prayers are "words without thoughts."

CHAPTER II

Our Father Which Art in Heaven

"Our father which art in heaven," Jesus tells us to pray. If we had only those six words we would have the Lord's Prayer. The other sixty words Jesus gave in the prayer are by way of explanation. Learn really to pray that first phrase and you need go no further.

The word "father" is a definition of God. For us it is an imperfect definition, because we as fathers are imperfect. A preacher who worked with boys in a slum area said he could not refer to God as a father. When those boys thought of father they pictured one who frequently was drunk and beat their mothers. We all put into that word the imperfections of our own fathers.

Thus Jesus could not use merely the term "Father." He must add, "which art in heaven." That phrase is not there to locate God or to tell us where God lives. Somehow, we have made up our minds that heaven is far distant. In one of our most beloved hymns, "The Old Rugged Cross," we sing, "He will call me some day to that home far away." And we think of God as being in that home far away. That is all wrong and not according to the teachings of Jesus. God is as near as the air you breathe.

Rather is "which art in heaven" a description of God. Heaven is synonymous with perfection. Jesus might have said, "Our perfect Father," and it would have been the same thing. And when you think of the term "father" immediately you think not of easy indulgence but of authority. In the very act of recognizing a father you are making yourself a son. And the father has the right of command over his sons.

Therefore, you surrender your own will to His will. It is not what you want but what He wants that becomes your controlling thought. We recognize the fact that God has established a moral order. Man does not create his laws, he merely discovers God's laws. By obedience to those laws we learn with Dante, "His will is our peace."

On the other hand, to fail to recognize the sovereignty of God is to fail in all of life. The seal of one of the Waldensian churches pictures an anvil and a number of broken hammers, with the motto: "Hammer away, ye hostile hands! Your hammers break; God's anvil stands." So, until you can say "Father," you need not attempt to pray further.

However, father means more than ruler or lawgiver or judge. Father signifies a rule of love, it puts mercy into the very heart of judgment. Because love begets love, thus our response to God becomes not one of fear, but of true sonship. St. Paul said it well: "For ye have not received the spirit of bondage again to fear; but ye have received the Spirit of adoption, whereby we cry, Abba, Father" (Romans 8:15).

"Heavenly Father" means not only authority and love, it also means holiness. Once, as Isaiah walked into the church, he heard the seraphims singing, "Holy, holy, holy, is the Lord of hosts." When he saw the spotless purity of God he was convinced and convicted of his own unrighteousness to the point he cries, "Woe is me! for I am undone; because I am a man of unclean lips," and he falls before God in repentance and consecration (Isaiah 6:5).

Why is it we close our eyes when we pray? Perhaps the reason is to shut out the world in order to be able to give our complete attention to God. However, true prayer opens our eyes.

A great Hindu said: "Why are you so anxious to see God with your eyes closed? See Him with your eyes open—in the form of the poor, the starved, the illiterate, and the afflicted." To pray, "Father," means to recognize our sonship, but it also means to recognize our brotherhood.

A young man came in to see me recently. He had spent two years in prison. Sometimes we do not realize the blessings of society until we are shut away from it. He said to me, "I do not want much in life. I only want to belong again." "To belong," that is what we all want. But to pray, "Our Father," means to remove all boundaries and barriers and to make every one of us a child of God.

In this first phrase of the Lord's Prayer is summed up the Christian life. The word "Father" expresses our faith. Not only does it mean that we believe in a God, but also the very word describes Him. "In heaven" includes all our hopes. Meaning perfection, the word "heaven" signifies the quality of life toward which sincere Christians are striving. "Be ye therefore perfect," said Christ, "even as your Father which is in heaven is perfect" (Matthew 5:48).

Man is never satisfied with himself. He is ever striving upward and onward. He can bear the failures of the past and present because he hopes to do better tomorrow. When a friend was looking over the work of William W. Story, the famous sculptor, he asked: "For which of your carvings do you care the most?" To which the sculptor replied: "I care most for the statue I'm going to carve next."

The word "our" means all inclusive love. Without that, prayer is futile. There is no such thing as a solitary religion, because unless we say "brother," we cannot say "Father." Ernest Crosby in his poem, "The Search," says it:

> No one could tell me where my soul might be;
> I sought for God, but God eluded me;
> I sought my brother out and found all three.

Faith—Hope—Love, they are all included.

How it would change my life to really pray, "Our Father which art in heaven." It would throw me on my knees in some Gethsemane in complete obedience to His will. It would lead me to sacrifice my life in serving and seeking to save my fellow man. Most important, it would bring God into my very soul.

Then, no matter what might happen, in complete confidence I could pray, even as my Lord prayed, "Father, into thy hands I commend my spirit" (Luke 23:46). Thus I would have the assurance that I could leave the results of my life in God's hands, knowing that even out of my seeming defeats in life would come glorious triumph. That out of the graves of my life would come resurrections and I would sing with the Apostle, "O death, where is thy sting? O grave, where is thy victory? . . . Thanks be to God, which giveth us the victory through our Lord Jesus Christ" (I Corinthians 15:55,57).

Rarely a week goes by that I do not conduct at least one burial service in West View Cemetery in Atlanta. Ten years ago now we laid my own father to rest there, and, before leaving, I usually go and stand at his grave and think about him. I always feel uplifted.

I think about how good he was to me. How that he gave all he had in a material way to his children, not just food and clothes and the necessities of life. Also balls and bats and the things with which boys wanted to play. He was happy in making us happy. I think about each night he would pray for us, one by one. There is a recording of his voice in my mind as he prays, "Lord, bless Charles. May he grow up to be a good man." "Bless Stanley," he would say. "Bless John—Grace —Blanche—Sarah—Frances." He would have a special prayer for each of us.

Standing there at his grave, I think of his deep honesty, of his high standards. I think of his humility. He was very unpretentious, never seeking much for himself. Our parsonage was usually next door to the church, where day after day people came seeking help. I think of how he always shared what we had, never turning anybody away. Sometimes I forget about time as I stand there thinking about him.

So I feel I understand, at least in a very small way, something of what Jesus meant when He told us to pray, "Our Father." Again and again, our Lord would go out into the mountains alone to pray. He would often stay all night. On one occasion he even stayed forty days, forgetting time, even forgetting to eat. There in the quietness He would think about His Father.

And He tells us that is the way to pray, "Our Father which art in heaven." We are not asking God for something, instead we open the way for the inflow of God into us. Norman Vincent Peale tells of his first visit to the Grand Canyon. He met a man who had spent much time at the canyon, so he asked which trip he should take in order to see the most possible of the canyon.

The wise old man told him if he really wanted to see the canyon he should not take any of the trips at all. Instead, he should come out early in the morning and take a seat on the rim, sit there and watch the morning pass into noontime and the noontime into afternoon, with the everchanging colors gleaming across the great canyon. Then get a quick supper and return to watch the purple twilight come over the vast abyss. The old man said that if one runs around, he merely wears himself out and misses the beauty and greatness of it all.

Well, that is what the old prophet said about God in the long ago, "They that wait on the Lord shall renew their strength" (Isaiah 40:31). What does it mean to "wait on the Lord"? It means to think about God, though "think" is hardly the word. To meditate better expresses it, to contemplate is still better. Or as the Psalmist put it, "Be still, and know that I am God" (46:10).

H. G. Wells said, "Until a man has found God he begins at no beginning and works to no end." So you are not ready to pray until first your mind has been possessed by thoughts of

God. For several years now I have watched hundreds of people kneel in prayer at the altar in the closing moments of the Sunday night service. Many have told me of amazing results of those prayers.

The reason why those altar prayers are so much more meaningful for many is because they come at the close of the service. For an hour or more the sacred building has been reminding them of the person of God. The hymns, the reading of the Bible, the sermon, the presence of other worshiping people, all work together to make one aware of the nearness of God. Then, when one kneels to pray his mind is properly conditioned, his thinking is Godly. Thus his prayer is natural and real. His words and his thoughts are the same.

"Our Father which art in heaven"—when those words become real to us we become quiet and confident. As the little verse expresses it:

> *Said the Robin to the Sparrow,*
> *"I should really like to know*
> *Why these anxious human beings*
> *Rush around and worry so."*

> *Said the Sparrow to the Robin,*
> *"Friend, I think that it must be*
> *That they have no Heavenly Father,*
> *Such as cares for you and me."*
> —ELIZABETH CHENEY

CHAPTER III

Hallowed Be Thy Name

JESUS TEACHES us that there are six things for which man should pray. But before man can begin the other five petitions he must pray. "Hallowed by thy name." Once Moses was out on a hillside watching the sheep. He saw a bush on fire which continued to burn without burning up. After a time Moses went over to see about it.

Actually, God was in that bush, ready to reveal His will for Moses' life, but as Moses approached he heard a voice saying, "Put off thy shoes from off thy feet, for the place whereon thou standest is holy ground" (Exodus 3:5). The meaning of this is that before God speaks to man man must have proper respect and reverence.

Many people never think of praying except in time of crisis. That is when we have a need which we ourselves cannot meet. And our prayers concern only ourselves, what we want God to do for us. That is why so few people really pray with power. Jesus says that first we must have God in our minds. To "hallow" means to respect and reverence.

But notice, Jesus does not tell us to hallow God's name. Rather is it a prayer, which means asking God to do something that we are unable to do. Thus we are asking God to hallow His own name. Profane man can do nothing for God until first God has done something for man. Suppose an artist, even the greatest artist of all time, said, "I shall go out and paint the sky." We would laugh at him. So man cannot hallow the name of God. If you tried to blacken the sky with a tar brush, you would succeed only in getting tar over yourself. The sky would remain as it is. So what does Jesus mean by this prayer?

The emphasis is not on the word "hallow" but on "name." The Bible is a book of names. Every name has a meaning, given to reveal the character of the person. For example, the name "Jesus" means "God is Salvation." Thus the angel said to Joseph: "Thou shalt call his name Jesus: for he shall save his people from their sins" (Matthew 1:21).

When Andrew brought his brother to Christ the Lord said, "Thou art Simon the son of Jona," which name means "shifting sand," which was descriptive of him. But under the influence of Christ he would become a different person. So Jesus says his name will be changed: "Thou shalt be called Cephas, which is by interpretation, A stone," something strong and unshakable (John 1:42).

To know a person's name was to know the person. Thus God's "name" means His nature revealed. So "Hallowed be thy name" really means, "Reveal thyself to me, O God." In the long ago Job asked, "Canst thou by searching find out God?" (Job 11:7). The answer is no. Man can know God only as God chooses to reveal Himself.

Walter de la Mare asks a question that we all sometimes ask. As he prays he wonders, "Is there anybody there?" Before you can pray you must be sure there is a Somebody to hear, and be conscious of His presence.

There are three ways—maybe four—in which God reveals Himself. First, in His marvelous creation. "The heavens declare the glory of God; and the firmament showeth his handiwork" (Psalm 19:1). That is the first revelation God made of

Himself. We stand at the seashore and are moved by the boundless expanse before us. When we remember that He can hold all the seas in "the hollow of his hand" (Isaiah 40:12), then we see something of His power. As we stand among great mountain peaks, His majesty is impressed upon us.

Jesus stood reverently before a wild "lily of the field" and saw the glory of God (Matthew 6:28,29). "Earth's crammed with heaven, and every common bush afire with God," sings Mrs. Browning. We look into the heavens and see the infiniteness of God, at a tiny snowflake and see His perfection. The sunset teaches us of His beauty.

Yet modern man is in danger of letting his own conceit blot out this revelation of God. Instead of praying for rain, we talk about making rain ourselves. We seed clouds, but who made the clouds? Jesus introduces us to a character much like ourselves. "The ground of a certain rich man brought forth plentifully; and he thought within himself, saying, What shall I do, because I have no room where to bestow my fruits? . . . I will pull down my barns, and build greater; and there will I bestow all my fruits and my goods" (Luke 12:16,18). I—I— I; My—My—My. There is no sense of God. God the creator he does not see.

Second, God reveals Himself through people. Through Moses we glimpse God's law, Amos showed us His justice, Hosea His love, and Micah His ethical standards. Someone was kind when we were sick, helped in time of trouble, was friendly when we were lonely. Someone we had wronged forgave in a spirit of love. In all such acts a little of God is revealed unto us. You better understand God because of the love of your mother, the consecrated life of some friend, the heroism of some Joan d'Arc. Corporate worship is so much more rewarding because we learn from each other.

God's supreme revelation of Himself is in Christ. "He that hath seen me hath seen the Father." As Harry Webb Farrington sang:

I know not how that Bethlehem's Babe
Could in the Godhead be.
I only know the manger Child
Has brought God's life to me.

I know not how that Calvary's cross
A world of sin could free.
I only know its matchless love
Has brought God's love to me.

I know not how that Joseph's tomb
Could solve death's mystery;
I only know a living Christ,
Our immortality.

As you read the four Gospels and see Jesus you begin to realize that you are actually seeing God.

One other way God reveals Himself. I have no name or explanation for it. We may call it the "still, small voice," or the impress of His spirit on us. But I can testify that there are times, perhaps rare times, when you feel you have received a direct word from Him. Samuel heard God directly.

As we know God, so can we pray, "Hallowed by thy name," that is "make us surer of Thee, O God, that we may understand Thee more fully." And as our minds are filled with God, as we steadily gaze upon Him, the little sins which so easily beset us lose their power over us, and we become both willing and able to hear and obey Him. That condition we must meet in order to pray with power.

CHAPTER IV

Thy Kingdom Come

"THY KINGDOM COME" is the second thing for which Jesus told us to pray. The very word "kingdom" is offensive to Amercans. "Democracy" is our word. We demand the right to govern ourselves. Kipling refers to us as a people among whom each man "dubs his dreary brethren Kings." Especially today do we rebel against dictators and totalitarianism. In fact, some of us assert the right of self-rule even to the point of dethroning God.

But we need to be reminded that in one sense God's kingdom has already come. His laws govern the universe with absolute authority. The scientist knows the law of God. He sees it in the precision of the cosmos. The physician will tell you there are certain laws of health. To obey them is to have health—to disobey them is to die. The psychiatrist understands that a man's pattern of thinking must be along right lines. To turn off the track is to become unbalanced. Even the sociologist teaches us that the good of one is the good of all. We are bound together in a common brotherhood, which is a law of God.

God established His kingdom on earth, which means His law and His rule. It is here right now. Whether we like it or not, His rule is upon us. As the prophet said in the long ago: "The soul that sinneth, it shall die" (Ezekiel 18:4).

We see the capitol building of our state. We know the governor and members of the legislature. We think of how man makes his laws. Yet every law of my state can be repealed or amended. There will be other governors and legislators.

Not so with the laws of God. I could rebel against God's law of gravitation and step out the window of a high building. But I would only destroy myself. I would not change the law. So I go down on an elevator. Is that not overcoming God's law with man's mechanical genius? No. Suppose the cable of the elevator breaks. It has happened. And the very fact that the elevator makers use such strong cables and regularly inspect them is a recognition of God's law and obedience to it.

This world is God's kingdom. It is under His sovereign rule and power, controlled by laws. However, in foolish disobedience, man rushes on to destroy himself. Will we ever come to our senses? Will we ever recognize the law of God to the point of surrender and obedience to it? There are many who say no. They are so depraved, so corrupted by egoism and so blinded by pride, that they cannot see the right way and have not the will to obey, even if they could.

Thus on every hand we hear destruction predicted for the world. We have eternal hell preached as our inescapable punishment. We are shouted at by would-be prophets who see no hope, but only the terror of an angry God's judgment. But Jesus said pray, "Thy kingdom come." Surely He believed not only in its possibility but in the actual event.

One night Jesus locked the door of His little carpenter's shop for the last time. He must be about His "Father's business." That business was to bring God's kingdom on earth. The text of His very first sermon was, "The kingdom of heaven is at hand" (Matthew 4:17). That was the one theme of His preaching all the way. He never lost His faith, and even on the resurrection side of the grave He talked to His disciples of the kingdom of God (Acts 1:3).

As we pray, "Thy kingdom come," it is well to underscore the word "come." It is so much easier to pray, "Thy kingdom go." It is not nearly as hard to pray for the conversion of Africa and to give offerings for missions as it is to face up honestly to the sins of our own lives, to repent and change our ways.

It is easier to crusade piously for world peace than it is to forgive someone who has done us wrong or whom we have wronged. David Livingstone sought out the savage with the word of God, but first he dedicated himself. Even the last day of his life he wrote in his diary, "My Jesus, my King, my Life, my All, I again dedicate my whole self to Thee."

There is a verse of Scripture that literally haunts me. I have the blessed privilege of preaching to many people. During the very week I am writing these words I am visiting in Columbia, the capital city of South Carolina, preaching in one of the largest churches of the state. Each night the great auditorium is being filled and many are being turned away. Yet there is something much harder than preaching to others. St. Paul said: "But I keep under my body, and bring it into subjection: lest that by any means, when I have preached to others, I myself should be a castaway" (I Cor. 9:27). If the greatest Christian preacher of all time was in danger of becoming a castaway, how much more so is it true for me.

"Thy kingdom come." It means that I look into my own heart and plead for God's cleansing power. It means that I bow before Him in faith and obedience.

Archibald Rutledge told the story of meeting a Negro turpentine worker whose faithful dog had died a few moments earlier in a great forest fire because he would not desert his master's dinner pail, which he had been told to watch. With tears in his face, the old Negro said: "I always had to be careful what I tol' him to do, 'cause I knowed he'd do it." That is what this prayer means.

Jesus said, "The kingdom of heaven is like unto a merchant man, seeking goodly pearls: who, when he had found one pearl of great price, went and sold all that he had, and bought it" (Matthew 13:45,46). The pearls he sold meant a lifetime of labor. They represented all he had. Yet the one pearl was worth all else. So, to really pray, "Thy kingdom come," means I am willing to surrender everything I possess in order to possess God. God demands our all or nothing at all.

It is so much easier for me to talk about the sins of the world, the corruption of government, for instance, or the evils of liquor, or the filthy literature and motion pictures, or the honky-tonks around town, or the heathens in China. But before I pray about where God's kingdom is needed, first let it come to me.

Jonathan Edwards, one of the most effective preachers America ever knew, so prayed. He said, "I go out to preach with two propositions in mind. First, every person ought to give his life to Christ. Second, whether or not anyone else gives Him his life, I will give Him mine."

The apostle said, "Let all bitterness, and wrath, and anger, and clamor, and evil speaking, be put away from you, with all malice: And be ye kind one to another, tenderhearted, forgiving one another, even as God for Christ's sake hath forgiven you" (Ephesians 4:31,32). That is what the coming of God's kingdom means for us, and when it comes, then we can spread it forth with power. Unrighteous people are not very powerful crusaders for a righteous world. As the spiritual tells us: "It ain't my brother, it ain't my sister, it's me, O Lord, standing in the need of prayer."

"Thy kingdom come." When that prayer is answered, then we shall have no doubt of the power of God's kingdom to cover the earth.

CHAPTER V

Thy Will Be Done in Earth, As It Is in Heaven

To PRAY with power, Jesus teaches us we must first get God in our minds and recognize His sovereignty. We must pray, "Thy will be done." Right there many people hesitate, lose their nerve, and turn away from God. I think I know why.

When I was studying psychology in college I worked out a number of word tests which I would use on my congregations. For example, say to a person the word "Christmas" and ask that person the first word which comes into his mind. I would get such answers as Santa Claus, decorations, gifts, etc. Rarely would Christ be mentioned. So I would conclude we had commercialized and paganized the Lord's birthday. I think the test was valid, with some limitations.

Well, let's try it on ourselves. I will name a phrase and check your first thought. "Will of God." What does that bring to your mind? The death of a loved one, or some great disaster, or severe suffering from some incurable disease, or some hard sacrifice. Most people will think of some dark picture in relation to the will of God.

Perhaps one cause is our Lord's prayer in Gethsemane, "Nevertheless not my will, but thine be done" (Luke 22:42). And from His surrender to God's will we see Christ walking up Calvary and being nailed to a cross. So God's will and crosses come to be synonymous terms for us.

However, we can go back further. There was Job. He lost his wealth, his children were killed, he suffered in body, and his wife deserted him. Job associated all those disasters with God, so he says, "The Lord gave, and the Lord hath taken away; blessed be the name of the Lord" (Job 1:21). So, when our hearts are broken we say, "It is the Lord's will." Naturally we shrink from such a will.

It seems to be a general belief that the will of God is to make things distasteful for us, like taking bad tasting medicine when we are sick, or going to the dentist. Yet we think we would be much happier if we disregarded God's will. We never say, "No, I forever turn my back on God's will." But we do say, "For the time being I will back my own judgment and follow my own will."

Somebody needs to tell us that sunrise is also God's will. There is the time of harvest, the harvest which will provide food and clothes for us, without which life could not be sustained on earth. God ordered the seasons, they are His will. In fact, the good things in life far outweigh the bad. There are more sunrises than cyclones.

I live comfortably during the winter in an automatically steam-heated house. Long before I was born God stored up the gas in the ground which is now being piped into my home for my good. I might say that cold winter freezes are God's will, but I must also know that the warmth God has provided is also His will. Whether you shrink from His will or gratefully surrender to it depends on how you look at it.

Jesus said, "Thy will be done in earth, as it is in heaven." "As in heaven," He said. What do you think of when the word "heaven" comes to your mind? You think of peace, plenty, perfect joy, the absence of pain and suffering and tears. John saw it all and recorded his vision in Revelation 21. That is exactly what we want here and now in our own lives.

Jesus says that is God's will for us.

Before you can pray, "Thy will be done," you must believe it is the best and happiest way. However, sometimes we surrender to the immediate, while God considers life as a whole. For example, here are two boys in school. The will of the teacher is that they spend hours in hard studying. One of the boys rebels against the unpleasant work. He wants to be happy, so he goes to a picture show. Maybe he quits school altogether to go his carefree way.

The other boy sticks to his studies, difficult though they may be. Look at those same two boys ten or twenty years later. The carefree boy is now bound and limited by his own ignorance. He endures hardships and embarrassments caused by his lack of training. The other boy is freer, happier, and finds life easier and more rewarding because he was properly prepared.

There was Joseph, the darling of his father Jacob's heart. Home was for him a place of great joy. But jealousy welled up in his brothers, who put Joseph in a dark well, and later sold him into slavery. Later those same brothers stood before him in need. Joseph said to them: "Be not grieved, nor angry with yourselves, that ye sold me hither: for God did send me before you to preserve life" (Genesis 45:5).

Surely Joseph's way was hard. But he kept his faith, never giving up, and at the end he could look back and see, as we read in "Hamlet," "There's a divinity that shapes our ends." Out of the surrender of our Lord in Gethsemane did come a cross, but beyond the cross lay an empty tomb and a redeemed world.

Sometimes it is not God who leads us through deep valleys and dark waters. It may be man's ignorance and folly. But even then we can feel His presence, for out of our mistakes God can make something beautiful. God did not bring Job's tragedies. But because of Job's faith God could use those tragedies for Job's final good. It is wonderful what God can do with a broken heart when we give Him all the pieces.

Not only is God's way the best and happiest, it is also within our reach. Many shrink from God's will because of a fear that God will ask them to do more than they can do. There was the man of one talent who buried it in the earth. In explaining his failure, his not even trying, he said to his master: "Lord, I knew thee that thou art an hard man . . . and I was afraid, and went and hid thy talent in the earth" (Matthew 25:24, 25).

He was afraid of unreasonable demands by his master. He felt that even his best could not please his master. There are some things we cannot do. Not many of us can be great artists. Conspicuous leadership is beyond the reach of most. We could list thousands of things we cannot do.

But of one thing we can be sure, we can do the will of God. Moses thought he couldn't. When God told him to lead the children of Israel out of bondage he made excuses. He sincerely felt it was beyond his abilities. But he did it. With complete faith and confidence, you can pray, "Thy will be done," because God is a loving father who knows His children better than they know themselves. He wants our best, but He expects no more.

To pray, "Thy will be done," is really an enlistment for action. In 1792 William Carey preached a sermon on the text: "Enlarge the place of thy tent, and let them stretch forth the curtains of thine habitations: spare not, lengthen thy cords, and strengthen thy stakes" (Isaiah 54:2).

It was one of the most influential sermons ever preached on this earth, because the result was the birth of the Baptist Missionary Society, the story of which a hundred books could not begin to tell. In that sermon Carey made his famous statement: "Expect great things from God, attempt great things for God."

But here is the important point. He not only preached about missions, he gave up all he had and went himself to India as a missionary. He prayed literally, "in earth as it is in heaven." He meant the whole earth and he dedicated his life in answer to his own prayer.

Recently a letter came asking me to pray that no child would ever again be born crippled. The letter quotes the Bible: "It is not the will of your Father which is in heaven, that one of these little ones should perish." (Matthew 18:14). Having three children of my own, certainly I can pray that no malformed child be born.

But we have got to work with God toward that end. We put into our national budget fifty billion dollars for armament. When we consider fighting diseases we talk about giving nickels and dimes. Who knows but that if the money we have spent on atomic bombs had been used in medical research, we would not now have the answers for cancer, arthritis, and many other diseases.

We feel compelled to maintain our vast program of defense. Yet whose fault is it? If we had spent on Christian missions in Japan the cost of one battleship which the Japanese sank at Pearl Harbor, we might never have had that war. If we had maintained a Christian spirit in Germany after World War I, Hitler might never have been heard of.

Actually, God's will is on earth. It is operating in your very life. For example, you did not decide in what century you would be born. You were not free to choose who your parents would be. The color of your skin, your sex, your physical appearance, all were decided by a higher will, God's will.

And God's will is in operation in our lives. There is a purpose for your life. I believe no person is an accident. Before you were born on the earth you existed in the mind of God. You can rebel against God, but ultimately you will be totally defeated. You can endure life as it comes, and find no joy and peace in it. Or you can choose the will of God and make His will your will.

As Tennyson put it: "Our wills are ours, we know not how; our wills are ours, to make them thine."

How can I know the will of God for my life? Many will never know, because God does not reveal Himself to triflers. No one can walk into His holy presence on hurrying feet. If you merely pray, "Lord, this is my will, I hope you will approve," you are wasting your breath. Only those who sincerely want God's will, and have faith enough in Him to dedicate themselves to His will, can ever know it. To pray, "Lord, show me Thy will. If I like it I will accept it," is a futile prayer. You must accept it before you know it. Whether or not you can do that depends on what opinion you have of God.

To the sincere, God reveals His will in many ways. Often we learn through the process we call insight. A psychiatrist said to me once, "Either a person has insight or he hasn't. It isn't something which can be learned." But it is something which God can give.

I have talked with people who have baffling problems. Maybe they have tossed many weary hours trying to sleep, but could not because of a problem. In the quietness of the pastor's study we have talked about God and His love and concern for us. After a prayer, we talked about the problem. And not once, but many times, I have seen a light on their faces, as suddenly the answer came, a solution came to mind. I say God gave them insight. Sometimes it is called the "inner light."

God may reveal His will through the advice of others, through circumstances, through the experiences of history, through the discovery of His laws by scientific investigation, through the voice of His Church. Certainly we see His will as we study the life and teachings of Jesus.

I have a little radio that I carry in my bag. At home I can hear any station in Atlanta I turn to. But if I get too far away the voice of the station is blotted out. It is the same radio—the station is broadcasting with the same power. But I have gone too far away. Many miss God's voice because they are too far away from Him.

The assurance that you are within the will of God does more to eliminate the fears and worries of life than any other one thing. I quote Dante: "In His will is our peace." Surrender to His will takes the dread out of tomorrow. We know, absolutely we know, that if we do His will today, tomorrow will be according to His will. I am not a fatalist, instead I can say with the Psalmist, "I have not seen the righteous forsaken" (37:25). Obedience to His will today means that God assumes the responsibility for our tomorrow.

So, Jesus teaches us that the first three petitions of our prayer must be with our eyes fixed firmly on God. There is a place in prayer to talk about our own needs, and our Lord assures us it is right to pray for ourselves, but first God must fill our minds before we come to our own problems. Then we are ready to talk about what we want Him to do for us.

CHAPTER VI

Give Us This Day Our Daily Bread

IN THE middle of the Lord's Prayer there is a distinct division. You see it in the pronouns. In the first three petitions we are taught to say "Thy," "Thy name," "Thy kingdom," "Thy will." But in the last three petitions are "us" and "our." First, we think of God, then we can rightfully think of ourselves.

And the very first petition our Lord permits us to pray for ourselves is the one we really want to pray. In fact, it is the one we must pray if we plan to stay alive. "Give us this day our daily bread." By that He means simply the physical necessities of life.

Many of the early church fathers, such as Jerome, Origen, and Augustine taught that this petition was for the same bread which Jesus refers to when He says, "I am the bread of life" (John 6:35). They felt it was wrong to pray for material blessings. And that idea persists to this day.

But why try to spiritualize this petition? After all, even a saint must eat. Even our very prayers would die on our lips if we did not have food to sustain our bodies. Jesus preached to the people, He healed the sick, He forgave their sins, and He also used his marvelous power to feed them real bread.

Study our Lord's life. You will see He knew something

about the everyday struggle to make ends meet. He knew the meaning of the widow's two mites, what a disaster the loss of a coin might be, wearing clothes which were patched. He knew about shopping in the grocery store to try to stretch a budget to feed the family. He talks about the housewife who must buy two birds which sold for a penny.

Even on the resurrection side of the grave our Lord was concerned with bread. We see Him walking home with two of His friends on that first Easter Sunday. He spoke hope to their hearts and He also took time to sit at the table with them. In fact, the Bible says, "He took bread, and blessed it, and brake, and gave to them" (Luke 24:30).

In the gray dawn of the morning we see Him on the seashore. His disciples had been fishing all night. Now they were coming in, and the Lord was prepared for them. What did He prepare? A prayer meeting? They needed prayer. A majestic and overwhelming revelation of Himself? They had lost faith in Him. No, He prepared breakfast.

The risen, resplendent Christ cooking breakfast! Though His feet were bruised, He walked over a rocky beach to gather firewood. Though His hands were nailpierced, He cleaned fish. He knew that the fishermen would be hungry.

He knows we have groceries to buy, rent or payments to make on our houses, clothes that are necessary, expenses for the children in school, bills of every sort to meet. Not only that, He knows we have desires and wants beyond our bare necessities. We are not wild beasts. We want some of the pleasant things of life.

Much better than we, He knew that the body and the soul are an inseparable unity. Just as worry and fear can affect the body and make one sick, so one's physical condition can affect a man's outlook on life, his religious faith, his moral conduct.

The God who made our bodies is concerned about the needs of our bodies and He is anxious for us to talk with Him about our physical needs.

Every morning the sun rises to warm the earth. If it were to fail to shine for just one minute, all life on the earth would die. The rains come to water the earth. There is fertility in the soil, life in the seeds, oxygen in the air. The providence of God is about us in unbelievable abundance every moment. But so often we just take it for granted.

Dr. John Witherspoon was a great American and a man of God. He was one of the signers of the Declaration of Independence and president of the College of New Jersey which later became Princeton. He lived about two miles from the college and drove over in his buggy each day.

One morning a neighbor came excitedly into his study and said, "Dr. Witherspoon, you must join me in giving thanks to God for His providence in saving my life. As I was driving this morning the horse ran away and the buggy was smashed to pieces on the rocks, but I escaped unharmed."

"Why," answered Dr. Witherspoon, "I can tell you a far more remarkable providence than that. I have driven over that road hundreds of times. My horse never ran away, my buggy never was smashed, I was never hurt. God's providence has been for me even more remarkable than it has been for you."

All of us know so well Maltbie D. Babcock's little verse:

> Back of the loaf is the snowy flour,
> And back of the flour the mill,
> And back of the mill is the wheat and the shower,
> And the sun and the Father's will.

The same is true of everything you have—the new television set you enjoy, or the nice car in which you take such great pride, or the home in which you live, or the clothes you are now wearing. All of those things come from the earth which God made. He put those things within our reach because He knew we would want them and would enjoy them. Long before you were born, God answered your prayer for material blessings. "Give us this day our daily bread" is a prayer that has truly been answered. It is also a recognition of what He has already done. I like to read that story of Jesus in the wilderness. Matthew tells us there were five thousand people with Him (14:21). They were hungry, and the Lord wanted them fed. The disciples surveyed the situation, and all the food they could find was a little boy's lunch of five loaves and two small fishes.

The disciples felt this was too little with which to bother. With such meager resources, there was no need to try. But watch the Lord's actions. No complaint from Him about not having more. Instead, the first thing He did was give thanks for it. Then He started using what He had. He began breaking and passing the food out.

To the astonishment of all, what He had was enough to feed everyone. In fact, they had more than they needed, and there were twelve baskets of food left over. The people were so amazed that immediately they tried to take Him by force and make him a king (John 6:5-15).

If today we would begin being thankful for what we have, and use it as best we can, God would give us insight as to how we could multiply what we have to cover every need of our lives, and have a lot left over. We would be so blessed that we would fall before Him as our Lord and King.

CHAPTER VII

And Forgive Us Our Debts, As We Forgive Our Debtors

JESUS GIVES us six petitions to make. Three concern God, and three are for ourselves. All six of them are of supreme importance, yet there is one of the six on which He turns the spotlight. He does not find it necessary to emphasize that we pray that God's name be hallowed, or that God's kingdom come, or that His will be done, vital as those are.

He does not emphasize our need for bread, yet without bread we would all die. But after the Lord's Prayer is completed, our Lord feels He should turn back and lift one petition out for special comment. "And forgive us our debts, as we forgive our debtors" is the prayer He spotlights. He says, "But if ye forgive not men their trespasses, neither will your Father forgive your trespasses" (Matthew 6:15).

It isn't that God forgives on an exchange basis. Our forgiveness of others is not a condition of God's forgiveness of us. Rather is it a condition of our ability to receive the forgiveness of God. We are told by Shakespeare, "The quality of mercy is not strain'd, it droppeth as the gentle rain from heaven." But I could cover a plant with a sheet of iron and the rain could not get to it. So, I can surround my soul with an unforgiving spirit and completely block the forgiving mercy of God.

A wrong spirit toward another person may or may not hurt him, but it is certain to destroy my own soul. Booker T. Washington understood it when he said, "I will not permit any man to narrow and degrade my soul by making me hate him."

I remember a scene from "Amos and Andy." There was a big man who would slap Andy across the chest whenever they met. Finally, Andy got enough of it and said to Amos, "I am fixed for him. I put a stick of dynamite in my vest pocket and the next time he slaps me he is going to get his hand blown off." Andy had not realized that at the same time his own heart would be blown out. The dynamite of hatred may inflict some injury on someone else and also blow out our own heart.

The words "forgiving" and "forgiven" are inseparable twins. They go together. They are never separated. At the death of Queen Caroline Lord Chesterfield said a sad thing: "And unforgiving, unforgiven dies."

On the cross our Lord prays, "Father, forgive them; for they know not what they do" (Luke 23:34). Often what we deplore is the innocent act of some person. But for us there is an even more important reason for not holding a grudge: "for *we* know not." If we understood the person, usually our judgments would not be so harsh.

With our limited understanding of each other, it is a fearful thing to set ourselves up as a judge. The Bible says, "Vengeance is mine; I will repay, saith the Lord" (Romans 12:19). If we are wise we will leave that business to God.

Somewhere I read these lines:

> *Has God deserted Heaven,*
> *And left it up to you,*
> *To judge if this or that is right,*
> *And what each one should do?*

I think He's still in business,
And know when to wield the rod,
So when you're judging others,
Just remember, you're not—God.

"As we forgive," He told us to pray.

A couple had gone to an orphanage to adopt a child. One little fellow particularly appealed to them. They talked to him about all the things they would give him—clothes, toys, a good home. None of these things seemed to appeal to the boy much. So finally they asked him, "What do you want most?" He replied, "I just want somebody to love me."

That is what we all want. Deep in every human heart is a hunger for love. Loneliness is a cross for more people than we realize. Yet people are hard to love. They have so many faults, they say things they shouldn't, many have antagonistic and unattractive spirits. Yet Jesus told us to pray, "Forgive as we forgive." This is the only petition He emphasized. Maybe it is the hardest one to say.

"For if you forgive not men their trespasses"—debts—sins—! Either of those words could be used, maybe all three better express what our Lord had in mind. Debts suggest failure to discharge obligations, not merely financial. There are also such debts as the debts of friendship, citizenship, etc.

"Trespasses" indicates the unlawful use of another's property. We see signs, "No Trespassing," and we know that the sign means to keep off. Our friends also trespass on our time, they trespass on our name and do it harm when they talk about us wrongfully. In many ways do friends trespass on us.

Sin indicates vice and wrong conduct. And we see a lot in our friends. In fact, the more you study the faults of your friends, the harder it becomes to offer this prayer, "as we forgive others." And sometimes we invest our love in friends only to be bitterly disappointed.

Sometimes we might feel like Sir Walter Raleigh, who just a few hours before his death, wrote his wife: "To what friend to direct thee I know not, for mine have left me in the true time of trial." Some people have been so deeply hurt that they cannot feel that Tennyson was right when he said:

> *I hold it true, whate'er befall,*
> *I fell it, when I sorrow most;*
> *'Tis better to have loved and lost,*
> *Than never to have loved at all.*

But notice carefully that Jesus said, "Forgive us our debts." He directs our attention first to our own debts—trespasses—sins. The faults of those about us are also in us. Maybe not exactly the same ones, but probably worse ones. He did not tell us to pray, "Forgive us *if* we have sinned." There is no *if* about it.

Let us honestly ask ourselves some questions and answer them: "What is my worst failure? That is, wherein have I not lived up to my obligations? Second, what is one way I have mistreated another person? Third, what is one sin I have committed?" Each of us has some answer for each of those questions. We all stand convicted.

But, also, do our friends have an answer for those questions? They, too, are guilty. Now, the supreme point is: If you will be willing to forgive them, then you will be able to receive God's forgiveness of you. It seems to be a good bargain for me. How about you?

CHAPTER VIII

And Lead Us Not Into Temptation, But Deliver Us From Evil

OUR LORD gives us three prayers to pray for ourselves. One is for the present, "Give us this day our daily bread." One looks both to the past and to the present, "Forgive us our sins." The third prayer looks to the future. As to our need to pray for bread and for forgiveness we are in agreement, but most of us take a view different from that of our Lord as to the prayer we should pray for tomorrow.

As we look to the future what is it we need to pray about? What do we fear and shrink from the most? For some the answer is sickness, so we ask God to keep us well, we are interested in preventive medicine, we take out sick and hospitalization insurance. We fear poverty, so we save for the rainy days. Others fear suffering. We worry about the possibility of being hurt.

We fear unpopularity and criticism, we fear old age, we fear death. But when Christ tells us what to pray about for the future, He mentions not one of these things. The one thing we need to pray about for the future is the possibility of doing wrong. The one fear we should have above all fears is that in the midst of temptation we shall slip.

But we take less seriously our Lord's prayer for the future than we take any of the other five petitions. We are not afraid of temptation. In fact, we are so confident of being able to command our own selves that we make temptation a constant companion.

There is an old story of a man who had been the victim of strong drink but had reformed and apparently was the conqueror of his evil habit. However, when he drove into town, he continued to hitch his horse at the post in front of the town saloon. Eventually he fell into his old ways again. Had he had a healthy fear of temptation he would have changed his hitching post.

Temptation most often comes first as thoughts. In the secret places of our minds we dramatize and act out the thoughts. We read books that describe wickedness, we play with emotional dynamite as if it were a harmless toy. We get ourselves into dangerous situations and enjoy being there. We keep the wrong company. When we go about work or pleasure some enticing voice may whisper, "Brother, lend me your soul." We might hesitate to give away a dime, even if we have a pocketful of coins, but we risk our souls though we know it may be for eternity. When it is temptation we face we are foolishly brave.

Not so with Jesus. He tells us to fear the temptation of the morrow more than any other thing. Our very strength is our greatest weakness, because the overconfidence in our strength leads to our downfall. We are afraid of our weaknesses and guard against them. But we take chances with our strengths, and that is where we lose. "Wherefore let him that thinketh he standeth take heed lest he fall" (I Cor. 10:12).

What is temptation? First, it is an inducement to evil. Read the third chapter of Genesis and you see a story that has been repeated in some form in the life of every person who has come after Adam and Eve.

The serpent says to Eve, "Hath God said, Ye shall not eat of every tree in the garden?" Eve replies, "All except one. If we eat of that one we shall die." The serpent tells her it will not hurt her. "In fact, if you eat of that tree you will know more, you will have a larger and freer life."

Here her inclinations began to struggle with her reason and conscience. The "Thou-shalt-not" of God and the bright alluring promise of forbidden pathways came in conflict. Thus temptation was set up.

Second, temptation means a test or a trial. It is like a fork in the roadway of life, where one must decide the direction to take, an action to carry out, a character to be. A mother whose son has been killed may be tempted to become bitter and harsh. One who is facing a difficult life situation may be tempted to escape by getting drunk.

One who is destined to a bed of suffering or the chair of an invalid may be tempted to self-pity. When someone has treated us unfairly there is the temptation to hate, spite, or resentment. One who has prospered is tempted to vanity and self-love. The successful is tempted to seek undue power.

When he was a boy in school Napoleon wrote an essay on the dangers of ambition. Yet his own ambition wrecked his life. Moses was noted for his meekness. In fact, the Bible says he was the meekest man on earth (Numbers 12:3). Yet, in a moment, when he tried to usurp the power of God by striking the rock, he lost his chance to enter the Promised Land. Simon Peter was noted for his impulsive courage. Yet it was through failure of his greatest strength that he denied his Lord.

A man is no stronger than his weakest moment, and every man has an Achilles' heel, a point of vulnerability. We cannot escape temptation because we are endowed with freedom of choice. And since no person has an iron will, every one is in danger of falling. We can choose between good and evil, between being true and false, between being brave and cowardly, between being generous and selfish. And the very freedom of choice becomes in itself temptation.

Many stumble at the interpretation of this petition, feeling that God would not lead one of His children into temptation. But God is concerned with the creation of character, and to create character He gives us freedom of choice. Otherwise we would be mere puppets.

Life would be much simpler if we had no such freedom. Thomas Henry Huxley once declared: "If some great Power would agree to make me think always what is true and do what is right on condition of being turned into a sort of clock, I should instantly close with the bargain. The only freedom I care about is the freedom to do right; the freedom to do wrong I am ready to part with." But one freedom requires the other freedom, thus our temptation.

God gave to each of us a free will, yet the very possession of our freedom should so frighten us that in every possible way we should throw safeguards around it. We should be very afraid of any circumstance that might mean our downfall.

Jesus tells us: "If thy right hand offend thee, cut it off" (Matthew 5:30). He may mean those words literally, for certainly it would be better to lose one's hand than to lose one's soul. However, I think He means by the hand the work of the hand—"Whatsoever thy hand findeth to do . . ." If your daily job brings you into situations which tempt you, better for one to give up the job even at the cost of sacrifice.

Again He says, "If thy right eye offend thee, pluck it out" (Matthew 5:29). Probably what He means by "thy eye" is the things you have your eye set on—your goals and ambitions. One can be so set on success, social or material, that he reaches the point where he demands "success at any price." If the direction of your life is a peril to your soul, better to try another road.

Elizabeth Barrett Browning understood it when she said:

> *I was too ambitious in my deed,*
> *And thought to distance all men in success,*
> *Till God came on me, marked the place, and said,*
> *"Ill-doer, henceforth keep within this line,*

Attempting less than others"—and I stand,
And work among Christ's little ones, content.

"Lead us not into temptation" is a prayer that makes us look at our choices, beyond our goals to the final destination of the road we would travel.

This is a prayer that can be answered and is answered in many ways. Sometimes it is answered by God's direct providence by what we call coincidence. Why is it you missed getting a certain job or opportunity? Maybe it was God intervening. At times this prayer is answered by what we call insight. In certain hard moments of decision we feel deep inside the right course to take.

Most of all is this prayer answered by the inner strength which God gives to all who sincerely desire it. In despair we sometimes throw up our hands. We feel caught in an entanglement of circumstances, or by the chains of some habit, or by our own inherent weakness. We say, "What's the use? I cannot do better." But when we sincerely desire to rise above our temptations and look to God for deliverance, a new inner strength becomes ours, a new spirit of confidence rises within.

One of the most sublime verses in the Bible is tucked away in the little book of Jude: "Now unto Him that is able to keep you from falling, and to present you faultless before the presence of His glory with exceeding joy" (verse 24). You begin to realize you are made for victory instead of defeat, that you are to overcome evil rather than to be overcome by it, and triumphantly you declare with the Apostle: "I can do all things through Christ which strengtheneth me" (Philippians 4:13).

The biggest lie of the devil is that we have to sin. "After all, you are human," he says, and thereby our high resolves are destroyed. We surrender and quit the struggle. One takes a very different view when he becomes acquainted with a power beyond human power. "I can do all things through Christ which strengtheneth me." That is a tremendously powerful truth, once we possess it.

There is a little story we read as children about the little engine climbing the hill. As it puffed and struggled it kept saying, "I think I can, I think I can, I think I can." Nothing is ever accomplished by the person who says, "I think I cannot," or "It is beyond me." Just to say, "I can," is to gain immediate power. But to add two words and say, "I can in Him," "I can in Him," is to multiply your power many fold.

I read recently of an experiment made by a psychologist. We are familiar with those gripping machines. You put in a penny and try your grip. Three men tried their grip, with no suggestion from the psychologist, and the average grip was 101 pounds. Then the three were hypnotized and the psychologist told each, "You cannot grip, because you are weak." Under the power of that suggestion their average grip fell from 101 pounds to only 29 pounds.

With the three men still under the power of hypnosis, the psychologist told them to grip again, but this time he told them, "Now you can grip." Their strength was five times greater when they said, "I can," than it was when they said, "I cannot."

Study the lives of those we call saints, those who have attained unusual spiritual power, and you will find their secret right at this point. They sinned, but they never surrendered to sin. They never accepted failure as final. They never ceased to look forward with confidence. They kept saying, "I can in Him." And to the utmost of their power was added His power.

The same power is available for any one of us. You may look into a past of shame and defeat, but I tell you that you can look into a future of peace and victory. "Only believe, only believe all things are possible, only believe." That is more than just a little chorus. It is the Christian faith.

What amazing confidence did our Lord have in us! C. F. Andrews reminds us of an old legend that tells us that when Jesus returned to heaven He was asked by an angel: "What have you left behind to carry out the work?" Jesus answered: "A little band of men and women who love me." "But what if they fail when the trial comes? Will all you have done be defeated?" "Yes," said Jesus, "if they fail, all I have done will be defeated."

"Is there nothing more?" "No," said Jesus, "there is nothing more." "What then?" Jesus quietly replied, "They will not fail."

With a confidence like that as we face tomorrow, we can triumphantly declare: "For thine is the kingdom, and the power, and the glory, forever. Amen." We see the complete victory of God in our own lives and our world.

PART IV

THE KEYS TO THE KINGDOM

The Beatitudes

And he opened his mouth, and taught them, saying,

Blessed are the poor in spirit: for theirs is the kingdom of heaven.

Blessed are they that mourn: for they shall be comforted.

Blessed are the meek: for they shall inherit the earth.

Blessed are they which do hunger and thirst after righteousness: for they shall be filled.

Blessed are the merciful: for they shall obtain mercy.

Blessed are the pure in heart: for they shall see God.

Blessed are the peacemakers: for they shall be called the children of God.

Blessed are they which are persecuted for righteousness' sake: for theirs is the kingdom of heaven.

Blessed are ye, when men shall revile you, and persecute you, and shall say all manner of evil against you falsely, for my sake.

Rejoice, and be exceeding glad: for great is your reward in heaven: for so persecuted they the prophets which were before you.

Matthew 5:2-12

CHAPTER I

Blessed Are the Poor in Spirit: For Theirs Is the Kingdom of Heaven

FREDERICK WILLIAM IV OF PRUSSIA once visited a school and asked the children some questions. Pointing to the stone in his ring, a flower in his buttonhole, and a bird that flew past the window, he asked to what kingdom each of them belonged. The children gave him the right answers: the mineral, the vegetable, and the animal kingdoms.

Then he asked, "To what kingdom do I belong?" That is really the supreme question facing every man. For some men the answer is the animal kingdom, because they live on the appetite level, and are controlled by their passions and physical desires. But most people rise above the animal level. They have a sense of right and wrong, a feeling of duty and decency, some ideals and purposes.

However, some rise to an even higher kingdom. No one can think of Christ as being animal. Though He took the form of man, the word "human" is insufficient to describe Him. Christ was divine. He belonged to a kingdom beyond the kingdoms of this world. The Bible tells us we can enter jointly with Him into His kingdom: "The Spirit itself beareth witness with our spirit, that we are the children of God: and if chil-

dren, then heirs; heirs of God and joint-heirs with Christ"
(Romans 8:16,17).

We can belong to the Kingdom of God! That is a thrilling
fact and gives to every life a thrilling mission. Recently someone asked me this question, "What do you want ten years
from now?" I might answer that I want to be preaching, to
be helping to build some church, some degree of comfort and
security, to see my children becoming established in life.
There are so many things I want.

But if I know my heart, as I think I do, I want, above all
things, to belong to the Kingdom of God. Well, Jesus gave us
eight keys to God's kingdom. The first key is poverty. Right
off, we are tempted to say, "I qualify so far as poverty is concerned. Let's look at the second key."

But are you really poor? So far as material possessions are
concerned, we are all poor. Even the man with a million dollars does not have enough to create one loaf of bread or to
buy one moment of real contentment or to keep his soul out
of hell. Yes, you are poor.

Also, the ten spies who went into the Promised Land were
poor. Whimperingly they reported: "And there we saw giants
. . . and we were in our own sight as grasshoppers" (Numbers
13:33). The man with one talent was poor. He buried his
talent in the ground. There are a lot of people who do not
have the courage really to amount to anything. They are very
poor, indeed.

On the other hand, one might possess a certain cocksure-
ness and yet be very poor. Peter typifies that type of poverty
when he says: "Though all men shall be offended because of
thee, yet will I never be offended" (Matthew 26:33). He was
not poor in spirit, yet he was poor, as it was proved when the
testing time came.

The first key to God's Kingdom is another type of poverty.

Two men went up to the Temple to pray. One said, "God,
I thank thee, that I am not as other men are." He listed all his
good qualities and was quite satisfied. He had a good eye for

himself, a bad eye for his fellow men, and no eye at all for God.

The other man prayed, "God be merciful to me a sinner." That man may have possessed great wealth, he may have had the courage of a conqueror, but he realized that he lacked something which only God could supply (Luke 18:10-13). The poverty which is a key to God's Kingdom is the realization that, though we possess all things, without God all our things are nothing.

My favorite story is of a boy who had received money from his father, and had a spirit which made him feel he could conquer the world. In spite of his wealth and his spirit, however, he remained poor until one day he fully realized his real poverty, and said, "I will arise and go to my father" (Luke 15:18). There is the poverty that makes rich—the realization of our lack of God and our desire for God.

"Blessed are the poor in spirit; for theirs is the kingdom of heaven." We sometimes interpret that word "blessed" to mean happy, but really it means a oneness with God. The "poor in spirit" have so emptied themselves of themselves— the pride of their accomplishments, the selfishness of their desires—that the Spirit of God has come into their emptiness. We sing, "What a joy divine, leaning on the everlasting arm"—that is it.

And what do we mean by the kingdom of heaven? Someone has said, "All that religion has to offer is self-denial in this life on the promise of some pie in the sky." But notice that Jesus uses the verb "is." His Kingdom becomes an immediate possession. It is not a place, it is an experience. It is not bounded by geographical lines, it is bounded only by our capacity to receive it.

Possessing the Kingdom, one possesses all things. The children of Israel were terrified. They had put their faith in Moses; he had died, and now they had lost everything. There are those of us today who put our faith in things which can die: rich one moment, we become poverty-stricken the next.

But not Joshua. Listen to his words to these fearful people: "Be strong and of a good courage; be not afraid, neither be thou dismayed; for the Lord thy God is with thee whithersoever thou goest" (Joshua 1:9). Joshua belonged in the kingdom of God.

Possessing God's power enables us to face life with enthusiasm; it gives us a deep inward peace because we are not afraid of tomorrow. There comes into our lives an inner joy that outward circumstances cannot reach. Because God is within us, and because God is love, there flows out from us a love for others that sweeps away all prejudice, jealousy, and hate.

In the light of the blessings of possessing the Kingdom of God, all our other possessions grow so dim that out of our very hearts we sing: "When other helpers fail, and comforts flee, help of the helpless, O abide with me."

CHAPTER II

Blessed Are They That Mourn: For They Shall Be Comforted

THE SECOND key to the kingdom of God is mourning. That is even less attractive to us than poverty, yet only those who can feel can mourn. There was Father Damien, for thirteen years a missionary to the lepers on Molokai. Finally the dread disease laid hold of him.

One morning he spilled some boiling water on his foot. But there was not the slightest pain. Then he knew he was doomed. He knew that death had come to his body and little by little would take possession. A hundred times better for him would it have been if that boiling water had brought pain.

St. Paul tells us of certain people who were "past feeling" (Ephesians 4:19). That is a horrible condition in which to be, yet, to some extent, each one of us is so afflicted. Socrates described a man's conscience as the wife from whom there is no divorce. Maybe we can't divorce our conscience, but we can stifle it until its voice is completely stilled.

A man whose feet were amputated told of his experience. He was caught out in the bitter cold of the far north. So long as his feet pained him he was happy, but after a while the

119

pain was gone, and he knew then that his feet were doomed. The pain diminished as they froze.

So with conscience. You have committed a certain wrong. Does it hurt? Then be glad. You become hopeless only when your soul becomes past feeling. Stuart N. Hutchinson tells of a small boy who, having been told by his father that conscience is a small voice which talks to us when we have done wrong, prayed, "O God, make the little voice loud."

"Blessed are they that mourn," said our Lord. He is not talking about the pessimist who constantly looks for the bad, nor of the selfish person whose ambitions have been thwarted, nor of the person who is bitter and rebellious over some loss. The first key to God's Kingdom, "poverty of spirit," tells us we should be conscious of our lack of God. Now, the second key tells us we should be so grieved over our moral and spiritual shortcomings that we cannot rest until we have found God, and our souls are satisfied.

Modern congregations have about discarded the old mourners' bench. It was a place where penitents came seeking divine pardon. In its stead we have a psychological clinic. Certainly I do not disparage the help of modern psychology. I have spent untold hours in counseling, but counseling by itself is not enough.

Today we want God's blessing without the pain of God's purging. We want sermons on how to win friends, how to have peace of mind, and how to forget our fears. But we must remember that Christ came to make men good rather than merely to make men feel good.

Each Sunday night in my own church I give people a chance to come and pray at the altar. An average of between six and seven hundred kneel there. Watching tears streaming down some praying face, I have felt like shouting for joy. The way of the Cross is not easy, but it is the way home.

Jesus told us, "And I, if I be lifted up from the earth, will draw all men unto me." Then the Gospel record adds, "This he said, signifying what death he should die" (John 12:32,33).

And as we see the suffering of the Saviour, surely it must bring suffering to us. Only a dead soul can see Him without mourning.

Let us remember that it is the sins of men that put Him there. If men had traveled less the paths of sin, His path up Calvary would have been less steep. If they had been less greedy and self-seeking, the nails in His hands would have burned less. If they had been less proud, His crown of thorns would have been less painful. If they had loved others more, they would have hated Him less.

On the cross He said, "Father, forgive them; for they know not what they do" (Luke 23:34). Surely Pilate and Caiphas, Herod and the soldiers did not know what they were doing. Greedy, selfish men were merely putting out of the way one who got in their way. Their very ignorance helped Him to bear His cross.

But we do know. We have the record which has been taught to us from childhood. We are the ones who grieve Him most, who make the pain for Him the hardest to bear. He died to heal our broken hearts, and, instead, we break His heart by our own sin and our indifference to Him.

"Blessed are they that mourn." Those who care—care to the point of a broken spirit and a contrite heart, care to a deep repentance.

When Jesus came to Golgotha they hanged Him on a tree;
They drove great nails through hands and feet, and made
a Calvary;
They crowned Him with a crown of thorns, red were His
wounds and deep,
For those were crude and cruel days and human flesh was
cheap.

When Jesus came to Birmingham, they simply passed Him
by,
They never hurt a hair of Him, they only let Him die;

For men had grown more tender, and they would not give
   Him pain,
They only just passed down the street, and left Him in the
   rain. (From "The Unutterable Beauty" by G. A. Studdert
   Kennedy, published by Hodder & Stoughton, Ltd.)

Maybe you are afraid. You dread to come into His presence. You are ashamed to face Him. You may feel miserable
inside. Then take heart and be glad, for your very shame
and misery and fear are a mourning that can lead you to His
comfort.

As you look at your life you may see your own broken
heart. Be glad that it is broken. Take it to Calvary. There,
under the warm glow of His love, your broken heart can be
welded together again, and your sorrow be turned into re-
joicing. Be thankful for your broken heart, if by becoming
broken we are led to Christ for the mending.

CHAPTER III

Blessed Are the Meek: For They Shall Inherit the Earth

ONE OF the keys to the kingdom of God is meekness. But we do not want to be meek. We prefer to be like the little boy whose mother kept calling him, "My little lamb." Finally, he said, "Mother, I don't want to be your little lamb. I want to be your little tiger."

We like to think of ourselves as being courageous and strong. We sing with inspiration, "The Son of God goes forth to war, a kingly crown to gain," but meekness does not appeal to us. We want to be conquerors, and meekness sounds too much like surrender. Meekness does mean surrender, but not surrender to men around us, not surrender to ourselves, not surrender to the circumstances of our lives.

For the true meaning of meekness turn to the Thirty-seventh Psalm. There you find it stated, "The meek shall inherit the earth." The Hebrew word which is translated "meek" really means "to be molded." The Psalmist says, "Fret not thyself because of evil-doers," do not be envious of the prosperity of the wicked. Instead, "Commit thy way unto the Lord." The Psalmist is saying, let yourself become as putty in God's hand, be molded by Him, yield your life to the purposes

123

of God, and eventually real success will be your reward.

Jesus lifted up that phrase of the Psalmist and made it one of the Beatitudes, a key to God's Kingdom. The New Testament writers used the Greek word *praos,* which we translate as "meek." Actually, it means to be controlled. It means submission to the divine plan of God.

The laws of God are already established when we are born. His ways are fixed. We have a choice in that we can accept God's way and live according to His law, or we can rebel against Him. But we cannot change what He has done. For example, the world is round and the sky is blue. Suppose you don't like round worlds and blue skies. There is nothing you can do about it.

Also did God make the laws of the universe, which are just as unchangeable as is the universe itself. There are the seasons. The farmer learns the laws of the seasons and becomes governed by them. He plants his crop when it should be planted and thus he reaps when he should be reaping. For him to rebel and plant out of season does not change the laws of God, it means only the failure of his crop. For the farmer meekness means planting when he should plant. It means submission to God's laws.

So with life. God has His will, and man has his will. Man has the choice of being meek or of being self-willed. He can say with Christ, "Nevertheless, not my will, but thine, be done" (Luke 22:42), or man can say, "I will do as I please." The Psalmist says, "Delight thyself also in the Lord; and he shall give thee the desires of thine heart" (Psalm 37:4). On the other hand, to fail to become molded or controlled by God's will is to destroy ourselves.

In the last chapter of the book of Job is a thrilling statement. Job's life had both sunshine and shadows. He had his successes and also his defeats. He had faith in God, yet there were times of doubt. It seemed that Job might "curse God," as he was advised to do. But in the end his faith triumphs and Job says, "I know that thou canst do everything" (42:2).

There are times when, with our limited vision, it seems that God's way is not the best way. We want material success on earth, we want happiness in our lives and peace in our hearts. If we believed, really believed, God would give us what we so much want; we would gladly be meek, that is, be willing to be molded and controlled by God. But it wasn't until he became an old man that Job knew without doubt that God is never defeated.

How wonderful it is to learn that lesson while there is still much of life to be lived. One of the sublimest statements outside the Bible comes from Dante, "In His will is our peace." The opposite of peace is conflict and the reason we do not have peace of mind and soul is that we are at war within ourselves.

There is the voice of duty and there is the voice of inclination, both within us demanding to be heard. We struggle to decide, and the struggle squanders our powers. We become weakened and exhausted. But when one decides to do the will of God, day by day, as best he understands it, the conflict is resolved.

Such a decision takes all of the dread out of tomorrow. The wise man of the Bible tells us, "In all thy ways acknowledge him, and he shall direct thy paths" (Proverbs 3:6). The very act of accepting the will of God for your life today places the responsibility of what happens tomorrow on God. So we do not worry about what the result will be. There is wonderful peace in leaving the results in His hands. An old Negro man once prayed, "When God tells me to butt my head against a rock wall it's my place to butt. It's the Lord's place to go through." As you study the lives of God-molded people down through the centuries you realize that every time God did "go through." In the long run, God is never defeated.

I think of how Mahatma Gandhi left Sabarmati on March 12, 1930, to go on the "salt march." He proposed to march to the sea, there make salt, which was a government monopoly, and thus precipitate a crisis. Gandhi explained that he would not return until he had gained independence for India.

It seemed absurd. A little man in a loin cloth and with a bamboo walking stick going out to do battle against the greatest empire the world had ever known. But seventeen years later the little man had won. Gandhi's power lay in the fact that his life was committed to the will of God as he understood it. Thus committed, he was totally without fear. And his freedom from fear struck fear into the heart of the British Empire and it dared not destroy him.

"Blessed are the meek," said Jesus. Those who surrender to God possess God. We are told, "The earth is the Lord's and the fulness thereof" (Psalm 24:1). Thus, possessing God, the meek do also "inherit the earth."

CHAPTER IV

---

*Blessed Are They Which Do Hunger and
Thirst After Righteousness: For They Shall
Be Filled*

ONCE A young man came to Buddha seeking the true way of
life, the path of deliverance. According to the story as Dr.
Ralph Sockman tells it, Buddha led him down to the river.
The young man assumed that he was to undergo some ritual
of purification, some type of baptismal service.

They walked out into the river for some distance and suddenly Buddha grabbed the man and held his head under the
water. Finally, in a last gasp, the fellow wrenched himself
lose, and his head came above the water. Quietly Buddha
asked him, "When you thought you were drowning, what did
you desire most?" The man gasped, "Air." Back came
Buddha's reply, "When you want salvation as much as you
wanted air, then you will get it."

Jesus would agree with that. He tells us that one of the
keys to the Kingdom of God is to hunger and thirst for it.
We get what we really want. The poet Shelley pointed out
that imagination is the great instrument of moral good. When
the imagination and the will are in conflict the imagination
always wins.

To imagine is to form mental images on the screen of our minds. It means to create in our thinking what we want created in our living. One's time, talents, and all other resources become organized and dedicated to the purpose of making real the objects of his imagination. As Georgia Harkness said, "Be careful what you set your heart on, for you will surely get it."

Jesus tells us that before we can possess God and the things of God we must first make God the center of our imagination. "Thou shalt love the Lord thy God with all thy heart, and with all thy soul, and with all thy mind" (Matthew 22:37), said Christ. And when God becomes the very center of our affection, our feeling, and our thinking, we shall find and possess and be possessed by God.

The greatest thrill this preacher ever has is to see some person attain a deeper experience of God. Every Sunday night, as I see hundreds pray at the altar of the church, I know that some are finding God there. But long before time for the altar prayers I can almost pick out those who will be blessed that night.

Watch a congregation during the organ prelude and you will see a lot of difference. Some are quiet in thought and prayer. They seem hardly conscious of their immediate surroundings. Others are chatting away with everyone around, they watch others as they come in, note their clothes, and wonder about them.

When the hymn is announced, some sing not only with their voices but also with their hearts. Others just say the words or don't even bother to pick up the hymnbook. During the sermon some are like blotters. They soak up every thought and mood of the preacher. Others seem utterly unresponsive.

What makes the difference? Some have needs that human resources do not supply. They have come to church feeling that need, hungering and thirsting for God, and it is they who find Him. You never find God until He becomes your deepest desire.

Two men were discussing New York City. One said it was a wicked place, filled with cheap sensations, with morally degraded people, with sin on every corner. The other said it is a grand place, filled with art museums, great music, and stimulating lectures. New York was the city that each inwardly desired.

We find in life what we want to find. So Jesus said, "Blessed are they which do hunger and thirst after righteousness: for they shall be filled."

It bothers me that the church seems to mean so little to many of its members, that in the church so many find almost no help. It is not the church, it is our own attitudes. Once a rather pious churchman was reproving his neighbor for profanity. The profane neighbor replied, "Well, my friend, I cuss a lot and you pray a lot, but neither of us really means what he says."

In one of his books Bishop Fulton J. Sheen says, "It is not uncommon to find Catholics who say: 'I knew I should not eat meat on Friday out of respect for the day on which Our Lord sacrificed His life for me, but I did not want to embarrass my host,' or, 'I was staying with some unbelieving friends over the week end and I did not want to embarrass them, so I did not go to Mass on Sunday'. . . . Such is the indifference of the world, a fear of being identified wholeheartedly with God, for whom we were made."

What he says of Catholics is, perhaps, even more true of Protestants. If we really desire God we will do those things which will cause us to experience God. Jesus says that we should hunger and thirst after God. I saw a picture show recently of a man lost on the hot sands of a desert, without water. His thirst whipped his weary body to the point of madness. His distorted mind was mocked with a cruel mirage of an oasis. He died frantically digging with his bare hands in the sand.

"Thirst" is a strong word, a driving word. And when the human soul thirsts for God, Jesus says he will be filled with

God. And not only will we find God for ourselves, we will bring God's Kingdom on earth.

Just suppose that there was only one real believer on earth and that during an entire year this one believer made one convert. Then there would be two. Suppose that during the next year these two made one convert apiece, then there would be four. Suppose that the next year these four made one convert apiece, then there would be eight. Suppose that they kept that pace of each winning one every year, how long would it take to convert every person in the entire world?

It has now been two thousand years since our Lord was on earth. Has that been enough time? Actually, there has been time enough, with just one winning one other per year, to convert sixty-five worlds like this. Starting with just one and doubling each year, at the end of just thirty-one years there would be 2,147,483,648 souls filled with God's righteousness. The next year they could convert another world the size of this one.

We can have God in our souls and in our world whenever we really want Him.

CHAPTER V

Blessed Are the Merciful: For They Shall Obtain Mercy

OF THE eight Beatitudes, the keys to God's kingdom, this one is the most appealing, the most important, and the most difficult. Most appealing because mercy brings to mind kindness, unselfish service, and good will. Everyone loves the Good Samaritan and Florence Nightingale, who are examples of mercy. We shrink from the justice of God, but we pray for His mercy.

Most important, for without mercy all of us are without hope. All of us have sinned and come short of God's glory. The only prayer we can pray is, "God be merciful to me a sinner" (Luke 18:13). As Portia said to Shylock, "In the course of justice none of us should see salvation."

When we come to the Communion table we pray, "We are not worthy so much as to gather up the crumbs under Thy table. But Thou art the same Lord whose property is always to have mercy." However, the key to God's mercy toward ourselves is the mercy we have toward others. If we are not merciful, then we are blocking God's mercy out of our own lives, and thus we become doomed men and women.

There is a saying, "All that goes up must come down," but

131

if nothing goes up, then nothing will come down. In physics we are taught that every action has a reaction, but if there is no action, then there can be no reaction. "If ye forgive not men their trespasses, neither will your Father forgive your trespasses" (Matthew 6:15). Without forgiving, forgiveness cannot be obtained. Be merciful, and ye shall obtain mercy.

The most expensive thing you can do is hold a wrong spirit in your heart against another. The price you pay is the loss, the eternal loss, of your own soul. In talking about the Kingdom of Heaven Jesus tells the story of a king who forgave his servant a large debt which he could not pay. That same servant met a fellow servant who owed him a trifling sum, and because he could not pay, the poor fellow was thrown into prison by the unmerciful servant. The king called back the servant whom he had forgiven, cancelled his forgiveness, and had him cast into prison.

Jesus concludes the story, "So likewise shall my heavenly Father do also unto you, if ye from your hearts forgive not every one his brother their trespasses" (Matthew 18:23-35).

Protestants do not regard Peter as the head of the Church as do Catholics, yet beautiful is the explanation a Catholic friend gave to me of why he believes Peter was chosen. James and John asked for the chief places, but they were passed by, as was the Virgin Mother, or one of the others. Peter was chosen because he sinned so shamefully but later wept so bitterly. Tradition tells us that Peter wept so much that even his cheeks became furrowed with tears.

So the Lord chose him who knew by experience the blessing of merciful forgiveness in order that his life should cause the Church to put at its very center mercy toward others, thereby saving itself as it saved others. Without being merciful, no one can enter the Kingdom of God. Not only is this key the most appealing and important, also it is the most difficult. When someone has done us wrong our natural human reaction is to seek revenge, to get even. We might refuse to commit any definite act of vengeance, yet cherish resentment and be glad if some misfortune happened to him.

Mercy requires not only a right spirit on our part against a person who has wronged us, not only that we must over-come all vindictiveness, jealousy, and littleness, but that we must do even more than feel a kind spirit in our hearts. Jesus wept, but He did more than weep. He gave Himself even unto death to serve and save those who had persecuted Him.

In his book, *High Wind At Noon*, Allan Knight Chalmers gives us the story of Peer Holm, who was a world-famous engineer. He built great bridges, railroads and tunnels in many parts of the earth; he gained wealth and fame, but later came to failure, poverty, and sickness. He returned to the little village where he was born and, together with his wife and little girl, eked out a meager living.

Peer Holm had a neighbor who owned a fierce dog. Peer warned him that the dog was dangerous, but the old man contemptuously replied, "Hold your tongue, you cursed pau-per." One day Peer Holm came home to find the dog at the throat of his little girl. He tore the dog away, but the dog's teeth had gone too deeply and the little girl was dead.

The sheriff shot the dog, and the neighbors were bitter against his owner. When sowing time came they refused to sell him any grain. His fields were plowed but bare. He could neither beg, borrow, nor buy seed. Whenever he walked down the road, the people of the village sneered at him. But not Peer Holm. He could not sleep at night for thinking of his neighbor.

Very early one morning he rose, went to his shed, and got his last half bushel of barley. He climbed the fence and sowed his neighbor's field. The fields themselves told the story. When the seeds came up, it was revealed what Peer had done, be-cause part of his own field remained bare while the field of his neighbor was green.

Mercy requires that we sow good seed in our enemy's field, even though it means that part of our own field will be left bare. It is not easy. It is the hardest possible action, but it is our key to God's Kingdom.

The way of the world was an eye for an eye and a tooth for a tooth. Hate always led to hate. Wrong always brought revenge. But one day the vicious circle was broken. One called Jesus came offering men a higher way and a better life, but men stood back to mock and to laugh and to crucify.

About His head was a bright circle, and when He uttered the word, "Forgive," that circle of God's love and approval became large enough to include others. A thief on a cross near by stepped inside that circle with Him and in so doing entered Paradise. The circle reaches to my own feet. To stay outside is to know hate, revenge, and destruction. Inside is to know God's healing love and eternally to possess His Kingdom.

The step into the circle is the step to mercy. "Blessed are the merciful: for they shall obtain mercy."

Blessed Are the Pure in Heart: For They Shall See God

THERE ARE many things I would like to see—the Grand Canyon, some of the great cathedrals of Europe, the paths in the Holy Land along which the Saviour walked. I want to continue to see my home happy and peaceful, I want to see my children growing mentally and spiritually as well as physically, and some day become established in some useful work in the world. I want to see always the difference between right and wrong. Most of all, I want to see God.

But all people have not the same ability to see. Many people have limited vision. Some are cross-eyed, the eyes of some are weak and diseased. Some people have a growth called a cataract, which shuts off vision. Some are nearsighted, others, farsighted; some are color-blind, others have blind spots in their eyes. Sidney Lanier looked at the muddy, crooked Chattahoochee river and saw in it a lovely poem; Joel Chandler Harris saw in rabbits, foxes, 'possums, and an old man named Uncle Remus, stories which will live forever. Woodrow Wilson could see a basis of lasting world peace, but tragically so few others saw it. Sir Christopher Wren could see a beautiful cathedral and made of that vision a temple to God.

135

There are at least three ways in which we see. St. Paul tells us that "eye hath not seen, nor ear heard, neither have entered into the heart of man, the things which God hath prepared for them that love Him" (I Corinthians 2:9). There we have pointed out three kinds of sight. There is the sight of the natural eye, with which we can see flowers and mountains, the printed words on this page, and people's faces. That is physical vision.

A teacher may explain to a boy a problem in mathematics or chemistry. As the teacher talks, the boy hears, and his mind takes hold of what he hears to the point of understanding. After he understands, he may say, "I see it." That is mental sight. In studying botany a student can reach the point of learning the various kinds of flowers and of their culture and development. Then he can see flowers with both his physical and mental eyes. If one understands what he reads, he sees with both his eyes and his mind.

But there is still a third sight, as when a truth has "entered into the heart of man." The heart has eyes, too. Robert Burns saw in flowers thoughts too deep for tears. Not only did he see flowers with his physical eyes, not only did he understand the growth and culture of flowers, also he felt their message. Jesus looked at people and had "compassion on them."

He saw them not only with His eyes and mind, but also with His heart. One can read the Twenty-third Psalm and understand the meaning of the words and phrases. But some read it and they feel the message and know the Good Shepherd. A boy can look at a girl and know that he loves her. He sees her not only with his eyes but with his heart.

A person sees God through the eyes of the heart. "Blessed are the pure in heart: for they shall see God" (Matthew 5:8). Jesus said: "He that hath seen me hath seen the Father" (John 14:9). Certainly not every person who saw Him with his physical eyes saw God. Mere physical sight of Him revealed only a man. It is not even enough to understand His teachings and His life. Many scholars have studied His words without seeing Him. Really to see God in Christ one must experience Him in the heart.

> *What a wonderful change in my life has been wrought,*
> *Since Jesus came into my heart.*
> *I have light in my soul for which long I have sought,*
> *Since Jesus came into my heart.*

When the heart sees Christ, then we see God. To see God is to realize Him, to feel Him, to center the affections of the heart in Him.

But one can have an indistinct and distorted picture of God. Read the story, "The Quest for the Holy Grail." The holy grail was the mystic cup used at the Last Supper, in which legend has it that Joseph of Arimathea caught the last drop of blood which fell from our Lord's side as He died on the cross. Sir Galahad, along with other Knights of the Round Table, set out in quest of it. In the story they found it, but each saw it through the mirror of his own soul.

To some it was swathed in mist and cloud. Their vision was very indistinct. Sir Lancelot saw it, but his heart was a sinful heart. He saw the holy grail covered with holy wrath and fire. To him it was a vision of stern and awful retribution. Sir Galahad also saw the grail. He was the knight with the white soul. Of him it was said, "His strength was the strength of ten because his heart was pure." For him the vision was clear and radiant and glorious.

How we see God depends on the condition of our hearts. To some He is a cloudy mystery, to others He is awful punishment, but to the pure in heart He is a friend and a glorious certainty.

Suppose one has lost purity of heart, can it be regained? Can a harlot become a virgin again? Yes, St. Augustine refers to Mary Magdalene as "the arch-virgin." Not content to call her merely a pure woman, he lifts her far above other women. She was a common prostitute of the streets. She was both vile and vulgar. But one day she came in contact with Him who was the purest. She so loved Him with her heart that all her affection was poured out on Him. She so completely took Him to heart that her evil desires were cast out. Being filled with the purity of Christ, she herself became pure.

In just a little while we see her standing at the foot of Jesus' cross. See who is by her side! It is Mary, the Lord's mother, the blessed Virgin. The two are standing together. Purity has been regained. Paradise lost has now been regained. And on Easter morning Mary Magdalene became the first vessel chosen by Christ Himself in which to send forth the blessed Gospel. If Mary Magdalene could become pure again, then there is hope for every one of us. She saw Christ with her heart.

"Blessed are the pure in heart: for they shall see God."

Blessed Are the Peacemakers: For They Shall Be Called the Children of God

WHAT DO we want most of all? Whenever I am in the vicinity of Warm Springs, I like to stop by the little cottage which Franklin D. Roosevelt loved so much. There he would come to rest and to think in the quietness of that lovely place. The night before he died he was there planning a trip to San Francisco to attend the organization of the United Nations. He was writing his speech—the last words he ever wrote. They were:

We seek peace—enduring peace. . . . We must cultivate the science of human relations—the ability of all peoples, of all kinds, to live together and work together, in the same world, at peace. . . . As we go forward toward the greatest contribution that any generation of human beings can make in the world—the contribution of lasting peace—I ask you to keep up your faith.

Above all things, peace was the desire of his heart, as it is of my heart and of yours. We want peace in our world—we want peace inside ourselves. The fact that the late Rabbi Joshua Loth Liebman's book *Peace of Mind* has now sold nearly a million copies is eloquent testimony that people are interested in peace.

139

The angel climaxed the announcement of the birth of our Lord with the words, "Glory to God in the highest, and on earth peace, good will toward men" (Luke 2:14). Peace was His mission. "Peace I leave with you, my peace I give unto you" (John 14:27). When we think of the Kingdom of God, we think of a kingdom of peace, where all strife has ceased. So we are not surprised that our Lord gave peace as one of the keys to the Kingdom.

As Rabbi Liebman pointed out at the beginning of his book, there are many earthly things we desire—health, love, riches, beauty, talent, power, fame; but without peace of mind all those things bring torment instead of joy. If we have peace, no matter what else we may lack, life is worth living. Without peace, though we may possess all things else, it is not enough.

What is peace? The mere absence of strife is not peace. At the moment Jesus was speaking of peace there was no war on earth, but neither was there peace. The Roman Empire had forced the world to its knees and the people had lost both the means and the will to fight. When Paris surrendered to the German fury without a struggle, someone said, "London lost her buildings, but Paris lost her soul."

Peace is a positive force. You may clear some plot of land of every noxious weed, but that will not make of it a garden. It will be only a barren field. It becomes a garden when flowers are growing there. The prophet of old reminds us that just to break up our swords and spears is not enough. Those swords must become plowshares and the spears pruning hooks (Micah 4:3).

To have peace in both the world and our souls, not only must hate, suspicion and fear be rooted out. Also must love, joy, patience and understanding be planted and cultivated. Peace is something to be made; thus we must be peacemakers if we are to enter the kingdom of God.

The place to begin making peace is within ourselves. Dr. Ralph W. Sockman in his book, *The Higher Happiness,* which is the most helpful book on the Beatitudes I know, lifts up the words of Christ, "And if a house be divided against itself, that house cannot stand" (Mark 3:25). Then he points out three ways by which a life is divided: between its inner self and its outer self, between its forward drive and its backward pull, between its higher and lower natures. Let's look at these a moment.

Inner and Outer Selves. The Pharisees became chiefly concerned with keeping up a front. All of their actions were "to be seen of men." They were worried about what the neighbors would think. Seeking to appear to be something outside which is one without peace. Unless our outward appearances which they were not inside, they became hypocrites. A hypocrite is one without peace. Unless our outward appearances and our inward character are in harmony with each other, we have no peace.

Forward and Backward. Physically, we are made to go forward. To walk backward is awkward. A little girl was trying to button her dress in the back. Finally, she gave up and went to her mother for help, saying, "I can't do it because I am in front of myself." But mentally we are just the opposite. We can think better backward than forward. We know what happened yesterday, we can only guess about tomorrow. Thus it is easier to live in the past, and reluctantly we turn it loose.

We load ourselves down with the futile regrets and mistakes of yesterday; thus the business of living becomes a hard pull. Instead of repentance, we know only the meaning of remorse. Remorse is futile worry and self-inflicted agony for some yesterday. Repentance is a redemptive experience which leads to forgiveness. It buries the past under the blessed hope of tomorrow.

Higher and Lower Natures. Finally, we make peace by the decisions of our souls. Elijah stood before the people on Mount Carmel and pleaded, "How long halt ye between two opinions? If the Lord be God, follow him: but if Baal, then follow him." He was pleading for a decision. The Bible says, "And the people answered him not a word" (I Kings 18:21).

Oh, the tragedy of one who cannot make a decision. There is marvelous inner peace which comes to one who completely decides for God. I suppose there is a peace, certainly a cessation of inner strife, which comes to one who decides against God. But to go through life undecided is to live in misery. "No man can serve two masters." Two thousand years ago Jesus said that, yet we have not learned it.

The oldest story of man tells how he sinned and then hid himself from God. Hiding from God is the most miserable experience the human soul can experience. Peace with God is the most blessed experience. One of the greatest thinkers of all time was Copernicus. He revolutionized the thinking of mankind in regard to the universe. The epitaph on his grave at Frauenburg is this: "I do not seek a kindness equal to that given to Paul; nor do I ask the grace granted to Peter; but that forgiveness which thou didst give to the robber—that I earnestly pray." That is the way to begin making peace.

The angel said, "Glory to God," before he said, "Peace on earth."

CHAPTER VIII

Blessed Are They Which Are Persecuted For Righteousness' Sake: For Theirs is the Kingdom of Heaven

THE sermon on the Mount recorded in Matthew 5, 6, and 7 is really the pattern of the Kingdom of God on earth. Jesus begins that sermon with the listing of the eight keys to that kingdom, the qualities of character of the Godly person. The climax of the Beatitudes and the sermon are really one and the same.

In the sermon He tells us how to live, and He concludes with a call to action, the expression of those principles in daily living. "Whosoever heareth these sayings of mine, *and doeth them,*" He says. At the beginning of the sermon He lists the qualities of character, as poverty of spirit, mourning, meekness, desire for righteousness, mercy, purity of heart, and peacemaking. Then He says, "Blessed are they which are persecuted." That is, actually to live these keys to the kingdom will cost something. But unless they are translated into life they are worthless.

Jesus never promised ease to those who follow Him. Never did He put a carpet on the race track or a bed of roses on the battlefield. He talked about self-denial, about crosses, blood-spattered, death-dealing crosses. To enter the Kingdom of God may mean decisions that are hard, consecration that leads to persecution. But it can be no other way.

In Revelation, St. John writes to the Christians, "Fear none of those things which thou shalt suffer: behold, the devil shall cast some of you into prison, that ye may be tried; and ye shall have tribulation ten days [indefinitely]: be thou faithful unto death, and I will give thee a crown of life" (2:10). Notice carefully one little word there. He does not say "until" death, but "unto" death. That means, be faithful, not merely until you die, but even though it kills you. Make whatever sacrifice is required, even die, before you be unfaithful.

A minister friend tells of going to a large church to preach at a special Good Friday night service. The weather was extremely bad and only a few people came. Apologetically, the pastor said to the visiting minister, "If it had not been for the bad weather we would have had a large crowd to hear you tonight."

At first, it angered the visiting minister, but quickly his anger turned to pity and contempt. Looking at his host, he said, "Do you realize what you have just said? If the weather had not been bad a larger crowd would have come to this Good Friday service. Jesus died on Good Friday, but His followers did not come to the service because the weather was bad."

When I started in the ministry I did not have a car. Sometimes I would walk to my little churches, sometimes I would borrow the horse and buggy of an old physician, Dr. George Burnett. One very cold and rainy Sunday morning I said to the doctor that I would not go to the little church out in the country because I doubted that anyone would be there. He looked at me with contempt. I will never forget the sternness of his voice. He said, "It is your duty to be there. Get the horse and go."

No person ever really lives until he has found something worth dying for. You can never really possess the Kingdom of

God until the cause of God becomes more important than your own life.

William L. Stidger told about a young lad he had baptized as a baby. The boy grew up, and when World War II began, he joined the Navy. One night his ship came into Boston, and the lad visited his former pastor and friend. During their visit together, Dr. Stidger said, "Bill, tell me the most exciting experience you have had thus far." The boy seemed to hesitate. It wasn't that he had difficulty in selecting the most exciting experience. Rather, the experience he had in mind was so wonderful and sacred that he had difficulty in putting it into words.

He was the captain of a large transport and, along with a big convoy, was making his way across the Atlantic. One day an enemy submarine rose in the sea close by. He saw the white mark of the torpedo coming directly toward his transport, loaded with hundreds of boys. He had no time to change course. Over the loud speaker he cried, "Boys, this is it!"

Nearby was a little escorting destroyer. The captain of that destroyer also saw the submarine and the torpedo. Without a moment's hesitation, he gave the order, "Full speed ahead." Into the path of the torpedo the tiny destroyer went and took the full impact of the deadly missile midship. The destroyer was blown apart, quickly it sank, and every man of the crew was lost.

For a long time the boy remained silent. Then he looked at his beloved pastor and said, "Dr. Stidger, the skipper of that destroyer was my best friend." Again he was quiet for a while, then slowly he said: "You know there is a verse in the Bible which has special meaning for me now. It is, "Greater love hath no man than this, that a man lay down his life for his friends" (John 15:13).

> *The Son of God goes forth to war,*
> *A kingly crown to gain.*
> *His blood-red banner streams afar;*
> *Who follows in His train?*

To be poor in spirit means to give up our pride; to mourn means to be penitent to the point of surrendering our sins; meekness means that we must surrender our very selves to the plans and purposes of God; our hunger for God means turning away from our ambitions for all things else; to be merciful means to pay good for the evil we have received; for purity we must give up all things impure; to make peace is wholly to choose God. Those are the seven ingredients of righteousness. They must be bought at a price. Blessed are those who pay the price, "for theirs is the kingdom of God."

... but

GOD

can

ROBERT V. OZMENT

GUIDEPOSTS ASSOCIATES, INC.

Carmel, New York

FOR
MY MOTHER AND DADDY
*whose wise counsel, unceasing prayers
and Christian example left an indelible mark
on my life*

Printed in the United States of America

Contents

CHAPTER 1

TEMPTATION: *The Challenge and the Choice*

TEMPTATION is a traveling companion of every person who walks down the corridor of life. It has no regard for custom, race, or heritage. It cuddles up to the rich and the poor. It stands beside the intellectual giant as well as the illiterate; it travels with those who ride in royal coaches, and walks with the peasants. It snuggles up to the saint and grabs the hand of the avowed sinner. Temptation slights no race, it skips no generation. Wherever you find human life, you may be sure temptation is near.

There is a little phrase in the prayer our Lord taught His disciples that has always disturbed me. It is the part which reads: "And lead us not into temptation." What does this mean? Are we to assume that temptation is a part of the divine purpose? If so, is it proper for us to pray that God will save us from anything that fits into His divine scheme?

Just what do we mean when we pray: "And lead us not into temptation, but deliver us from evil"? The word "tempt" means to entice or seduce. We must dismiss at once the idea that God would induce or entice us to sin. I do not believe that God would ever seek to lead His children down a trail of moral disaster or chaos. It also appears wholly inconceivable seriously to entertain the thought that God would seek to draw us astray and in any way design a trap that would place the soul in jeopardy, and cause us to surrender our noble aspirations to beastly desires, or to switch our allegiance from the eternal to a passing pleasure. In the little Epistle of James we read, "Let no man say when he is tempted, I am tempted of God: for God cannot be tempted with evil, neither tempteth he any man: But every man is tempted, when he is drawn away of his own lust and enticed" (James 1:13-14).

Now I believe this about temptation: God leads us into temptation only in the sense that He has created a world in which temptation is inevitable. Even then, we must hasten to remember that out of these unavoidable temptations we can emerge as stronger Christians and more stalwart men and women in the faith.

Let us consider some possible interpretations of this baffling phrase, "And lead us not into temptation." First, the Greek word which is commonly translated *temptation* is, to say the least, confusing. It is exceedingly ambiguous. It could be translated to mean *trial,* or *test.* Therefore, it is altogether possible that Jesus taught His disciples to pray, "And lead us not into trial," or "And lead us not into spiritual tests."

Second, we could interpret this phrase to mean something akin to the first, yet different in degree. For example, it could mean this: Do not let us be exposed to situations in which we are likely to sin. Give us wisdom and spiritual insight to discern areas and situations which would cause us to stumble.

Finally, I do not believe we can lift a phrase out of its context and give it a wise and intelligent interpretation. We must read into its meaning the statement which precedes the phrase as well as that which follows.

Think with me about another prayer Jesus prayed. The scene was underneath the olive trees in the Garden of Gethsemane. Eight of Jesus' disciples were found just outside the garden engaged in friendly conversation. Peter, James, and John were deeper in the garden, only a few yards away from the Master, fast asleep. Jesus was faced with the greatest struggle of His entire career. He was lying stretched out, His face to the ground, His fingers buried deep in the dirt. The silence gave way to His agonizing prayer: "Oh my Father, if it be possible, let this cup pass from me." Now, if Jesus had ended His prayer at this point, we would interpret it thus: Take away this cruel cross; get Me out of this horrible situation; provide some legitimate substitute for the cross; create a morally acceptable detour around this dreadful experience. But the prayer did not end there. Jesus took no more than a short breath before He was praying again. The very next phrase reads: "Nevertheless not as I will, but as thou wilt" (Matthew 26:39).

The latter prayerful plea changes the picture. It throws a different light on the whole scene. Jesus was human enough to want to avoid the cross, yet He was divine enough to endure it if God had provided no alternate route. The scene is no longer that of Christ praying for an easy path. Now, Jesus is praying, "Oh God, if the cross cannot be removed, give me the strength to face it and remain faithful. Deliver me from the evil possibilities of this ugly cross."

Let us again turn our attention to the phrase, "And lead us not into temptation." The phrase preceding it reads: "And forgive us our debts, as we forgive our debtors." Here we truly see a picture of a man at prayer. He has just prayed for and has received God's divine forgiveness of his past sins. In an effort to remain in this forgiven relationship, in an effort to keep his soul clean, in an effort to follow faithfully he prays: "And lead us not into temptation." He does not end his prayer here, but continues, "but deliver us from evil." Is not this a parallel of the prayer Jesus prayed in the garden? Temptation, like the cross, is inevitable. We cannot avoid it. Therefore, we can only pray, "If temptation cannot be removed, when life places us in the midst of temptation, deliver us from its evil clutches. Keep us from yielding. Keep us faithful, even in the face of life's strongest temptations." I believe a true interpretation of this baffling portion of our Lord's prayer might read as follows: "Lord, when temptation is near, keep my soul from becoming contaminated; deliver me safely out of the possible evil that is involved."

In any consideration of temptation, we must take into account the following two facts. First, temptation is an inevitable certainty. A man or woman can no more live without facing temptation than one can breath without lungs. Second, God has endowed human personality with a free nature. That is to say, man has in life a freedom of choice. He can choose to court temptation, play with it, cultivate its friendship, become engaged in its evil scheme, and eventually become trapped in its morally degrading web.

The very fact that temptation exists and, further, that man is free to choose, opens the gate to possible moral disaster. This is not strange, because all of life is lived within certain unalterable laws. If you stand on a bridge and drop your car keys over the deep chasm below, the keys will be drawn to the bottom by the force of gravitation. One of the most common mathematical laws is illustrated in the fact that two plus two equals four.

Life is also governed by spiritual laws. No man can defy the laws of God and enjoy a large measure of spiritual peace and confidence. To do so is as incongruous as trying to mix water and gasoline. In view of inevitable temptation and man's freedom, here is a spiritual law which we ought to remember: God will give us the necessary moral fortitude to conquer and to be victorious over temptation.

Let me suggest some things that can be said about temptation, no matter in what form it appears.

God is both aware that we are being tempted and He is present during periods of temptation. He stands near to encourage us to take the right turn, and to urge us to make the right choice.

Paul wrote to the church at Corinth and said two significant things about temptation. First, he assured the Corinthians that God would never allow them to be tempted beyond their ability to remain true and faithful. That is to say, if we apply Paul's writings to our own situations, if we yield to temptation, we sin and become estranged from God by our own choosing. We may try to justify our actions by logic and rationalizations, but to yield to temptation is a sign of human weakness and not a deficiency in divine power. Poet Nathaniel Willis wrote, "No degree of temptation justifies any degree of sin."

In a second statement to the people of Corinth, Paul expressed in unequivocal terms his belief that God provides a way through which we may safely pass during temptations. "God," wrote Paul, "will with the temptation also make a way to escape, that ye may be able to bear it" (I Corinthians 10:13). Paul did not say that God would build a detour around temptations. God will never curb human desires. He will give us power to control them, and He will help us to consecrate them, but He will never remove them. God promises us that He will give us strength to overcome temptation and open a door whereby we may escape.

A few weeks ago, a successful businessman came to see me. He had been a faithful member of a church in another state. In his spiritual life he had developed a vital and wonderful relationship with God. He was promoted and moved to our city. His position almost demanded social drinking. He lived by the philosophy that anything that caused so much hardship and sorrow as alcohol was morally wrong. He was nervous and tense.

One day he went to the hospital for a physical checkup. The doctor told him he should quit drinking. "Now," he said, "I've got an excuse and I have quit drinking. When my friends offer me a drink, I simply tell them the doctor has ordered me to stop."

I told my visitor about another man I know who is the

president of his company. There was a time in this man's life when he drank excessively. He finally came to the conclusion that drinking was ruining his life; therefore, he quit. He is still tempted to drink when his old friends and associates are around, but God has opened a door that permits him to escape during these temptations. He simply says, "No, thank you, I don't drink any more." God opened for him the door of courage. It takes a lot of courage for this man to say what he does, but God has given him that courage.

When we are tempted, God will furnish an open door by which we can escape. It may be the door of courage, or the door of common sense. It may be the door of fair play, the application of the old adage "Do unto others as you would have them do unto you."

Think about the lonely hours Jesus spent in the Garden of Gethsemane on the night of the arrest. These were difficult hours for the Master. He was lonely, yet not alone; His soul was protected by His overwhelming desire to please His Father. His commitment to God's will saved Him. Do you suppose Jesus was tempted? I think so. Surely, He was tempted to escape. The shadow of an ugly cross must have covered His soul with mystery and despair. His soul was troubled, He trembled with fear. In this dark hour Jesus must have said to Himself, "I could run. I could get the disciples together and get out of Jerusalem. We could go back to Capernaum and work around the shores of Galilee. It was around the shores of Galilee that I healed Peter's mother-in-law, the lepers, and many others. We will be among friends. They will love and appreciate us."

During Jesus' mighty struggle in the garden, God came upon the scene. Above the rustle of the olive leaves, and beyond the clamor of personal desire, Jesus heard the voice of God. I think God must have said something like this, "My son, be not afraid. I am with you. The cross is cruel. It will be humiliating and painful. But it will stand for eternity as a symbol of my love for man. It will inspire and challenge the human family as long as men march across the stage of life. By the cross, men will be lifted from their lives of spiritual poverty to the riches of my grace. From the cross there will flow an unceasing stream of fresh and healing water, where thirsty men and women, boys and girls, may quench the deep thirst of their souls. Go to the cross, my son. I will open a door of love through which you may pass and not be polluted by the evil this temptation suggests."

Jesus passed through the door of love that night in the garden. He loved God with all His heart and soul and mind. He loved an undeserving humanity even more than He loved Himself. He was no longer tempted to run. God opened a door for Him.

Temptation is only an invitation to sin. Within itself, it is neither good nor evil. It brings neither honor nor shame. It was William Shakespeare who said, "It is one thing to be tempted, and another thing to fall." No man is ever divinely condemned by meeting temptation; we are condemned only when we make out of temptation a personal friend. Temptations from without can never harm the soul unless there is an overpowering and corresponding desire within. I like the first verse of an old hymn which was written by H. R. Palmer:

> Yield not to temptation
> For yielding is sin;
> Each victory will help you
> Some other to win;
> Fight manfully onward,
> Dark passions subdue;
> Look ever to Jesus
> He'll carry you through.

Temptation serves, I believe, as a testing ground for the soul. Some time ago I visited a factory where huge airplanes are manufactured. I was especially interested in the "endurance tests" the planes had to undergo. Undue stress and strain were administered to the plane, the purpose being to make the plane safe and to determine its limitations. Temptations sometimes try our strength and they reveal unto God something about our dependability or unworthiness, as the case may be.

Temptation in life is some ways like the testing of a ship.

A ship cannot be tested if anchored safely in the harbor of calm and protected water. Yet send this ship on a voyage, and in the middle of the ocean it encounters a great storm. The ship did not seek the storm; the storm is the result of certain atmospheric conditions. Nevertheless, the storm would try the strength of the ship and test the skill of the captain.

The tests of life are like that. There are times when we find ourselves surrounded by the mighty waves of temptation. We do not seek them. They are the result of conditions beyond our control. Nevertheless, these temptations challenge our spiritual strength and test our ability to mount the mighty waves of temptation and sail toward some noble and worthy harbor. One of my favorite little poems was written by R. L. Sharpe:

> Isn't it strange
> That princes and kings,
> And clowns that caper
> In sawdust rings,
> And common people
> Like you and me
> Are builders for eternity?
>
> Each is given a bag of tools,
> A shapeless mass,
> A book of rules;
> And each must make,
> Ere life is flown,
> A stumbling-block
> Or a stepping-tone.

Our ability to choose is a part of the tools, and our temptations represent a part of the shapeless mass out of which we will either make "a stumbling-block or a stepping-stone."

Temptation is a battleground upon which man's selfishness challenges God's divine will. Temptation is a conflict between that which I want to do and that which I know I ought to do.

Man is in grave danger at this point in life. We have been endowed with great strength. We can succeed in getting our way in life when we face many of life's temptations. Herein lies the danger. God will permit us to follow our foolish and selfish ways, rather than to restrict our freedom and force His will and wisdom upon us. We have seen people ruin their lives by insistence on getting their own way in life. They yield to one temptation after another. They satisfy one sinful desire after another until they find they have cast themselves on the scrap pile of broken dreams and empty hopes.

The challenge belongs to you and me. The decision is ours to make. Will we let Christ be at the center of life? No one can make this decision for us. We make it over and over again when we face temptation. May God help us to give Him first place.

The old saying, "There are two sides to everything," is certainly true regarding temptation. No discussion of this subject would be inclusive unless we look at both sides. Usually, when we think of temptation we think of some evil trap set for the righteous. However, there are also temptations, or righteous impulses—call them what you will—which emerge quite naturally along the trail of life. There are times in every life when we are overwhelmed with an inner longing to live on a higher plane. God places within us a feeling of discontent with the petty, mediocre, and lewd. He tempts us to leave the low road and travel the high way that leads to noble living.

Let us never stifle the temptation that incites righteousness. Poverty on the part of our neighbors tempts us to do something about it. Injustice stirs us to action. Wrong and suffering will not permit the sensitive soul to rest until some effort has been exerted to right the wrong and to relieve the pain. Such noble and righteous temptations flow from the heart of God through the stream of humanity.

Here is a strange note about temptation. The saint is far more sensitive and is aware of more temptations than those who are spiritually less mature. Think about this. The most difficult plateau upon which mortal feet can walk is the spiritual peak of sainthood. Some persons who are only half-dedicated to God dream about the ease and uninterrupted life of the saint. Yet a casual study of the lives of the saints tells us that they are not tempted less than others. A saintly person's keen perception of God's will keeps him constantly in the arena of temptation.

The average man measures his actions by what is socially acceptable; the saint measures his by divine standards. The average person is content to live in the boundaries of respectability; the saint is never quite satisfied with his life. The average man prays spasmodically; he repents occasionally. The saint marches through life with a prayer on his lips and unceasing repentance in his heart. The average man feels the need of God only during a crisis. The saint lives constantly in an awareness of his utter dependence upon God.

Once Paul wrote to the church at Corinth indicating his fervent desire to visit there. In Corinth he would get some needed rest. He would be among friends and they would care for his needs. In Ephesus, however, he saw a great opportunity to expand the boundaries of the Kingdom. He forgot himself and his wishes and thought only of God's will. He was tempted to go, but found the courage to stay. Paul wrote, "There are many adversaries" in Ephesus. Now, no one would have criticized Paul for continuing toward Corinth, which was a part of his plans. The halfhearted person would not have been aware of temptation at this juncture. But Paul, who had dedicated and conquered his desire for soft, comfortable living, recognized that his wish to visit Corinth was in opposition to a door of opportunity that had been opened.

The mountain peak of sainthood is not beyond the long and persistent arm of temptation. The saint must constantly crucify his opinions, his preferences, his tastes, and his will. Temptation appeals to man's selfishness. It comes in many forms. Let me suggest four.

1. Temptation attacks the powerful urges of our physical bodies. We have certain responsibilities toward this body. It makes continued demands upon us. It demands food, air, and water, as well as other things. Now, it would be foolish to assume that any kind of food is sufficient. Any good doctor or dietitian will tell you that it is not the amount of food you eat that counts as much as it is the type of food you eat. It is not satisfactory to give your body unclean air; it must be reasonably pure. We spend uncounted millions of dollars each year in an effort to purify the water we drink. The body could not survive on polluted water. These simple facts about the demands of our bodies should reveal to us some important truths: namely, the body needs constant care, regular attention, and intelligent management. It is common knowledge to the refined soul that many demands of the body must be curbed, controlled, and mastered.

Consider the sex instinct, for example; it is one of the most powerful urges of life. To live by the philosophy that it must be satisfied on our own terms will ruin civilization and bring the soul to moral chaos. This desire, like many other desires, must be kept under constant guard and wise supervision. The sex life of an individual must be consecrated and satisfied only in the framework of God's eternal will.

The Bible tells us that after the baptism of Jesus, He fasted forty days and forty nights. "And when the tempter came to him, he said, If thou be the Son of God, command that these stones be made bread" (Matthew 4:3). This temptation represents a real struggle, a struggle between a weary soul and the power of evil. Jesus must have said to Himself, "I cannot fail. To yield would be to lose everything." This temptation appears to be an innocent one; Jesus was hungry. It is no sin either to be hungry or to satisfy this basic need in life. Jesus' friends were hungry, and our Lord was well aware of the fact that men suffered in poverty because of the heavy burden of the Roman taxes. The tempter must have emphasized the hunger of Jesus, and I suspect he said, "If thou be the Son of God, command that these stones be made bread. Feed the hungry; help wipe out some of this poverty." But Jesus would not be tricked. He was weak from fasting, but He was spiritually alert.

Jesus' temptation born of hunger goes deeper than simply feeding an empty stomach. It was an occasion to scar a pure soul; it was a temptation to doubt God. Jesus could have turned stones to bread, but in doing so He would have been saying, "I must prove to Myself that I am truly God's Son." The tempter began, "If thou be the Son of God. . . ." Jesus knew He was the Son of God. He would not doubt that for a single minute.

The temptation to ease His hunger encouraged Jesus to misuse the power of God. He was hungry, and He needed to eat; therefore, He was tempted to use His power to satisfy His own personal need. This He would not do. When others were starving, they could not turn stones to bread and satisfy their inner craving for food; neither would Jesus do so to satisfy His hunger. Jesus taught a lesson we need to learn as He answered the tempter, "It is written, Man shall not live by bread alone, but by every word that proceedeth out of the mouth of God" (Matthew 4:4).

For the individual, it is not enough to own two cars and belong to the country club. Happiness does not come from drinking out of sparkling crystal or eating with glittering silver. We must not live for things that pass away. We need to anchor our hopes upon things eternal. The abundant life is found not in things, but in obeying the commands of God.

For the nation, it is not sufficient to have more missiles, muscles, and satellites. If we survive and live together in peace, we must live by understanding, forgiveness, and respect for the dignity of man.

2. Temptation spurs man's desire for popularity. We all

have the desire to be "somebody." In the New Testament there is a very interesting story of an ambitious mother. She asked Jesus to give her two sons a favored place in the Kingdom.

The desire to be popular must be guided. There is nothing wrong with the desire to be a congenial, well-thought-of and popular person. In fact, I think Jesus wanted this kind of relationship with people. The important question we need to ask is this, "What will it cost us to gain popularity?" If we must lose our self-respect, degrade our souls, or yield to earthly temptations, then popularity is too costly.

When Jesus was tempted to jump from the pinnacle of the temple, He must have thought of the effect this would have on the crowd. Surely this would gain Him a great following. Such a stunt would prove to the crowd that Jesus not only trusted God, but in this exhibition men could see the power of God at work. Yet Jesus knew that the Kingdom of God would not come out of some miracle, but would grow gradually. It would come not because of the spectacular, but as the result of hearts and minds being captured by His unswerving loyalty to God, His unceasing love to man, and His unwavering faith in the goodness and wisdom of God.

3. Man's thirst for power is another form of temptation with which we must deal. Power rightly used will bring honor and progress. Power used selfishly brings dishonor, shame, and misery beyond man's ability to imagine. The greatest tragedies ever to befall the human race have come as the result of men who let power corrupt their sense of man's worth. Because ungodly men have stood at the helm of governments, civilizations have been destroyed, talents squandered, justice trampled, and unnumbered millions have entered prematurely into the silent halls of death.

The third temptation of our Lord was probably the greatest crisis He faced until the night of His arrest. The tempter took Jesus to the peak of a high mountain; here, he showed Him all the kingdoms of the world and asked for a compromise. "All these things will I give thee, if thou wilt fall down and worship me" (Matthew 4:9).

Evil has a way of taking what it can get. If it cannot get all of a man's devotion, it will endeavor to get a little. Consider the man who has experienced the evils and heartaches of alcohol. With the help of God he stops drinking. The tempter does not urge him to get drunk; he knows this approach will not work. He simply says, "Just take one drink. What harm can that do? Just take one to be sociable." This is the compromise.

As Jesus surveyed the countryside from the top of the mountain where He had been bidden by the tempter, His mind must have been full of thoughts of how much He wanted the kingdoms that were spread out below. The Hebrews had been ruthlessly treated for decade after decade; at the very time of the temptation, Roman soldiers marched in every town of any size. Jesus must have reviewed His purpose in life. He decided once and for all that He must work with His Father if a new Kingdom were to be ushered into the pagan world. He fully committed Himself to walk under the sway of God's will. Jesus never misused His power; He never compromised with evil. He was always ready to say, "Thy will be done." He repeated again and again that He had come to do the work of His Father.

4. Our desire for material things is another form of temptation that we need to conquer. Suppose someone were to ask you to name the one thing among your possessions that you consider priceless. What would you name? You may have some expensive jewels, or antiques. Even if these objects could not be replaced, there is something more valuable. When I look at my own situation in the light of this question, I say without hesitation that my little son is the most important thing that has been entrusted to my care. I don't know of anything on the face of the earth that excels in importance over life. It may denote a little egotism on the part of man to feel that he is so significant, yet the writer of the story of cre-

ation reminds us that human personality is made in the image of God.

In our busy pace of living it is easy to allow our goals to be mixed and our purposes confused. I have talked to many people who have let this happen. Peter let it happen in his life. Jesus told His disciples that He would be rejected by the elders and scribes, that He would be killed by ruthless and indifferent men. Peter interrupted at this point. According to the Bible, he began to rebuke Jesus. I can imagine Peter's saying something like this, "Master, this will not happen. No one will dare lay a hand on You. I will take the personal responsibility to see that it does not happen. You can count upon me to protect You with my very life."

Then Jesus spoke to Peter, saying, "Thou savourest not the things that be of God, but the things that be of men" (Mark 8:33). Jesus was saying to Peter, "I know you mean well, but you are confused. You have placed your own wishes and hopes above the will and wisdom of God."

When Jesus saw the shadow of the cross in the Garden of Gethsemane, He cautioned His disciples. They were in danger of deserting Him in His time of need and, thereby, deserting themselves. Jesus knew the disciples would be tempted to run. Therefore, He said to the three sleeping disciples, "Watch ye and pray, lest ye enter into temptation. The spirit truly is ready, but the flesh is weak" (Mark 14:38).

Let us be determined not to court temptation. Many people find themselves engaged in a mighty struggle with temptation simply because they have opened the door and invited it to come in for a visit. For instance, let us think of the businessman who intends to be honest in filling out his expense account, but who soon discovers his associates are taking advantage of the company. The tempter whispers, "Go ahead, it's only a few dollars." The businessman rejects the suggestion. But the tempter comes again, "You work as hard as the others. Everybody else is doing it. You might as well get your share." He yields.

There are five questions which we ought to ask ourselves in the presence of temptation.

1. If I engage in this activity, will it degrade human personality? Human personality at its best is noble. It is sacred. It shines with a spiritual lustre that denotes divine worth. It is never ashamed. When temptation sends us an invitation, we ought, before we accept, to be certain that we will emerge from the experience with a high regard for ourselves. Jesus must have asked Himself this question as He faced temptation, "Will I be less than what God expects of Me if I turn stones to bread, jump from the pinnacle, or worship Satan?" The answer came back strong and clear, "Yes." If after objective scrutiny, you get an affirmative answer to the question of degrading personality, reject the invitation.

2. Another question by which we can test temptation is this, "Where will it lead me?" Every deed is a step leading somewhere. It may be toward the land of gladness and holy living or it could be in the direction of misery and moral degradation.

Using one curse word will not make you an habitual user of profanity; it is only one short step in that direction. Betting on one race horse will not make you a gambling addict; it simply opens the door to that possibility. No one ever became an alcoholic by sipping one cocktail; on the other hand, there are no alcoholics who have never taken the first drink. Unless the activity sends us on the road that leads to worthy habits, we ought to conquer the temptation.

3. Still another question we should consider in the presence of temptation is this, "Will my engaging in this activity cause another to stumble?" We do not live unto ourselves. I believe God holds us responsible for our influence upon other people. In the light of the life and death of our Lord, we have come to believe that the answer to that ancient question, "Am I my brother's keeper?" is definitely "Yes."

We must not forget that our relationship with others will, in no small measure, determine our relationship with God.

The two cannot be divorced. The Christian attitude is to shun temptation if the results would adversely affect another.

4. Then, we ought to examine temptation in the light of this question, "Would I be willing to permit those I love most to enter into this activity?" We may be sure that anything that would not be good for those we love would not be good for us. One of the greatest commandments, according to Jesus, is this: "Thou shalt love thy neighbour as thyself" (Mark 12:31). In view of the question under consideration we could turn this commandment around and be determined to love ourselves as much as we love others.

5. Finally, let us give this acid test to the temptations we face: "If I yield to this temptation, will it meet the standard of God's will for my life?" In all His relationships Jesus lived by the rule, "Not my will, but thine be done."

Remember two things about temptation: First, you cannot escape it; second, God will give you the power to be victorious and overcome the strongest and most insistent temptations.

CHAPTER 2

BURDENS: *Hold Fast to the Eternal*

ON MY DESK there is a stack of letters that have come to me during the past few months. In a way, these letters are very special to me; they represent the heartaches, broken dreams, crushed hopes, wasted lives, and, in general, the tremendously heavy burdens the writers have been called upon to shoulder. In reading these letters I have noticed that this little phrase, "Please pray for me," appears in each of them.

Consider, for instance, this letter: a woman writes, "I have been in the hospital for over two long years. I have known many sleepless nights and at times the pain is almost unbearable. Please pray that God will give me strength to remain a faithful disciple until the end."

Another person writes, "My wife and I have tried to live a good life; we have always gone to church and have done everything we knew that a Christian ought to do. In spite of this, our only son has been stricken with an incurable disease. He is now at the point of death. Please pray for us. I am about to lose my faith in God. I cannot understand why God let this happen to us. Could you give me the answer to the question *why?*"

Now the question *why* is exceedingly difficult to answer. It is much easier to answer other questions, such as: when did it happen? where did it happen? how did it happen? Human wisdom can usually supply the answers to the latter questions. Only God will be able to give us an answer to the *why* of the baffling and sometimes agonizing experiences that cause many of us to cry out in utter desperation.

When I was a freshman in college I was appointed to serve six rural churches in the beautiful mountains of western North Carolina. Soon after I arrived, someone asked me to visit a sick member of one of the little churches for which I had been given the responsibility. I was given a little of the man's background: he was almost fifty years old, and he had spent the last twenty years of his life in one room, flat on his back. I was frightened at the thought of seeing this man. The thought that came to my mind was this: Suppose he should ask me this question, "Why did this happen to me?" What would I say? Would I be adequately prepared to represent God in a situation such as this? I must admit that I felt rather insecure. I prayed that God would put the words in my mouth that should be expressed in case the sick man questioned me.

My fears subsided as I entered the house, and they vanished completely as I walked into the room. I could see the faint shadow of a smile across his pain-racked face. "Come on in, Preacher," he said. "I am glad to see you." We talked for a long while and before I left he said something like this to me, "Twenty years in this little room is a long time. There are times when I feel like screaming because the pain is so intense. But God helps me through each day. I am not complaining, but a man cannot help but wonder at times why he must bear such a heavy load. Then, I think of Christ. He never asked *why*. He only asked God for strength to live life to its fullest. When you come to think about it, twenty years is a mighty short time compared to eternity. Somehow, I know that I was born, not for a few years of suffering, but for eternity. I have stopped asking *why*—I just pray for the courage and strength to be faithful."

I left that room with a new song upon my lips. I said to myself, "I may never understand why some people struggle under the weight of many burdens, but I know God stands in the shadows keeping watch over His own. No man could stay in a little twelve-by-fourteen room for twenty years and grow such a radiant spirit unless God is with him."

When we learn to carry our burdens, it seems so unnecessary to find the answer to the question *why*. Jesus had some questions in His mind as He looked at Calvary from the Garden of Gethsemane. ". . . Now is my soul troubled," said Jesus, "and what shall I say?" (John 12:27). Was Jesus trying to understand the cross? Was He asking God to tell Him *why?* Whatever the reason, Jesus did not hesitate for long. He whispered to His Father, "Father, glorify thy name . . ." (John 12:28).

The miracle of *how* stands at the center of the stage when we accept our burdens. How can one shoulder the heavy load and stand with a noble spirit and proclaim as his daily litany the words of the psalmist, "The Lord is good to all: and his tender mercies are over all his works" (Psalm 145:9). The answer is found when we come to know the truth of the words of Moses as he blessed the twelve tribes of Israel before his death. "The eternal God is thy refuge, and underneath are the everlasting arms . . ." (Deuteronomy 33:27). When we feel the presence of God and know that His strong arms are around us, we have found the source of strength that enables us to walk through the dark nights toward the dawn with an unwavering faith in both His goodness and His wisdom.

The questions which keep raising their heads in many minds are these: Does God send the storms of life; and, are these heavy burdens divinely appointed? These questions have a magnitude that is far-reaching. They are important and need to be analyzed.

There are those who contend that God sends the storms of

life and causes the waves to beat upon the sides of our little ships. These storms, they reason, are not without a divine purpose; they come in order to make us look at our lives and alter our courses and head toward some noble harbor. These people give sustenance to the idea that we must walk across the chasm of sorrow, suffering, and disappointment before we reach the summit of our spiritual development.

One of the most thought-provoking incidents in the New Testament is the story of the blind man who had never seen a lovely flower, the blue sky, or a majestic sunrise. He was born blind. The disciples asked Jesus this question, ". . . who did sin, this man, or his parents . . .?" (John 9:2). They took for granted that the blindness was payment for either the man's own sins or the mistakes of his parents. This is clear evidence of the early conception that man's burdens were the fruits of evil living. It should go without saying that many of our heavy burdens are due to our own selfish ways. Some are due to our neglect. However, we cannot account for all the difficulties we encounter by writing them off as the result of sin.

Jesus spoke quickly and clearly after the disciples posed the question as to whether the blind man's handicap was due to somebody's sin. ". . . Neither hath this man sinned," said Jesus, "nor his parents . . ." (John 9:3). There can be no doubt in our minds that many of our burdens come from sources other than sin.

The next remark Jesus made gives some evidence to the position held by many people that God is directly responsible for sending our burdens in order for us to achieve a higher good. That is to say, the burdens we bear are mere training exercises that will enable us to become stronger in the faith and more effective in our Christian witness. However, this does not explain the many experiences people endure that tend to drive them away from God. Jesus indicated that the man in question was born blind for a divine purpose. He is blind in order ". . . that the works of God should be made manifest in him" (John 9:3). How shall we interpret this baffling remark of our Lord? First, we can interpret the statement of Jesus to mean that the man's burden of blindness was sent to him directly from God's throne. Therefore, he is blind according to a divine order and God will be glorified through his blindness. This would be a simple answer to all the burdens, heartaches, and suffering we feel in life. In days of agonizing pain and crushing sorrow we could explain them by saying, "God has given them to us for a divine purpose." This view satisfies some people, but it leaves me with an even greater conflict.

How can I reconcile the love, goodness, and mercy of God with so much suffering in the world? The innocent suffer; some enter this life and suffer from the door of birth to the door of death.

I stood, some months ago, by the bed of a little seven-year-old girl. She had a smile on her face, but an ugly disease was gradually sapping her strength and would eventually take her life. Medical science, up to this time, has not found the answer to this problem. One day scientists will conquer this disease, but it will be too late for this little girl. I could neither satisfy myself nor the grief-stricken parents by saying, "Don't worry about this, God sent this disease and something good will come out of it." I do not doubt for one minute that God can transform all our burdens and as a result of His presence and power make something good out of them; on the other hand, I fail to see God as the instigator of many tragedies that men experience.

Jesus taught us that God is like a good shepherd. Now, a good shepherd loves his sheep. He counts them at the end of the day to be sure that all of them are safely in the shelter he has provided. He checks each sheep to see if it has wounds that need his attention. If he discovers one sheep missing from the fold, he returns to the pasture in search for the lost. The shepherd may be weary, but he refuses to think of himself; he thinks only of the welfare of his sheep. When he finds the lost sheep, he gently lifts it to his shoulders and carefully takes it to the fold. Now, I believe God is like that.

In the course of a week I go in and out of many hospitals and see many people with burdens that are almost unbearable. I am forced to conclude and say with Plato, "Of our troubles we must seek some other cause than God."

Second, we can interpret the statement of Jesus to mean that without this man's blindness the glory of God could not be made manifest in him. That is to say, God did not send the burden to him; he is blind because of other circumstances. However, because of his blindness and Christian spirit, God will be glorified. In this situation man's weakness gives expression to God's strength and greatness. The man's blindness made him the object of a great miracle. God could not have used a man with twenty-twenty vision to manifest His glory in this way. This is a truth we forget or fail to see at all when we travel under the load of heavy burdens. It is conceivable that God can use us with greater effectiveness when we walk under the shadow of sorrow and disappointment. Most people will be remembered not because of the ease with which they sailed the sea of life, but because of the storms they faced and the struggles over which they became conquerors. This has been true many times.

I know a man who will be an inspiration to his friends as long as they live and remember him. He suffered more than any other person I have ever been privileged to know. For month after month he endured excruciating pain. Yet, in all of this, he waved high the flag of faith. No one could look at him even in his dying days and not be able to see that he was victorious. It was not play-acting; men do not play-act when the certain hands of death are on the scene. That man's gentle spirit, his kind thoughts, his unwavering courage, his unrelenting patience, his unflinching belief in God's unceasing love and infinite wisdom will serve to remind others that God will help His children to live above the burdens of life.

Think of David Livingstone. He spent thirty-three long

years in the jungles of Africa. He broke away from those he loved in order to tell Africa's native people about God's love. Several times Livingstone barely escaped death, but this did not discourage him. Injustice and sin stalked the earth and he dedicated himself to replace man's ignorance with knowledge; man's suspicion with understanding; and man's hate with boundless love. Livingstone traveled through the jungles of Africa with a few black friends proclaiming the goodness of God. His body was weak from sickness, yet he bound up the wounds of others, started a school, and planned a church. He never retreated; he died on duty, and in recognition of his courageous missionary work against such death-defying odds the British empire saw to it that Livingstone's abused body was laid to rest in Westminster Abbey.

David Livingstone's bruised body and heavy burdens have caused many young missionaries to light their torches of faith and travel to the corners of the earth to tell others about the love of Christ. Had Livingstone refused to take God's hand and fight to his death under the weight of such opposition, God's glory could not have been reflected in him.

I know there is a reason behind the burdens we bear, and frequently we do not understand that reason. The source of our burdens lies sometimes within ourselves. This is true, even though we may be ignorant of the cause. Then, we bear some burdens because we are the victims of circumstances beyond our control. Try as we may, there is absolutely nothing we can do to change the situation. Finally, I would be willing to admit that in the great wisdom of God He may lead us down a rough road where there are many burdens. If this be the case, we are assured of the victory through the power of God even before the journey begins.

Hanna Whitall Smith, who wrote *The Christian's Secret of a Happy Life,* lived by this philosophy. Sometimes the Good Shepherd leads us in pastures not of our own choosing. We find there opposition and earthly trials. When God leads us in a situation such as this, we will grow and become strong.

There may be times when He feels that it is best to lead us not by the still waters, but beside boisterous waves and streams of sorrow and troubled waters. Even here, He will give us courage to lie down beside these waters and receive from them a spiritual blessing. "The Shepherd," writes Hanna Smith, "knows what pastures are best for his sheep, and they must not question nor doubt, but trustingly follow him."

When our burdens cast a shadow of confusion over our souls, we should remember the wise words of the writer of the Proverbs, "Trust in the Lord with all thine heart; and lean not unto thine own understanding. In all thy ways acknowledge him, and he shall direct thy paths" (Proverbs 3:5, 6).

There is an old hymn I like to sing. The Lord did not give me much talent in the area of singing, but I enjoy trying. E. W. Blandly wrote this hymn and the chorus ought to be the theme song of every Christian. It is an expression of complete trust in God. The chorus goes something like this:

> Where He leads me I will follow,
> Where He leads me I will follow,
> Where He leads me I will follow,
> I'll go with Him, with Him all the way.

When we come to the place in life where we trust Him unreservedly, the burdens of life are lifted. It matters not how many troubled waters cover our souls, life will be both beautiful and abundant. God will see to that.

Let us look at Calvary; it is a cruel and ugly scene. The taunts of evil men, the slurs of the crowd, and the indifference of a host of people are sufficient enough to make a sensitive man sick to his stomach. At the center of the stage, yea, even at the center of history, there is a stalwart Man, weary with the burdens of the world. The spirit of this Man demands our attention. He is exhausted; He looks defeated; yet, He is kind and gentle. His heart seems to go out to the crowd. His lips move slowly, as if He is praying. The rough soldiers carry out their orders: steel spikes are driven through Christ's hands and feet; His side is pierced. The blood gushes down His legs and drips to the ground from the ends of His toes. A crown of sharp thorns is pressed onto His head. His body is racked with pain. Finally, His strength is gone; life ebbs away; He draws His last breath and dies.

What a horrible sight! Here was the only Man who ever lived without participating in the evil of the world. His life was spotless, His hands were clean, His heart was pure. Yet, God was glorified on Calvary more than at any other place in history. God took this ugly picture of His Son, struggling under the heaviest burden that the human mind is capable of imagining, and made out of it the most magnificent expression of God's love, concern, and forgiveness of mankind.

Thank God there are people who permit their burdens to be used to speak of God's love rather than to cast a shadow of doubt and skepticism over the lives of those who watch us struggle in the arena.

When Moses began the exciting and challenging task of releasing the Hebrews from slavery in Egypt and leading them to the Promised Land, God gave him some clear instructions. First, God assured Moses that he could accomplish such a great feat. "Come now therefore, and I will send thee unto Pharaoh, that thou mayest bring forth my people the children of Israel out of Egypt" (Exodus 3:10). God expected Moses to succeed. He knew Moses could do the job. He did not say, "I want you to go and try to deliver the Hebrews." God sent him to "bring them forth." Second, God assured Moses that He would be with him. No man ever walks down the road of life by himself. God is always near to give strength. God said to Moses, ". . . I will be with thee . . ." (Exodus 3:12). Finally, God promised to show Moses what to do and to teach him what to say. The Lord said to Moses, "I . . . will teach you what ye shall do" (Exodus 4:15).

Sometimes, perhaps by circumstances or perhaps by divine orders, life has a way of pushing us into a corner. The cares and burdens of life press hard upon our souls. Our strength at its best becomes weak; our courage at its height fails, and suddenly we become aware of our miserable plight. Everyone who reads these lines must have sailed down the river of crushed hopes, broken dreams, and unrealized aspirations. Could we not all say that there are times when life is not as fruitful as we had expected. Life is like an electronic computer; if you get the right answers, you must feed it the correct information. The harvest we garner from life is completely dependent upon the seed we plant and the virtues we cultivate.

What shall we do when we find our burdens more than we can bear alone? Do you recall these words of Washington Gladden?

> In the bitter waves of woe,
>   Beaten and tossed about
> By the sullen winds that blow
>   From the desolate shores of doubt,
> When the anchors that faith has cast
>   Are dragging in the gale,
> I am quietly holding fast
>   To the things that cannot fail.

When burdens are heavy, I can at least do this: I can hold fast to the things that cannot fail. But what are the things that cannot fail? Let me suggest three things to which we can anchor our hopes during the days when burdens press upon us.

1. God knows that we can face all of life and be victorious. He never places us in a hopeless situation. We may stumble and fall, but God will provide the strength for us to get up and walk again. If we fall under the weight of heavy burdens and give up the struggle, it is not God's fault, it is our own.

2. We can hold fast to this eternal truth: God walks down the path of life with us. We are never alone.

The *Saturday Evening Post* published a story entitled "The Marvelous Mayos." In this story the writer tells about a patient who went to the Mayo Clinic for a physical check-up. After the examination, Dr. Charles W. Mayo frightened his patient when he gave his verdict: "You need an operation immediately."

The patient nervously twisted her hands and remarked, "But I'll be all alone."

Dr. Mayo gently tapped her on the hand and said, "No you won't, I'll be with you."

This very thing happened to Moses. He was afraid; he thought his task was beyond his own strength, and he was right. Moses could never have lifted the burden alone. God tapped him on the shoulder and gave him assurance of His presence.

Somewhere in the Garden of Gethsemane Jesus felt the tap on the shoulder. God gave Jesus strength to face the cross. An awareness of this truth caused the psalmist to say, "Yea, though I walk through the valley of the shadow of death, I will fear no evil: for thou art with me; thy rod and thy staff they comfort me" (Psalm 23:4).

Such an experience can be ours. God is constantly tapping us on the shoulder and whispering in our ear, "Do not be afraid. I will stand beside you to guide and help you through this situation."

3. Third, we can hold fast to the knowledge that God is on our side. Once the psalmist cried, ". . . for God is for me" (Psalm 56:9). Let us not become confused at this point. God is always on our side, but we are frequently found playing for the opposing team. Our task is to make sure that we are on God's side. If we accomplish this, we will certainly succeed.

The psalmist asked a question that we ought to entertain when our burdens become heavy, "Who is so great a God as our God?" The psalmist thought about the greatness and goodness of God. He talked about God's power and strength. He reminded us that God is adequate for all our needs. This is something we forget. God is on our side and His strength is sufficient. What else do we need to know? It appears to me that this is sufficient. When a man comes to believe, and anchors his hopes on the following truths, there is no problem he cannot solve, and no burden he cannot bear. First, God believes in me, therefore my situation is not hopeless. Second, God walks with me, therefore I am never alone. Third, God is on my side, therefore I cannot lose.

The difference between spiritual success and failure is not so much how many storms we face, but rather how we face them. The record book is filled with illustrations that reflect the truth of this statement.

Several years ago a friend told me about two people whom we knew during the depression: both were very wealthy; both lost their fortunes. One man went home and took a gun and ended his own life; the other went to the altar of his church and prayed. He asked God to give him the courage to face reality and the wisdom to meet the uncertain days ahead with Christian fortitude. One man took his life during the storm, and the other man found his.

Look at the two men who were crucified with Jesus. One of them turned to Jesus and said, ". . . If thou be Christ, save thyself and us" (Luke 23:39). The thief was saying, "I don't believe you are the Christ. If you were, you would do something about our situation. You are only pretending." This is a cry that God hears daily.

The other man rebuked his companion, for he saw in his own death a bit of justice. He was ready to confess his sins. "We receive the due reward of our deeds: but this man hath done nothing amiss" (Luke 23:41).

The second man turned to Jesus after rebuking his friend and said, ". . . Lord, remember me when thou comest into thy kingdom" (Luke 23:42). This man knew that his plight could not be changed. He was reaping the harvest of an evil past. Jesus was his only hope.

The Master said unto him, ". . . Verily I say unto thee, today shalt thou be with me in paradise" (Luke 23:43).

The penitent thief caught a glimpse of an eternal truth as he hung on the cross. I think this man must have had a good mother. She surely must have taught him that God does not change. He knew this eternal truth: Pain and sorrow can never obstruct God's love and concern for us. He also knew that man must pay for his sins. He recognized in Christ the only person who could redeem his past. He did not ask to have his immediate situation changed; he merely wanted the courage to face the descending clouds of pain and death. This he could face if God would forgive his sins.

Job knew that God never deserts His people. Job refused to distrust God during his days of darkness. We need to learn this truth. There is no reason to doubt God during moments of sorrow or days of struggle when heavy burdens bear down upon us. God is still God, no matter what happens.

Paul labored in the face of overwhelming opposition. He wrote, "We are troubled on every side, yet not distressed; we are perplexed, but not in despair; persecuted, but not forsaken; cast down, but not destroyed" (II Corinthians 4: 8-9). Paul faced prison, shipwrecks, and beatings, not asking God *why,* but thanking Him for the privilege of suffering with Him.

Heavy burdens may try our strength, but they need not weaken us; they may cause us pain, but they need not distress us; they may rest heavy upon our hearts, but they need not crush us. The question that remains is this: "How shall we react to the burdens of life?" Let me suggest five things to remember when the burdens of life press upon us.

1. *We must learn to accept our burdens as a part of life.* The burdens of life, as well as the joys of life, represent a part of the price we must pay for the privilege of living. The quicker we realize this truth the more victorious we shall be in dealing with life's perplexities. Someone has written:

> We are not here to play, to dream and drift,
>   We have work to do and loads to lift,
>   Shun not the struggle, face it, 'tis God's gift.

Job came to the conclusion that trials are a part of life. "Yet man is born unto trouble," said Job, "as the sparks fly up-ward" (Job 5:7). That is to say, we cannot avoid the tribula-tions of life, therefore, we must accept them.

For many weeks, I visited a man who was in great pain; naturally, he was depressed. The doctors had not been able to find the cause of his pain. One day he seemed better, and I asked him if the cause of his suffering had been found.

"Yes," he replied, "the cause has been found, and there is nothing that can be done to help me. The doctor told me the diagnosis, and after he left I asked God to give me the grace to accept this as a part of my life. He has already given me that strength." When a man learns to accept the things that life brings which cannot be changed, he is well on the road to overcoming his burdens.

2. *We ought to make up our minds to be faithful.* You do not become a competent doctor, an effective preacher, or a good parent by accident. You have to work at it. The people who succeed are the folks who make up their minds to suc-ceed. "I have found," wrote Lincoln, "that most people are about as happy as they make up their minds to be."

To be completely faithful is not as easy as it sounds. Sup-pose a young high-school student hears the call of God to enter the ministry to become a missionary to some foreign land. Then, suppose the student makes up his mind to re-spond. The decision is only the first step; there are many years of preparation. He must go to college and attend a theological school. He will be required to study the language of the people with whom he will live and serve. All this re-quires determination, discipline, and effort.

Moses warned Israel about the temptations they would en-counter in the strange lands through which they would pass. He tried to prepare them for the difficult journey. In days of tribulation if you seek God, you will surely find Him. Moses assured the Hebrews that this is the only door of hope that would always be open to them. When tribulations are upon you, ". . . turn to the Lord thy God, . . ." said Moses, "For the Lord thy God is a merciful God; he will not forsake thee . . ." (Deuteronomy 4:30-31). When we make up our minds and submit ourselves to God, no burden is unbearable.

Just before his death, Joshua called the tribes of Israel together and talked to them. Joshua challenged the people to make up their minds about whom they would serve. Pagan gods had attracted them at times. In Joshua's valedictory he reminded the children of God's goodness and urged them to choose whom they would serve. Then, Joshua told the people that he had made up his mind; ". . . We will serve the Lord" (Joshua 24:15).

I know a man who at one time in his life had just about become a slave to alcohol. He soon discovered that he was losing his family and that alcohol was ruining his health. One day he made a covenant with God to stop drinking. "I'll furnish the effort," he told God, "if you'll furnish the strength." He had made up his mind to stop drinking. This was the first step, and for week after week he struggled. It was a tremendous battle, but God kept His end of the bargain. One day the man failed to put forth the effort and slipped back to the bottle. Again, he promised God he would try if God would help him. He asked God to forgive his sins. The struggle within this man is still going on, but I know God will help him and I believe that together they will win the struggle.

3. *Let us grab hold of our hopes and take God as our partner.* Mr. R. L. Middleton, in his book *Thinking About God,* tells a story about Clarence Powell, Jr., a construction worker who lived in Philadelphia. There was a time in the life of this man when he found his financial situation most alarming. As a young married man Powell made an adequate salary as long as he worked, but there were periods when the company had no work to be done. The Powells were the parents of six children, and one fall just before school was due to begin, they discovered that three of their children had

worn out their shoes. They had worn them out skipping, and using their feet for brakes as they coasted down a hill in their wagons. In the meantime, the family washing machine had broken down hopelessly and Clarence Powell searched the newspapers in an effort to find a second-hand machine for sale. He found one advertised and went to the address which was listed.

The house was large and beautiful, so much so that Powell was reluctant to enter. When he rang the doorbell, a kind-looking gentleman answered. Powell told him that he had come to look at the washing machine and he was invited into the house. As he walked to the kitchen to see the machine, he looked in astonishment. Everything was so convenient and beautiful. The man and his wife offered to sell the machine for such a small amount that Clarence, in an effort to express his gratitude, thanked them kindly and at the same time told them that he was in financial difficulty, explaining that he had no work and three of his children had completely worn out their shoes. As he finished speaking, the lady left the room, sobbing as if her heart would break. "Did I say something wrong?" asked Clarence.

"No," replied the husband, "you didn't say anything wrong. You were talking about children's shoes being worn out. We have only one child, a little girl, and she's never walked a step in her life. A pair of worn-out shoes would make us very happy."

After this experience Clarence Powell said, "I went back home and went up to my room and closed the door. I got down on my knees and asked the Lord to forgive me for fretting about little things. I got those three pairs of shoes and looked at them and smiled. I was so thankful for three pairs of worn-out shoes. . . ." We would forget some of our burdens if we focused our attention on the many good things we enjoy from God instead of brooding over our burdens.

When David received word that "the hearts of the people of Israel are after Absalon," he placed his life in the hands of

God and said, ". . . let him do to me as seemeth good unto him" (II Samuel 15:26). Instead of spending our energy rebelling against God, we should seek His will and in this search we shall find His peace.

4. *We should resolve to live each day to the best of our ability.* I am convinced that marriages break up, men fail in business, and people fall under the weight of pressing cares, all because we do not practice what we know is best. Men do not fail because of lack of knowledge: They fail because they do not do the things they know they ought to do in their daily lives.

The prophet proclaimed a long time ago that we know the rules of life; ". . . and what doth the Lord require of thee, but to do justly, and to love mercy, and to walk humbly with thy God?" (Micah 6:8).

I frequently give people two bits of advice; I believe it is good medicine. Most of us need this advice. First, do your best. Let each of us search his heart and ask himself the question, "Am I doing my best to make life what it ought to be?" Most of us would have to answer *no.* Then, I advise many people to slow down. We do our best work when we take time out and give all our talents and energies to the task at hand. The only animal that can do its work more efficiently while in a hurry is a race horse.

Thomas Carlyle, Scottish historian, wrote in one of his essays: "You should not worry about the dim, unknown and unknowable future, but you should view the duty that is closest at hand and accomplish as best you can the task that needs to be done this day." It was Jesus who said, "Take therefore no thought for the morrow: for the morrow shall take thought for the things of itself . . ." (Matthew 6:34). Jesus also taught His disciples to pray, "Give us this day our daily bread."

"It has been well said," remarked George Macdonald, a Scottish novelist, "that no man ever sank under the burden of the day. It is when tomorrow's burden is added to the burden of today that the weight is more than a man can bear. Never load yourselves so, my friends. If you find yourselves so loaded, at least remember this: it is your own doing, not God's. He begs you to leave the future to Him and mind the present." Take one step at a time. Remember that "the longest journey begins with a single step."

5. *Finally, let us cast our burdens upon the Lord.* The psalmist wrote, several hundred years ago: "Cast thy burden upon the Lord, and he shall sustain thee . . ." (Psalm 55:22). This means that we can be sustained. Most of us look for bargains in life and here is a bargain that we can't afford to miss. God will provide the strength, and we furnish the burdens. God promised the children of Israel that they would be equal to the burdens they might encounter on the long journey through the wilderness. ". . . as thy days, so shall thy strength be" (Deuteronomy 33:25). Surely this means no less than to place our burdens upon the strong shoulders of God and He will help us bear them.

Iona Henry tells a moving story in her book *Triumph Over Tragedy* about losing her fourteen-year-old daughter Jane, with a brain tumor. A month later Mrs. Henry, her husband Pete, and Jack, their ten-year-old son, decided to visit Pete's father. They began the journey early one morning. On the third of the trip they met tragedy. A fast-moving freight train hit their car as they attempted to cross the railroad track near St. Louis. Pete and Jack were killed instantly, and Iona Henry was critically injured. Would Iona Henry live? This was the big question that trained doctors and nurses could not answer. If she knew that her son and husband were dead, would she want to live? Could she find the strength and courage to pick up the broken dreams of life and make out of them a new life? Would she be able to find in her sorrow a purpose that would challenge her? Only time would tell; these were questions that she would have to answer for herself. Many weeks passed, and then months; the struggle was on. It was not between God and Iona Henry. God loved her; she belonged to Him. He was standing by to help her. The struggle was between Iona Henry and God. It was her move. How would she react?

There were lonely days when Iona felt alone. Her mind and heart became a great battlefield. Iona won; she cast her burden upon the Lord, and the Lord lived up to His promise. He sustained her. This is the answer Iona Henry heard from God; she tells it in her own words. God said, "Iona Henry, put your hand in the hand of the God you know is there. Stop insisting that you will do what you want to do, like a spoiled, sulking child, and do what you must do. What must be done may seem impossible, but God has a way of working out the impossible." Under the weight of a broken body and the loss of her entire family, Iona Henry found the strength and presence of God sufficient. God built a bridge to span the vast chasm of sorrow over which she walked to a new life.

When she had received this word from God, Iona Henry said, "A strange new peace and relaxation flooded over me such as I had not known since the fearful trial began. . . . The little questions turned and ran; they were not important any more. The tension went out of me; the strain eased. I was completely relaxed."

Let us take our burdens trustingly to the Father. He will either remove them or give us courage to bear them. It was Jesus who said, "Come unto me, all ye that labour and are heavy laden, and I will give you rest" (Matthew 11:28). Do you believe that? I do.

CHAPTER 3

TROUBLE: *God, the Light Eternal*

ONE OF THE greatest lessons one can learn in the schoolroom of life is how to face trouble successfully. One very fine definition of trouble is this: "Touble is that which disturbs or agitates us mentally or spiritually." Trouble finds its way into the millionaire's mansion as well as the peasant's hut. It comes to the intellectual giant as well as the illiterate. It visits the saint and the sinner alike. No man travels the road of life without passing through the dark tunnels of trouble.

Trouble travels in many costumes. Frequently it comes wearing strange garments: some persons have mental troubles; others know physical trouble; still others are faced with spiritual troubles.

Since all trouble is not alike, it stands to reason that the springs from which trouble flows are many. For example, none could intelligently deny that we ourselves are the cause of many of our heartaches. I talked with a man once who was being discharged from his position. He was a junior executive and had been very successful. One day one of his superiors discovered several thousand dollars missing. The auditors could not find a record of expenditure to account for the money; the man finally and regretfully confessed that he had stolen it. The man explained that he had become involved in gambling and had lost his savings and decided to take some of the company's money to win back his losses; he had every intention of paying the money back to the company; however, not only did he fail to win, he lost the money he had taken, and as a result could not repay it. "My life is in a mess," he said, "and I know that I am responsible for the troubles I am facing." It is clearly evident that much of our trouble is a result of our own stubbornness, stupidity, and selfishness.

Others bring trouble upon us, and we are frequently responsible for the trouble others bear. I know a man who has been a source of constant worry to his parents. He left school when he was in the eighth grade, and he is habitually in trouble with the civil authorities. He has already served one term in prison. The casual observer would recognize that by this man's determination to satisfy his evil desires and his flagrant disregard for the rights and feelings of others, he has placed a bag full of trouble upon the shoulders of his parents.

In addition, there are unannounced troubles that come unexpectedly. They seem to come from beyond the realm of human activity. We cannot discover a motivating force behind them. With all our intelligence and wisdom, try as we may, we cannot evade them. We, therefore, must come to the conclusion that some troubles must be faced.

My telephone rang late one night and on the line was a nurse calling from one of the large hospitals in my city. "We have a patient here who would like to see you. The doctor tried to reach you earlier. The patient will undergo major surgery in the morning. Can you come tonight?" I told the young lady that I would be there within thirty minutes. It was almost midnight when I arrived on the hospital floor and the nurse took me quietly and quickly toward the patient's room. On the way down the hall she said, "You may call the surgeon if you like, and he will bring you up to date; the only thing I can tell you is that this gentleman is critically ill." She opened the door of the room and whispered, "Stay as long as you like."

I found in that room a man whom I had known and loved for a long time. He twisted the sheet and tossed nervously on the bed. "I apologize for getting you out so late," he said, "but I cannot go into that operating room feeling as I do. I had to talk with you," he continued.

We talked for a long time and then we prayed together. Something strange and marvelous happened. The look of anxiety and fear left the man's face. In its place one could see confidence, serenity, and assurance. I knew he would be able to face the sunrise with an unfaltering trust in the goodness of God. He was no longer restless. When I stood up to leave, he said, "I want to thank you for coming. You will never know how much you have meant to me. I am not afraid any more."

My visit did not change the circumstances; the man went through difficult surgery and died several days later. Yet death somehow was more of a triumph than a tragedy. God had become real to him. As soon as he had placed his life in the hands of God, he had a different attitude toward his trouble. God took the burdens he could not bear himself; he knew that God was his refuge and strength. With God's help he discovered that he could face life and even death with a song of faith in his heart that enabled him to say with the psalmist, "The Lord is my light and my salvation; whom shall I fear? The Lord is the strength of my life; of whom shall I be afraid?" (Psalm 27:1).

Sometimes trouble weaves a confusing web. It offers no clue to a pattern. Things happen to us that do not make sense. With all our theology and wisdom we find ourselves completely perplexed when we try to take the pieces of trouble and make out of them a logical and sensible picture. During days of trouble I have seen people cry out in utter despair, "Where is God? Why doesn't God do something? Why did this happen to me?" As a pastor I have had to tell people that there is no pat answer to much of the tragedy we experience in life. In spite of this, we must believe that life is good.

One of the finest young couples I know have an afflicted boy. His body is well developed; he looks like a little angel; but he is mentally retarded. There are times when he does not recognize his mother and father, yet they love and care for him with all the tenderness and gentleness of which they are capable. They have a fine Christian spirit toward God. They refuse to be bitter. They have been able, with God's help, to accept their son's handicap with an unwavering faith in the goodness of God.

Some of our troubles do not make sense. An unknown author expressed this truth in the following lines:

> Not till the loom is silent
>   And the shuttles cease to fly,
> Shall God unroll the canvas
>   And explain the reason why
> The dark threads are as needful
>   In the weaver's skillful hand
> As the threads of gold and silver
>   In the pattern He has planned.

Jesus expressed one of the deepest thoughts of His heart when He said: "Now is my soul troubled . . ." (John 12:27). The shadow of a cruel cross erected by a ruthless humanity had fallen across the mind of our Lord. Here we see Him in the arena of struggle. It displays His humanity as much if not more than any other record we have regarding our Lord.

The fact that Jesus was troubled does not reflect a divine weakness; rather, it expressed His likeness to you and me. Here we get a glimpse of our Lord behind the curtain, before He marches out on the stage. This is the battleground for the shining victory we see as Jesus hangs on the cross. As Jesus faced this frustrating hour He asked: "And what shall I say? Father, save me from this hour?" That is the cry that often comes from the hearts of men. We do not like to bear burdens or face trouble. "God take us around this experience," we say. Jesus did not linger with this thought. He could see His divine mission mirrored in the cross. "No," He said, "for this purpose I have come to this hour. Father, glorify thy name" (see John 12:27).

In the book, *Days of Our Years,* Pierre van Paassen tells about his sixteenth birthday when his Uncle Kees escorted him upstairs and handed him a set of keys which would open a mysterious blackpainted set of bookcases. His old uncle ran his fingers across the back of the books and said, "Here are the lamps that never go out."

God is one of the lamps that will never go out. Jesus walked in the light of that lamp that will never flicker even in the darkest night. When Jesus saw the ugly cross, the lamp seemed to burn brighter. It gave forth its radiant light by which Jesus could walk unfalteringly to His death.

I tell people who face trouble that they can walk in the rays of the eternal light and say with the psalmist, "Thou hast enlarged my steps under me, that my feet did not slip" (Psalm 18-36). We should make every effort to avoid trouble, but at the same time we must concede that there is no detour around many troubles; they are inevitable. Like Jesus, if we are to live successfully, we must face troubles with unquenchable courage.

Ernest Fremont Tittle, famous preacher and author, tells the story of a young man who received a spinal injury during World War II. The doctors told him that he would never walk again. Since the dreadful days of 1944 he has been paralyzed from his waist down. In spite of this tragedy he has learned how to be grateful and happy. He has been able to make a go of life by praying this prayer of St. Francis of Assisi each day: "Grant me the serenity to accept the things I cannot change, courage to change the things I can, and wisdom to know the difference." This is a wise prayer. If circumstances cannot be altered, we have no alternative but to face them with courage if life is to be worthwhile.

I want to suggest six things that we would do well to remember while we are walking under the black shadow of trouble. Perhaps from these suggestions we can find some light that will guide us safely through the storm to the safety of God's harbor.

1. *Do not be afraid to face trouble.* It is impossible to solve any problem if we are afraid. Jesus was constantly telling people not to be afraid. He knew that we cannot do our best work if fear fills our minds. Jesus did not ignore His troubled mind; He was not afraid to face it. He examined it and decided on a course of action.

When Arthur J. Gossip's wife died, he was left with an emptiness people know only when they lose someone very dear to them. Dr. Gossip was sustained during those days of sorrow by his dauntless faith. On the first Sunday that he mounted the pulpit to preach to his congregation after his wife's death, he spoke with reassuring authority: "I do not think you need to be afraid of life. Our hearts are very frail and there are places where the road is very steep and very lonely, but we have a wonderful God."

The man who believes in the integrity and power of God and repeats as his daily litany the words of the psalmist: "The Lord reigneth; let the earth rejoice . . ." (Psalm 97:1), will never be afraid to face his troubles.

2. *Remember that God has created a universe in which He permits trouble.* This is not to say that God is the instigator of the trouble we know, but it is conceivable that God would send us trouble in order for us to achieve a higher good. Now, according to our interpretation, some experiences that help us achieve a higher good might be called trouble, but in God's view they would be called something else.

Christianity does not solve for us the problem of suffering and trouble. On the contrary, it accentuates the problem and makes the solution difficult to find. For example, to join the church and live a righteous life will not make us immune from trouble. Jesus lived the will of God to perfection, yet, at the end of His brief life, He found a cruel cross. If righteous living assures one of a life without sorrow, suffering, and disappointment, Jesus would have experienced endless joy without as much as a single trouble.

3. *Remember that God is in our troubles.* Again we cannot contend that God is responsible for our troubles; however, I am sure that God is in them. Author James Stewart writes, "God is not outside the tears and tragedy of life. In every dark valley of trouble and suffering, God is always present." Some people seem to think that God is outside the battleground of human struggle. More than we realize it, God is in the midst of the struggle, commanding His forces.

Benjamin Franklin once said, "I have lived a long time; and the longer I live, the more convincing proofs I see of this truth, that God governs in the affairs of men."

It is difficult, sometimes, to discover God in our troubles. For the disciples, it was next to impossible to see God in the cross. They could see almost everything else in it but God. It was cruel; it was ruthless; it was flagrant injustice. How could God be a part of this? The disciples must have said to themselves, "Certainly, God is not in this ugly picture." But we know that God was there. He was hidden to the disciples by their sorrow and self-pity. Despair covered their souls and all they could see was defeat. Then, Easter came. Standing on this side of Easter, one is likely to forget about the savagery that attended the crucifixion. The victory of Easter overshadows the suffering and shame of the cross. It was not until the first day of the week that the disciples realized that God had been in the cross and had transformed it into an eternal spring from which flows God's mercy and forgiveness.

When I was a boy at home, we sang an old song that has more meaning for me now than it did then:

> Farther along we'll know more about it,
> Farther along we'll understand why,
> Cheer up, my brother, live in the sunshine,
> We'll understand it all by and by.

Job could not make sense out of his trouble; it just simply did not add up. The Bible tells us that Job was a "perfect and upright" man. He had a large family of seven sons and three daughters. He was also a very rich man. Job lost his wealth, his loved ones, and his body was covered with boils; yet in all of this he managed to express his profound belief that God was in his troubles. "Though he slay me, yet will I trust in him . . ." (Job 13:15).

4. *Know that God will supply the strength we need to face life cheerfully during periods of trouble.* We read in the Psalms, ". . . call upon me in the day of trouble; I will deliver thee, and thou shalt glorify me" (Psalm 50:15).

I talked with a very sick man recently and asked him to pray with me about his condition. "I don't believe it would do any good for me to call upon God. I am in a tight place now and He probably would not hear me." I told him it was never too late to ask God for strength to bear the load. I reminded him that others have prayed during days of trouble and God heard them. The psalmist said, "I called upon the Lord in distress: the Lord answered me . . ." (Psalm 118:5).

Have you ever come to the place in life where your troubles seemed so much greater than your strength that you felt you had no place to turn? I have seen a great many people face this dilemma. When Jesus became aware of the cross, He was troubled; I suppose many questions came to His mind: Will I have the strength to face the cross and be true to My Father? If the cross cannot be avoided, will God help Me face it? These questions did not tarry long in the mind of Jesus; He regained His poise and knew beyond any doubt that God would give Him the strength to stand unflinchingly before the cross.

There is one thing that I always try to remember about trouble. If there is no way around it, God provides a way through it. If one door is closed, God opens another for us. We all need to know that God will not let us down. We are not always dependable, but God's power is available to us.

The psalmist said, ". . . the Lord is the strength of my life; of whom shall I be afraid?" (Psalm 27:1).

Paul talks about his "thorn in the flesh." No one knows exactly what Paul was talking about, but all the scholars agree that it troubled Paul. He prayed about it. He asked God to remove it three times. God did not take this "thorn in the flesh" away. But He did tell Paul this: ". . . My grace is sufficient for thee: for my strength is made perfect in weakness . . ." (II Corinthians 12:9).

Paul was shipwrecked, cast into prison, and beaten many times. Some would have given up, but Paul never retreated. He wrote to Timothy and told him that during the hardships he had endured ". . . the Lord stood with me, and strengthened me . . ." (II Timothy 4:17).

Once there were three Hebrew men who believed in the power of God so strongly that they defied the commands of a pagan king. Nebuchadnezzar, the king of Babylon, ordered all people to bow down when they heard the sound of music and worship a golden image which he had erected. Shadrach, Meshach, and Abednego refused to worship the pagan gods, and the king ordered them to be thrown into the fiery furnace. The Hebrews were not afraid. ". . . our God," they said, "whom we serve is able to deliver us from the burning fiery furnace . . ." (Daniel 3:17). In other words, these men were saying, "God is able to save us from the evil temptation. He could even deliver us from the furnace. Therefore, we are not afraid." They also faced the possibility that God would not deem it wise to save them. What if they should be called upon to die for the faith? "But if not," said these courageous men, "be it known unto thee, O king, that we will not serve thy gods, nor worship the golden image which thou hast set up" (Daniel 3:18). The three men firmly believed that God would give them the strength to remain faithful in temptation and even in death. When you face some overpowering trouble, remember the words of the Hebrews, ". . . our God is able . . ." (Daniel 3:17).

My wife's father owns a beautiful farm in the mountains of north Georgia. Near the house there is a huge spring, where water gushes out of the ground. It is fresh, cool, and pure. The family carry water from the spring to the house in buckets, and the buckets are emptied many times each day. They must be refilled each time. Now these buckets are not sufficient unto themselves. They are simply instruments in which the water is transported. In a sense, you and I are like the buckets. We are not strong enough to bear all the troubles of life alone. We must return frequently to the eternal spring where God's source of strength continually flows. No trouble is too big for God. If we dip our buckets deep into the endless spring of God's power, we can face all our troubles with confidence.

5. *Remember that God can use our troubles for our own good as well as for the good of others.* The psalmist said, "It is good for me that I have been afflicted . . ." (Psalm 119:71). You will note that I said God can use our troubles; it does not always happen this way. I know a woman who lost her husband unexpectedly; he went to the office one day to work, and was dead before lunchtime. This experience turned the woman against God; she became sullen and bitter. She stopped attending church and lost her faith in God. I know another woman who lost her husband in a tragic automobile accident. She did not take a great interest in church work before this happened, she told me. Now she is found in her pew every time there is a worship service; this tragedy turned her to God. She is gentle, kind, and thoughtful to everyone she meets on the road of life.

Once a lovely lady lost her only son. He was about five years of age. Life, for her, was empty and lonely. In her sorrow, she looked to God for help. God gave her strength to bear her sorrow and faith to carry on. Today, she is a great inspiration to others who face a similar experience. Whenever she hears of a mother who has lost a child, she writes to her with encouraging words. These words are some that she might write: "I know something about the sorrow you feel and the loneliness your heart knows. I, too, lost my only child. He was just a lad. I have found strength to lift my heavy burden and live again. Only God can give you that kind of strength and courage. He has helped me, and I know He will help you. I will be praying for you." Many people have been inspired by this woman's faith. She walked in the darkest night, and found light for living.

Paul wrote, ". . . all things work together for good . . . ," and this is where many people end the quotation. Paul said more than this; he knew that all things do not work together for good. There is too much evil in the world for such a statement to be true. There are too many broken hearts and too much sorrow for us to believe such words. Paul continued, ". . . all things work together for good to them that love God . . ." (Romans 8:28). That little phrase, "to them that love God," makes the difference. I believe Paul was saying that if we love God and remain faithful to Him, He can use our troubles to glorify His name.

Katherine Mansfield, the British writer and poet, let God use her suffering. Before she died, she wrote: "I do not want to die without leaving a record of my belief that suffering can be overcome. For I do believe it. Everything in life that we really accept undergoes a change. So suffering becomes love." Her Christian spirit ripped off the tear-stained garments from the monster of trouble and revealed the noble virtues God can produce if we give Him a chance to use our troubles.

George MacDonald, in one of his books, wrote about a woman who had experienced a sudden tragedy. The heart-ache was so crushing and her sorrow so bitter that she spoke aloud, "I wish I'd never been made." Her friend, in what appears to be divine wisdom, whispered, "My dear, you are not made yet. You're only being made and this is the Maker's process." This is but another expression of how we can let God take our troubles and make out of them a garment of Christian fortitude which will not only warm our souls, but will serve to inspire others.

God took Paul, with his disappointments, thorn in the flesh, and opposition, and made out of him a champion of the faith. God took the ugly cross and transformed it into a flowing stream of mercy and forgiveness. I am convinced that God can take each of us with our fears and troubles and make out of us a faithful and worthy disciple.

6. *Finally, always remember that we are never alone.* Jesus said to His disciples, ". . . I am with you alway, even unto the end of the world" (Matthew 28:20). It is true that we can never drift out of the channel of God's love and concern. His help is always accessible. He is near to guide us through all the valleys of uncertainty.

I am expressing a well-known truth when I say, "God is with me alway." But God does not help me unless I give Him a chance. I must do my part and ask Him to guide me during periods of trouble. "For I am persuaded, that neither death, nor life, nor angels, nor principalities, nor powers, nor things present, nor things to come, nor height, nor depth, nor any other creature, shall be able to separate us from the love of God, which is in Christ Jesus our Lord" (Romans 8:38-39). This is what Paul wrote to the church at Rome.

David Livingstone gave his life to a people whose language was strange to him and whose attitude toward him was always uncertain. He never retreated: he died on duty. Before his death Livingstone said the thing that sustained him as he went into one hostile group after another was the knowledge that God was with him. He was constantly among strangers, but he never felt alone.

It is truly a source of courage to discover that we are not alone in our troubles. God stands with us. The psalmist was not afraid, because he knew God was near. "Yea, though I walk through the valley of the shadow of death, I will fear no evil: for thou art with me . . ." (Psalm 23:4).

Epictetus, the Greek stoic, said, "When you have shut the doors and made a darkness within, remember never to say that you are alone, for you are not alone, God is within."

The cross loomed before Jesus with unprecedented clarity as He prayed in the Garden of Gethsemane. He knew the rest of the journey would be difficult. He left the garden with a resolute heart. Jesus had gained the assurance that the cross would not be an obstacle too big for Him. "God," Jesus must have thought, "will be glorified in the cross." Jesus knew that He was not alone as He trudged to Calvary under the heavy burden of the cross.

As Jesus approached the final days of His earthly life He said to His disciples, "Behold, the hour . . . is now come, that ye shall be scattered, . . . and shall leave me alone: and yet I am not alone, because the Father is with me" (John 16:32).

I have heard the late Dr. W. E. Sangster tell about the terrible days of World War II. Dr. Sangster was minister of Westminster Central Hall in London during those dark days in world history.

One day I was having lunch with Dr. Sangster and he told me that during five long years of the war he never slept once in his own bed; he was busy day and night serving others. In spite of this, he never missed preaching a single Sunday in his church. He said, "For many months I did not have time to prepare a sermon, but when I mounted the pulpit to preach, God was there with me, and He always gave me a message."

Louise Haskins, in "The Gate of the Year," wrote,

And I said to the man who stood at the gate of the year:
"Give me a light, that I may tread safely into the unknown!"
And he replied:
"Go out into the darkness and put your hand into the Hand of God.
That shall be to you better than light and safer than a known way."

We are never alone in our troubles. God is always with us. He is able to help us. It seems to me that such knowledge is sufficient for us to live all of life with confidence.

CHAPTER 4

DEATH: *Live Life With God; Face Death Without Fear*

CHURCHES EVERYWHERE ARE thronged on Easter Sunday. I dare not say that these masses of people wish only to parade in their Easter finery. Underneath the lovely clothes, buried deep within the soul, there lurk sincere longings. Through the ages, from the first Easter to the present day, man has hailed the message of the risen Christ, and has thrilled anew to the story of the resurrection. In contrast, in the innermost sanctum of his mind, man has pondered the fact of death, and longed for the answer to the many questions which plague his thoughts concerning death—his, and the deaths of those whom he loves.

Most of us have stood beside an open grave to bid farewell to some loved one or close friend. When this earthly pilgrimage is over and when those we love set sail upon that silent sea of death, there emerge within the soul many questions regarding the destiny of man. These longings of the heart cry out for the answer to the eternal question concerning what happens to man at the end of his earthly journey, as a thirsty man cries out for a cool drink of water to ease the discomfort of a parched tongue.

Those of us who stand upon the sandy shores of earthly life look with eager hearts upon the mighty ocean of death. If, with human eyes, we could see the other shore, we could go about our business with peaceful hearts; but the expanse is too wide. We cannot see the other side with human eyes. How happy we would be if we were assured that those we love have anchored their little ships in God's eternal harbor.

I have seen men, after they have mustered up all the hope and courage at their command, permit doubts to flood their minds, fear to capture their powers of reason, and despair to capture their hopes. These enemies of Christian faith have, at times, pushed the devoted and faithful disciples into a room temporarily filled with suspicion and doubt about life after death.

I would be less than intelligent if I were to assume that on the following pages I could convince the atheist, agnostic, or cynic that life is eternal. It appears to me that any intelligent view of the universe, the nature of man, and the reality of God would lead one to recognize the necessity for belief in immortality. We are learning more and more about the orderliness of the universe. The harmony of planets as well as a learned explanation of our surroundings tell us that some intelligent Creator must be behind this creative activity.

The most reasonable explanation of human life points to immortality. There are some obstacles to overcome to reach this conclusion, but the alternatives present mountain after mountain of perplexing problems which cannot be solved.

Immortality is more than a product of man's wishful thinking. It is a divine reality. It is not a soothing tonic that we take to camouflage death and to comfort with a brave illusion the broken heart; it is as much a fact as life itself.

The average person finds it difficult to break away from the common experience of judging the reality of a thing by the standard of the five senses. We place a lot of importance on the appearance of things. We believe more quickly the things we are able to see and touch. Conversely, we find it difficult to believe in the things beyond our limited world of experience with the five senses.

Here is the major problem in accepting, without any doubt, eternal life. All our experiences speak against it. We have never been permitted to look beyond the grave. We have seen no traveler who has returned from the unknown land which we call death; death looks like the end. Our loved ones, whom we have known in the flesh, are limp and lifeless. They cannot speak. There is no evidence of survival.

To doubt life after death because there seems to be no outward appearance to support this fact is actually unscientific. If science has taught us one thing about the world around us, it is that the outward appearance of a thing is deceiving. You cannot depend upon your five senses to reveal the reality of a thing.

My family and I live in a lovely brick house. It looks secure and solid. I have no fear of its collapsing. Every brick is in its place; yet the fact remains, according to scientific truth, that every brick in my house is a moving mass of electrons. Therefore, as this one instance shows, it is a scientific fact that we cannot ascertain the reality of a thing by its appearance.

Sir Arthur Eddington, the English astronomer, wrote, "We are no longer tempted to condemn the spiritual aspects of our nature as illusory because of their lack of concreteness. We have traveled far from the standpoint which identifies the real with the concrete." The greatest part of life and the things that make life real are composed of that vast store of intangibles. Character is invisible, yet it marches in the army of reality. Love is not as concrete as a cookstove, but no intelligent person would deny its reality. Truth cannot be seen, yet we know that truth exists. Death may look final, but this is only an illusion. In reality, death is only the elevator that takes us to a higher floor in the building of life.

Harry Emerson Fosdick has reminded us, ". . . that unless Germany denies that men like Kant are her deep-seeing prophets; unless England chooses lesser souls than her Wordsworth, Browning and Tennyson to represent her loftiest spiritual insight; unless America says to Emerson, Whittier and to their like that they are not our seers; man must confess that with marvelous unanimity the most elevated and far-seeing spirits of the race have most believed in immortality."

Every Sunday millions say, "I believe in the resurrection." Do we really mean this? Is it something we say glibly without any real meaning? Men of all ages have asked, "If a man die, shall he live again?" That agonizing question raises its head when we stand by the open grave with a feeling of irreparable loss and it disturbs our faith. Unless Jesus was a hoax, a sneaky imposter, a designed cheat, and a deceiving liar, He gave us the true answer when He said, "I am the resurrection, and the life; he that believeth in me, though he were dead, yet shall he live. And whosoever liveth and believeth in me shall never die . . ." (John 11:25-26).

Can we believe these words of Jesus? The answer is "Yes." When these words are written upon the heart, we can march to the sunset of life, not with sad words of parting upon our lips, but with a triumphant song of Easter in our hearts.

The greatest message God ever sent to the world was spelled out upon the cross. It tells us of a love that is unfathomable and which defies description. The cross was only a part of the message.

The Cathedral of Winchester in England holds a story that has become tradition; it tells of how the news of the Battle of Waterloo was first received in London. The news came to the south coast by ship, and was sent on to London by signals. As the message reached Winchester it was spelled out by signals, "W-E-L-L-I-N-G-T-O-N D-E-F-E-A-T-E-D . . . ," and then the fog rolled in and the signals were no longer visible. The news of supposed defeat spread quickly. The whole country was saddened by the message, which actually was incomplete; yet it looked final. When the fog lifted, the signals on Winchester Cathedral were busy spelling out the complete message: it read, "WELLINGTON DEFEATED THE ENEMY." This news changed the picture. It changed the situation from defeat to victory and from gloom to gladness.

God finished His message to humanity three days after Calvary. On Easter morning the friends of Jesus found the tomb empty. Their lives of gloom were changed immediately to happiness. At a casual glance the message of the cross looks like defeat, but this is only a part of the message. Death also looks like the end; but I believe Easter morning gave us the only answer we need to know to assure us that beyond the gate of death is a land filled with the living. The Christian church has conclusive evidence that men live after death. The claims for eternal life rest squarely upon the resurrection of our Lord. The entire structure of the Christian faith has its foundation on the truth of Easter.

Ralph Turnbull, in his book, *The Pathway to the Cross*, relates the story of a Moslem who approached a Christian with these words, "We Moslems have one thing you Christians do not have."

"What is that?" replied the Christian.

"When we go to Medina," continued the Moslem, "we find a coffin and know that Mohammed lived because his body is in the coffin. But when you Christians go to Jerusalem, you find nothing but an empty tomb."

"Thank you," commented the Christian. "What you say is absolutely true and that makes the eternal difference. We find in Jerusalem an empty tomb because our Lord lives and we serve a risen Christ."

The critics have failed to explain away the fact of the resurrection. Every effort has failed. Let me hurriedly suggest some of the attempts to explain away the fact of the resurrection.

1. Some people say that Jesus was not dead when He was removed from the cross; they maintain that He was only in a state of unconsciousness. The seasoned Roman soldiers knew when their job was finished. They examined the body of

Jesus and took a spear and pierced His side until blood and water streamed to the ground. The enemies of Jesus were on hand to see that the execution was completed; they wanted to make certain that He would cause them no more trouble.

When Joseph of Arimathea came to Pilate to request the body of Jesus in order to give Him a decent burial, Pilate marveled that He was dead already. Therefore, he sent word asking the soldier, who was probably in charge of the crucifixion, if Jesus was dead and even inquired as to how long He had been dead. Pilate refused to release the body of Jesus until the soldier assured him that Jesus was dead. He was dead. No historian would sincerely question that fact.

2. Others have fostered the idea that the chief priests and elders bribed the soldiers who had been stationed at the grave and charged to watch the body for three days to say that they fell asleep, and the disciples stole the body of Jesus. How absurd! If they were asleep, how did they know the disciples took the body? What would the disciples have done with the body? Could the lifeless body of Christ have inspired them to preach and even give their lives for the Kingdom? No one was convinced of the truth of the resurrection more than the disciples.

3. Still others say that the Jews disposed of the body of Jesus. The Jews did not want more trouble than they already had. Yet, when Peter began preaching the resurrection of Christ, they were disturbed. The Sadducees, the priests and the Captain of the Temple arrested the disciples and held them imprisoned overnight. The next day, Annas, Caiaphas, and the elders and scribes held a council. ". . . What shall we do to these men? for that indeed a notable miracle hath been done by them is manifest to all them that dwell in Jerusalem; and we cannot deny it" (Acts 4:16). They decided to reprimand the disciples and caution them not to mention or teach in the name of Jesus. If they had taken the body of Jesus, they would have revealed this fact in order to clip this new movement in its infancy.

4. Finally, there are those who say the body was buried in a common burial ground, and the women went to the wrong tomb. This is contrary to all available evidence. In the first place, Joseph, a friend of our Lord, buried Him. Then, the Jewish leaders persuaded the authorities to place a guard at the grave. The burial spot was a well-known place and the close friends of Jesus as well as His enemies knew the spot. There could be no mistake about this.

Life at its worst is good, and I believe death will be even better. The eyes of faith will lift the soul above the intellectual confusion that places obstacles in the path of reason regarding life after death. Tennyson wrote, "My own dim life should teach me this, that life shall live forevermore."

We are about as weak as we think we are, but when God holds our hands, we are stronger than we ever dreamed. If someone told Iona Henry at Christmas time, 1951, that the future would bring her untold suffering and sorrow she would not have believed him. Suppose someone had whispered in her ear and said, "Iona, before the spring flowers are in full bloom you will have lost your daughter Jane, your son Jack, and your husband Pete; and you will be flat on your back with indescribable pain." Could a weak human stand so much pain and sorrow? No one whispered that message in Iona's ear, but it happened. She tells the moving story in her book, *Triumph Over Tragedy.* The last sentence in that book reads, "For I have walked far in the valleys of the unknown land, and I have come safely through." Death is like that. I believe when we reach the other side, we will greet those we love by saying, "I have walked through the valley of death. There was no need to doubt or fear. God was there to show me the way and I have come through safely."

It is not strange that the disciples made no effort to prove the resurrection of Jesus. This was a fact that needed no additional proof. They knew Jesus had conquered death and their job was to spread the news rather than to explain the details of the event. For them, it did not need an explanation. The great joy of the victory overshadowed the question of *how*.

It would seem like an incredible proposition to the disciples to waste an ounce of energy on proving the resurrection. Someone asked William James, famous Harvard psychologist and author, if he believed in infant baptism. He looked utterly amazed as he replied, "Believe in it. Why, man, I've seen it." It would, therefore, represent the height of foolishness to ask the disciples, "Do you believe that Jesus conquered death?" They would look surprised and respond by saying, "Believe in it. Why, man, I saw it." What other proof do you need in order to believe in it?

The various denominations of the Christian church are out of step at many points regarding theology, ritual, and doctrine. We do not all agree, for example, on the form of baptism or the manner of observing the Sacrament of the Lord's Supper. Yet, when it comes to the resurrection, every denomination of the Christian church falls into step. Here we march by the music of the same drummer. We all proclaim without apology, "Hallelujah, Christ Arose!" This is the basic and fundamental fact of the Christian church.

A little five-year-old boy named Eddie was told that his father had been killed. Eddie loved his father. There must have been, in his home, expressions of Christian love and evidence of Christian faith; for Eddie took his father's Bible to the funeral home and placed it in the casket and was heard to remark, "I know Daddy will want his Bible in heaven." Many questions came to the mind of this lad as he stood before the body of his father: "Will he ever come back? Will my Daddy be in heaven? Is he in the ground? Will I ever see him again?"

I want to say this to Eddie and others who have pondered similar questions about loved ones. "Your Daddy won't ever come back in flesh and blood, but I am convinced that our dead are closer to us than we can ever imagine. Your Daddy is not in the ground. His body, which is only the temple of his soul, is in the ground; but the soul and personality of your

Daddy, which are your real Daddy, are safe in the loving hands of God. Oh yes, you will see him again. Somehow, somewhere, by the goodness and grace of God, you'll see him, know him, and love him."

We base our claim for eternal life on the resurrection of our Lord. He lived; He died; and He rose from the dead and lives eternally in the hearts of men and in the presence of God. I believe in the resurrection, and here is why. I believe in the resurrection because apart from it, we cannot account for the Christian church. The birth of the Christian church came out of the belief that Jesus was the long-awaited Messiah. The church was organized around a living Christ, not a dead Messiah. The service of Holy Communion symbolizes both the death of our Lord and His resurrection. Here we testify to His power to forgive sins and fill the future with hope and peace. A dead Christ could not do that.

The fact that the day of worship was changed from the seventh day of the week to the first day of the week is evidence of His resurrection. The traditional sacred day that was set aside for worship was the Sabbath or seventh day of the week. The followers of Christ changed this day when they were certain that Christ rose from the dead.

Unless Jesus conquered the grave, the Christian faith and indeed the Christian church are based upon illusions. After nearly twenty centuries, it scarcely seems possible that this could represent the truth. Sometimes men become the victims of illusions; we measure life by false values. Yet, history clearly shows us that the end is misery and certain death. Illusions let you down; they deceive you. Only the real truth holds you up and brings you to the goal.

The truth of the resurrection and the power of the risen Lord have stood the test of time. They are just as powerful today as they were on Pentecost. Ernest Fremont Tittle has reminded us that where men have really tried and lived by the power of the risen Christ, it has brought new life. "It has lifted men out of despair into hope, out of selfishness, pettiness and meanness into lively concern for others. . . . It has brought forth the idea of a universal brotherhood of man and a vision of a world redeemed from hunger, poverty, chaos, and war. . . ." A church with a heart and conscience such as this cannot be accounted for other than through the risen Lord. This is the only adequate explanation. We need to recognize that the resurrection story did not grow out of the church; rather, the church grew out of the resurrection. The living Lord brings power to the church of this century.

Then, I believe in the resurrection because of the reliable reports of those who saw the risen Lord. The Gospel according to Matthew records two appearances made on earth by Jesus after the resurrection.

As Mary Magdalene and the other Mary approached the tomb early the first day of the week, they were told by an angel that Jesus had conquered the grave. They were instructed to take the news to the eleven disciples. While on the way, ". . . Jesus met them, saying, All hail. And they came and held him by the feet, and worshipped him" (Matthew 28:9).

After the disciples received word that Jesus was alive, they went into Galilee and to a mountain where Jesus had appointed them. It was here, according to Matthew, that the disciples received their first glimpse of the risen Lord. ". . . they saw him, they worshipped him: but some doubted" (Matthew 28:17).

The Gospel of Mark, the oldest of the gospels, mentions several appearances of the risen Lord. However, it is felt by biblical scholars that the last part of the original chapter of Mark was lost. The last twelve verses of the present sixteenth chapter seem to have been written by some later author. However, the resurrection was reported in the section of the last chapter which was a part of the original. It seems probable that the writer of the last verses of Mark was familiar with the original document.

In its present form, Mark's Gospel reports that Jesus made

three appearances. First, He appeared to Mary Magdalene (Mark 16:9). Then, ". . . he appeared in another form unto two of them, as they walked, and went into the country" (Mark 16:12). Finally, ". . . he appeared unto the eleven as they sat at meat, and upbraided them with their unbelief and hardness of heart, because they believed not them which had seen him after he had risen" (Mark 16:14).

Luke's Gospel records the risen Lord as having made three appearances. First, Jesus appeared to two disciples on the road to Emmaus. Jesus talked with them as they journeyed and visited with them when they reached their destination. As Jesus broke bread and gave it to them they recognized Him, then He vanished out of their sight. Too, there is a reference indicating that Jesus appeared unto Simon Peter. Finally, He appeared before the eleven disciples and they were invited to touch His body. They talked together and Jesus ". . . did eat before them" (Luke 24:43).

John, in his Gospel, speaks of four appearances made by our Lord. When Mary Magdalene found the tomb empty, she reported this to the disciples. As she stood in the garden weeping, Jesus spoke to her, ". . . why weepest thou? whom seekest thou? She, supposing him to be the gardener, saith unto him, Sir, if thou have borne him hence, tell me where thou hast laid him, and I will take him away. Jesus saith unto her, Mary. She turned herself, and saith unto him, Rabboni, which is to say, Master" (John 20:15-16).

On the same day Jesus appeared unto the disciples; Thomas was absent. The disciples examined Jesus. They knew He was their Lord. Then He appeared to the disciples again and Thomas was present. When Thomas looked upon Jesus, he said, ". . . My Lord and my God" (John 20:28). Finally, John reports that Jesus appeared to seven of the disciples on the shores of Galilee. When Peter heard one of the disciples say, "It is the Lord," he jumped into the sea and made his way toward Jesus.

These chosen few experienced the risen Lord; they reached

a new level of joy and gladness as they discovered that Jesus had conquered the grave. I believe in the resurrection because of these reliable reports.

Finally, I believe in the resurrection of our Lord because of the attitude of the disciples and friends of Jesus. One must go back to Calvary in order to get a true picture of the attitude that was common to the friends of our Lord. Despair and hopelessness were written all over the faces of the disciples. Their dreams were crushed, their hopes shattered. They looked at each other with a stare of indescribable emptiness: Jesus was dead, His body was limp. The summer sun sank below the horizon and the shadow of three crosses played on the hillside. The shadow of one cross reached backward to God and it has played across the hearts of men in every century.

The attitude of Peter reflects the feelings of the others. Suppose, in fancy, we travel back across the centuries and talk with Peter. The stage is set. The scene is just after the crucifixion, nineteen centuries ago. The first speaker asks, "Peter, what do you think about the future?"

"Future, you ask," replies Peter. "There is no future without Christ. He was our hope, and now He's dead. Who cares about the future? We fought a losing battle." Peter turns to walk away. "I don't want to talk about it. I am going fishing." That is the prevailing attitude. Doubt, fear, and sheer hopelessness are evident in the lives of the disciples.

The disciples did not expect Jesus to conquer death. This is a strange note, yet, I believe, a true one. Not a single disciple accepted the truth of the resurrection at first without the shadow of doubt covering his mind.

Let us look at the record. According to Matthew's Gospel, when Jesus appeared to the disciples they saw Him and worshiped Him; ". . . but some doubted" (Matthew 28:17). It was a difficult truth to accept, not because they did not want to believe it, but because they lacked faith.

As written in Mark's Gospel, when the disciples heard that

Jesus was alive and had been seen by a woman of integrity, they ". . . believed not" (Mark 16:11). Why did these disciples find doubt so easy and faith so scarce? They were like men of this century; when we stand by the grave of one we love, we want to believe, but sometimes it is difficult to believe.

According to the writer of Luke, when the women told the disciples that Jesus had come back to life, the attitude of the disciples was recorded in these words: "And their words seemed to them as idle tales, and they believed them not" (Luke 24:11). Again when Jesus appeared before them, they were terrified and believed that they had seen a spirit.

According to John's account of the resurrection, when Mary Magdalene went to tell the disciples that Jesus was alive, she found them behind locked doors, trembling with fear. This is evidence that they did not expect Jesus to return from the halls of death. Thomas, one of the twelve, refused to believe even after the other disciples, all of whom were honest, told him that they had seen the Lord. Thomas said, ". . . Except I shall see in his hands the print of the nails, and put my finger into the print of the nails, and thrust my hand into his side, I will not believe" (John 20:25).

Finally the disciples accepted the truth of the resurrection. They believed what their hearts wanted to believe because they experienced the power and presence of the living Lord. Their doubts were changed to faith, their despair to joy, their fears to courage, their weakness to strength, and their gloom to assurance.

The disciples came from behind their locked doors. They preached in the streets, for they were no longer afraid of the Jews. They were persecuted and beaten, yet they continued to proclaim their undying faith in the power of the risen Lord. They even died for the faith they preached. Death held no terror for them, for Christ arose from the dead and this was all the assurance they needed. They, too, would live for eternity.

Apart from the complete acceptance of the resurrection of Jesus the attitude of the disciples and friends of Jesus cannot be explained. There is in every soul a divine spark which all the winds of earth and devils of hell cannot extinguish. I believe that life is eternal.

The injustices of earth support my belief in everlasting life. Think of the uncounted thousands of youths from every land who, in battle, have been cut down in the prime of life. There is a vast army of children who have died because of the evils of war. Millions have entered an early grave because of disease, lack of food, and because of accidents, storms, and other tragedies. Think of the millions who live in Asiatic lands for whom life is a constant struggle against poverty and disease; they must struggle even to stay alive. What about the people who live in every land, including our own, who are compelled to live from birth to death in ugly surroundings without hope of an opportunity to enjoy proper food, housing, and clothing?

Mozart promised the world great music; yet the end of his earthly pilgrimage came at thirty-five. Keats wrote beautiful poetry which could calm restless hearts; yet he died at the age of twenty-six. Jesus was in the prime of life; yet He died on the cross at the age of thirty-three.

Surely man is not created simply for the little speck of life he knows here. For many, life is misery; for all of us it is a mixture of joy and sorrow, victory and defeat. God did not make man to cast him on the scrap pile after a few fleeting years. Death is not the end. Our dreams, for the most part, are unrealized; our aspirations are unfulfilled, and our talents not yet developed.

The character of God supports my belief in life after death. There are many things that we do not know about God. Yet, we know enough about Him to believe that He loves us. God knows all about us. He cares for us and heals our broken hearts. God is completely honest and trustworthy. The world about us teaches that man is somehow tied to the eternal.

God has placed within us a restlessness which cannot be satisfied by anything except the divine. God has placed within us a spark that believes in and longs for life eternal; He will not deny the satisfaction of that spark.

Death, if we can trust the character of God—and I believe we can—is not a dead-end street; it is a passageway to God's eternal throne. James Stewart reminds us that "if the great Father has loved His children enough to go into the far country after them, to climb the terrible slopes of Calvary for them, to send the urgency and passion of His Holy Spirit to revive and rescue them, . . . If God so loved the world—do you imagine that He will consent to have His love balked and thwarted and robbed by death at the end of the day?" This endless and unrelenting search for man supports my belief in eternal life.

Then, I believe in eternal life because I see death as a part of God's divine and intelligent plan for man. Our existence follows a natural pattern. We are born, we live for a while, and then we come to the close of our earthly pilgrimage. Someone has rightly said, "This is the world of the dying and the next is the world of the living."

Life is like the day and death is like the sunset. The day, like life, begins in the morning. The hours and minutes tick away until finally, darkness comes; the sun sets; we see it no more. Our loved ones die and we bid them farewell. Yet, those of us who know anything about geography and the nature of the universe know that as the sun sets for us it is shining on another continent and lighting the way for other people. It follows that those of us who look at life through the eyes of Christian faith know that our loved ones are not dead. They are living on another continent, with God and His people.

When we learn to accept death as God's plan, we lose our fear. Death must be good, because all of God's plans for us are good. They are worked out in God's laboratory of wisdom and in the presence of divine love. Jonathan Swift wrote, "It is impossible that anything so natural, so necessary and so universal as death should ever have been designed by Providence as an evil to mankind."

Not too long ago I stood by a hospital bed and looked into the face of a young man who had been the tragic victim of an automobile accident. He was as helpless as a baby, yet at times so violent he had to be tied to his bed. The doctor said he would never be normal again; he had received a severe brain injury and would always be helpless. It was sheer agony for the loved ones of this man to see him in such a condition. Only a few days before, he was a strong healthy young man. Death finally took him. Standing outside the room in the corridor of the hospital, one could almost hear the loved ones say, "Thank God for death." In this case, death was a good friend.

Death does not always appear as one's friend. At times, it looks like a cruel enemy coming to crush our hearts. I remember standing by the grave of a little seven-year-old girl who had died suddenly. Her life was just beginning. It was almost an impossible task to comfort her distraught parents. I was frank to tell them I was baffled and did not pretend to have an answer to the question *why*. "There is one thing I know," I told them, "death is a part of God's plan, and while we do not understand it, I know it is a good plan. God sees life in its entirety, and we see only a few fleeting years. God knows best and we must trust Him in a tragedy such as this, a tragedy so perplexing that all human wisdom cannot hope to give a satisfying answer."

I believe in life eternal because of the teachings of our Lord. When Jesus went to Bethany, where His friend, Lazarus, had died, He was greeted by Martha and Mary. They did not expect Jesus to raise their brother from the dead, but Jesus looked at Martha and said, ". . . I am the resurrection, and the life: he that believeth in me, though he were dead, yet shall he live" (John 11:25). Then Jesus prayed and called Lazarus from the dead.

Jesus tried to prepare His disciples for the events they

would experience near the end of His earthly ministry. He told them He would suffer many things and even die, but they should not be troubled. Then He said, ". . . I will come to you. Yet a little while, and the world seeth me no more; but ye see me: because I live, ye shall live also. At that day ye shall know that I am in my Father, and ye in me, and I in you" (John 14:18-20).

Death is the experience of going to God rather than a time of ceasing to live. It is a door by which the Christian enters the Father's house, rather than some dead-end street. As some anonymous author has written:

> The tomb is not an endless night,
>   It is a thoroughfare, a way,
> That closes in soft twilight,
>   And opens in eternal day.

Jesus trusted His Father in death. As He hung on the cross, He knew His life was not over and He kept His serenity and faith even though indescribable pain pierced His body with every heartbeat. Above the noise of the crowd, the darkness was filled with the voice of One who was confident as He cried, ". . . Father, into thy hands I commend my spirit . . ." (Luke 23:46). Jesus was simply saying, "Father, life for Me on earth is over. Now, I am coming home."

Then, I believe in life everlasting because it is a universal belief. Men of every age and circumstance have believed there is some form of life after death. When Michael Faraday, the British chemist and physicist, was on his deathbed someone asked him, "Dr. Faraday, what do you speculate concerning the future?" The old man, with one eye on the earth and the other looking in on heaven, said, "I have been speculating in my laboratory for nearly fifty years; I will no longer deal in the area of speculation. I will deal with certainties from now on." Earth was real to him, but heaven was even more of a reality.

"When I go down to the grave," wrote Victor Hugo, "I can say, like so many others, I have finished my work; but I cannot say I have finished my life. My life will continue. My tomb is not a blind alley. It is a thoroughfare."

Robert Ingersol, the avowed infidel, said at his brother's funeral, "From the voiceless lips of the unreplying dead there comes no word. But in the night of Death, Hope sees a star, and listening Love can hear the rustling of a wing."

William Thackeray wrote, "Life is the soul's nursery—its training place for the destinies of eternity." Henry Wadsworth Longfellow wrote:

> There is no death! What seems so is transition.
>   This life of mortal breath
> Is but a suburb of the life elysian,
>   Whose portal we call Death.

The final and undebatable evidence of eternal life for me is found within my soul. It is an experience, not a doctrine or a belief. This experience has been born out of a struggle and prayer. I have come to know Jesus as a living Lord and not a dead figure of the past. You might shake my beliefs; you might change doctrine, but you will never be able to destroy this experience.

I belong to God, not only for the few fleeting years we call life, but for eternity. He is on both sides of the river. I am in God's presence in life, in death, and even forever. I like the story that I read many years ago, as told by another minister.

Once a father and his son went mountain climbing. There were some steep and dangerous places on the path they chose. As they were climbing one of these treacherous places, someone called out to the little boy, "Do you have a good hold on your father, lad?"

The little lad replied, "No, but he has a good hold on me." This exemplifies a significant truth. If I depend upon my grip on the Father for security, I will be likely to stumble and fall. The thing that keeps me going is the knowledge that my Father has a good grip on me. I know that in death He does not loosen His grip.

There are a good many mysteries about death, but I press

on with confidence, believing that death is only a graduation from one schoolroom to another, where I shall be ready to begin my advanced studies.

Death is not the final blast on the trumpet of life. It is the prelude to a musical composition that exceeds our most noble hopes and our highest aspirations. Face life with God, and you can face death with undefeatable hope and confidence. Poet Thomas Parnell wrote: "Death's but a path that must be trod—If man would ever pass to God." This, I believe.

CHAPTER 5

GRIEF: *Surrender to God*

SORROW, GRIEF, AND their companions come to every life. Tennyson wrote, "Never morning wore to evening, but some heart did break." The most difficult thing I have to do as a minister is to pour the refreshing water of comfort upon the hot tears of sorrow. I do not mean that this is distasteful; I find joy in helping people find a rainbow of peace in the dark clouds of sorrow. My heart is crushed and my tongue is almost paralyzed as I stand in the presence of sorrowing souls and broken hearts. Yet when it is my golden opportunity to try to comfort the grief-stricken, I must pray diligently that God will give me the serenity and power to say with convincing sincerity what my heart knows to be true.

Grief can leave the soul desolate and blot out the hopes of the future, or it can draw the soul into the presence of God and enrich life with new dreams and golden hopes never before entertained. The avenue down which the grief-stricken soul will travel depends for its choice upon the ability of the individual to open his heart to the promises and assurances of God.

During my ministry, I have seen grief choke noble aspirations and strangle efforts that would later serve a struggling humanity. Once a man lost his only son with whom he had had a most satisfying relationship. Both the father and his boy seemed to radiate with joy and gladness when they were together. This close relationship was even more pronounced as the boy became a man. One day tragedy struck without warning; the young man was killed instantly. The shock was so great that the father lost all interest in life. He sat in his little world of grief and refused to assume his place of responsibility in a world that needed his talents. He lived only in the past. The future was no longer a challenge or an adventure; it was simply a time to dream about happy memories of a golden past that was gone forever. This man has existed for the last ten years in his secluded room of grief, making absolutely no contribution to the world around him. His life points up the folly of permitting grief to shut out the sunshine of the present, and making the future look dark and hopelessly sad.

In contrast to this man, I have known uncounted dozens of people, both men and women, who have emerged from the valley of grief with a basket full of God's richest blessings. Some respond to sorrow in such a way that it brings them nearer to the heart of God.

I was out in Mississippi preaching a series of services some months ago, and I met a deeply religious man. He gave himself as well as his resources to God's Kingdom in a selfless and generous manner. Every time the doors of the church were open, this man was there. Whenever something needed to be done in the church, he was among the first to volunteer. His sincerity and loyalty impressed me. Before I left, I asked the host pastor about him. His reply was, "He has not always been a good man. There was a time when he ignored God, flouted truth, and looked only to material things for his happiness. He was a very successful man, in material things. Life was a pleasure and he lived in a little selfish world of his own. One day the clouds of trouble darkened his blue sky, and when the storms were over, he had buried his wife and a little girl. That was several years ago, and since then he has been God's man." I like that phrase, "God's man." There is a thrill that cannot be explained about being "God's man or God's woman."

Sometimes it takes a shocking tragedy to cause a person to look up and recognize God and the hopelessness of life without Him. That man in Mississippi walked deep into the chasm of grief. He came out with a true perspective and a high purpose of life. God can take the darkest night and make out of it a temple of praise where one can see in every star the changeless love of a Creator who cares for His people.

Many have walked the road of sorrow and found the truth of the little poem written by Robert B. Hamilton:

> I walked a mile with Pleasure,
>   She chattered all the way,
> But left me none the wiser
>   For all she had to say.
>
> I walked a mile with Sorrow
>   And ne'er a word said she;
> But, oh, the things I learned from her
>   When Sorrow walked with me!

It is difficult for most people to prepare their hearts in anticipation of grief in such a way that the burden that grief brings does not leave its heavy load of loneliness, despair, and sadness upon the soul. Yet we can, in some measure, analyze grief during our sober moments. An objective analysis of grief will give one some help and guidance in dealing with it when it descends upon him. It is not a question of "Will grief come?" but, rather, "When will it come?"

Grief is inevitable. Man, no matter upon what rung of civilization he finds himself, will one day come face to face with sorrow. The savage beats his breast in an effort to fill the empty feeling left by sorrow. The saint knows the same sadness, but through the eyes of Christian faith he is convinced that every dark night is followed by a beautiful dawn. You may sail down the sea of life for many years without the slightest ripple in the calm water, but remember, soon or late, the storms come and the mighty waves cause the ship of life to lurch to and fro. These experiences test the anchors of faith and try our Christian skills.

Physical pain can be relieved by many of our wonderful drugs. Our loved ones can approach the sunset of life without unbearable pain. Yet, there is no pill or antibiotic that can ease the anguish, loneliness, and suffering of a broken heart.

It is comforting to remember that while no man walks through the sunshine all his life, God makes available a light of faith that keeps us from losing our way.

Grief is the price-tag we find on the bag of love. God made us in such a way that we can both love and respond to love; if man did not have this ability there would be no sorrow in the world. Therefore, it follows that those who love most usually bear the heaviest load of sorrow.

Grief mirrors the deep qualities of the human soul; it reveals the concern we have for those in distress; it expresses the compassion which the soul is capable of extending because it senses the spiritual worth of man. Sorrow is evidence that man is a product of God.

Alfred Tennyson wrote:

> I hold it true, whate'er befall;
> I feel it, when I sorrow most;
> 'Tis better to have loved and lost
> Than never to have loved at all.

I have come to the unswerving conclusion that the aching heart, no matter how great the hurt, is a mighty small price to pay for the joy, gladness, and love we know in life.

I know a young couple who, for six years, loved a little boy. His life was full of hope and promise. One day, he contracted an incurable disease, and death took him to the Father's house. The feeling of loss for the parents cannot be expressed by human lips. Their grief seemed more than they could bear. In spite of this, they would prefer bearing their sorrow and holding in their hearts precious memories than never to have loved and held that little boy. He brought them six of the happiest years of their lives.

We ought to remember that there is no immediate cure for grief. I do not believe that it is consistent with God's nature to relieve sorrow instantaneously. Therefore, we should not be embarrassed or ashamed to display in an emotional way the deep hurts of the heart. Do not be afraid to give expression to your sorrow; to do so helps break the nervous strain, and it brings some relief.

In the eleventh chapter of John's Gospel there is an interesting story concerning the raising of Lazarus from the dead. Jesus and Lazarus were good friends. When Lazarus became critically ill, Martha and Mary, the sisters of Lazarus, sent word to Jesus. Before Jesus reached Bethany, Lazarus died. The writer of John tells us, "Now Jesus loved Martha, and her sister, and Lazarus" (John 11:5). Mary and Martha were crushed with this great sorrow and when Jesus arrived, He found the Jews trying to comfort them.

Jesus was troubled when He found the Jews weeping. He asked, ". . . Where have ye laid him? They said unto him, Lord, come and see" (John 11:34). As Jesus walked toward the grave, He found it impossible to control His emotions. "Jesus wept" (John 11:35) as He neared the place where His friend was buried.

Why did Jesus weep? Jesus knew that in the matter of a few minutes He would replace the sorrow with unimagined joy. He would soon heal broken hearts by raising Lazarus from the dead. Perhaps Jesus was overcome with sorrow as He saw so many hearts filled with sadness. Every sensitive life is touched at the sight of many broken hearts. Too, Jesus may have been weeping because His friend had entered the heavenly glories of his eternal home, and now he would be called back into a world of hate, greed, and hardship. Jesus may have been weeping because Lazarus had already heard the perfect harmony of heavenly music, and must give up the goal of life, for a time, and become again a part of the music where discordant notes fill the song of earthly existence.

It seems strange that Jesus would weep. Yet, I am glad that He did. In this lovely story we see revealed some of the deep qualities of our Master. The fact that Jesus wept teaches us that sorrow is natural. There are those who proclaim, "If I had assurance, beyond any reasonable doubt, that there is life after death, sorrow as a result of death could be banished." This, of course, is not true. Jesus knew that life is eternal. There was no hesitation or question mark in the mind of Jesus when He said to Martha, ". . . I am the resurrection, and the life: he that believeth in me, though he were dead, yet, shall he live: And whosoever liveth and believeth in me shall never die. Believest thou this?" (John 11:25-26). Even the sure knowledge of eternal life will not take all the grief out of the human heart when we lose our loved ones. It is natural that we should want to hold on to those we love as long as we can.

In some measure, the fact that "Jesus wept" tells us that God's heart is moved when we feel the piercing pain of sorrow. The writer of Hebrews wrote, "For we have not an high priest which cannot be touched with the feeling of our infirmities . . ." (Hebrews 4:15). Here we get an insight into another facet of God's nature. He has compassion upon us. The hurt hearts and crushed hopes of man are not unnoticed by the Creator.

There are times in life when people seem to think that man is alone with his heavy load of sorrow. Have you ever felt like that? It seems, at times, that no one is near to help carry the load and keep man from stumbling. We forget that after every night comes the sunshine. Jesus experienced the dark and lonely hours of Gethsemane and trudged slowly up the hill of Calvary before Easter came.

Whatever else we learn, as we journey through life, we ought to come face to face with this truth: we cannot go through a room which is darker than those our Lord has gone through before us. Look at His life: He was born in a stable. When His birth was announced, evil men became jealous and set out to take His life. He faced more opposition than any man who ever lived. His temptations were intense. He did more good than all the kings who ever ruled and received less praise than the modern garbage collector. Jesus was subjected to all sorts of humiliation. False charges were brought against Him. He was despised, spat upon, and stoned. He was doubted, deserted, betrayed, and denied. He was mocked, beaten, and abused, and men laughed at Him. He was unjustly tried by perverted men and unmercifully sentenced to die on the cross. His hands and feet bore the marks of steel spikes and His side was pierced with a sword. Jesus lived about thirty-three years. No man has suffered more in body or spirit than our Lord. Therefore, it would be impossible for you and me to experience greater pain, to know more sorrow, to bear heavier burdens, or to pass through a darker room than did Jesus Christ. These words of the prophet seem to fit our Lord: "He is despised and rejected of men; a man of sorrows, and acquainted with grief; and we hid as it were our faces from him; he was despised, and we esteemed him not" (Isaiah 53:3).

The psalmist was aware of God's presence as he said, "O Lord, thou hast searched me, and known me. Thou knowest my downsitting and mine uprising, thou understandeth my thought afar off . . . and art acquainted with all my ways" (Psalm 139:1-3). I am glad the psalmist said that God is acquainted with all our ways; it means that God knows when our hearts are broken.

I want to suggest four things that will be helpful when the human heart faces sorrow.

1. *Commit your feelings to God in prayer.* The soul is never out of place when it is found upon its knees in the presence of God. David endured some great tragedies in his life. Once he said, "The sorrows of hell compassed me about; In my distress I called upon the Lord, and cried to my God: and he did hear

my voice out of his temple, and my cry did enter into his ears" (II Samuel 22:6-7). God hears the prayer of the broken heart.

When I was a young boy, it was always a thrill to go without shoes during the hot summer months. It was also cheaper that way. Many times I ran to my mother with a stubbed toe. Somehow, she had the magic power to ease the pain, but even if the pain did not go away, my mother's presence gave me the assurance that all was well. I think this is true also with God's presence. There is no question but what He can ease some of our hurt. I would be foolish, however, to indicate that God will take all the hurt away. The miracle is found in the fact that in spite of the hurt, God will give us the feeling of security that tells us in no uncertain terms that all is well.

After you have committed your feelings to God, I believe you can say with David, ". . . when I cried thou answeredst me, and strengthenedst me with strength in my soul" (Psalm 138:3). This is the place where we need courage and strength, in the soul.

2. *Talk to some trusted and understanding friend about your sorrow.* A lot of people come to see me. Many of them are not members of our church. Just the other day a lady called and said, "I called you once before; I don't know whether you remember me or not, but I have read many things you have written. I am sorry to take up your time, but I wanted to talk to someone and I thought you would understand." Her life was heavy with sorrow. She shared her burden with me and we had a prayer on the telephone. Before she put down the receiver she remarked, "You will never know how much these few minutes have meant to me." The lady did most of the talking, and I listened. You will find some relief simply in sharing your grief with some understanding and trusted friend.

3. *Keep this vital truth clearly in mind: God will not let you down. He will give you the strength to face sorrow.* I live by the philosophy that God will see His people through life's

inevitabilities. Since there is no way around grief, I am convinced that God provides a way through it. This has been substantiated in the lives of other people. We see it more clearly in the life of Jesus. When Jesus faced the cross, it was His wish to avoid it. If, however, He stood true to His purpose, He could not evade it. God gave Him the strength to face the inevitable with unyielding courage.

Paul referred to his "thorn in the flesh"; he mentioned this in his prayers on several occasions. He tells us, "For this thing I besought the Lord thrice, that it might depart from me" (II Corinthians 12:8). I suppose that one could assume that Paul prayed fervently about this infirmity three times. God did not remove the thorn in the flesh for Paul; this was one of life's inevitabilities. God assured Paul that he could live with it. ". . . My grace is sufficient for thee . . ." (II Corinthians 12:9). It is impossible to be free from grief, but God will provide the strength to see a rainbow of peach-colored hues through the tears of sorrow.

4. *Finally, when grief descends upon you, read with a believing heart the wonderful affirmations of faith and promises found in the Bible.* The psalmist said, "I will say of the Lord, He is my refuge and my fortress: my God; in him will I trust" (Psalm 91:2). And, "I will lift up mine eyes unto the hills, from whence cometh my help. My help cometh from the Lord, which made heaven and earth. . . . The Lord shall preserve thy going out and thy coming in from this time forth, and even for evermore" (Psalm 121:1,2,8). Paul proclaimed, "For we know that if our earthly house of this tabernacle were dissolved, we have a building of God, an house not made with hands, eternal in the heavens" (II Corinthians 5:1). "The Lord is my shepherd; I shall not want" (Psalm 23:1). I read an interpretation of this verse which I like. Actually, it was a misquote. A little girl said, "The Lord is my shepherd; and that's all I want." When we come to realize that the Lord is our Shepherd, looking after us and caring for us, that is all that is necessary to bring the heart comfort.

Before Jesus faced the cross, He confidently said to His disciples, "Let not your heart be troubled: ye believe in God, believe also in me. In my Father's house are many mansions: if it were not so, I would have told you. I go to prepare a place for you" (John 14:1-2). The Bible offers comfort to those who read it with faith.

Now, let me suggest some things we should guard against when sorrow comes. In every area of life a person must have some guards. Unless we stand watch over all of life, we fail to be responsible disciples who push back the boundaries of God's Kingdom.

1. *Do not give way to excessive grief.* By this, I do not mean that one should not weep; it is often through tears that one finds relief. I mean simply that we ought to make it our business to master sorrow. To store grief inwardly could seriously injure your health. I know a lovely lady whose heart was crushed because death claimed one she loved most. She has buried herself in a life of grief: her talents are dormant; her usefulness to society is stifled. She is alive only to herself and the sorrow her heart knows. Excessive grief makes life miserable and it will destroy your health as well as your peace of mind.

2. *Do not sit and brood over your sorrow.* You can cultivate grief, and it will master your life. Your loved ones would not want their passing to rob your life of joy. This is a time to face life with courage. The challenge here ought to be to try with all your power to live up to the highest ideals of the person you loved. Somewhere, I read the lines about a minister who lost his son. After the service he said, "Now I shall have to laugh twice as much"; and he did. When grief strikes, here is the time to think and act positively.

When David received word that his son Absalom was dead, he went to his room and wept. The soldiers of David had defeated the enemy and Absalom had been killed in the process. The writer of II Samuel tells us, "And the victory that day was turned into mourning unto all the people: for the people heard say that day how the king was grieved for his son" (II Samuel 19:2).

It was Joab who came to David and encouraged him to stop brooding over his deep sorrow. There is one evident truth the people recognized. He could not be effective serving as their king unless he moved out of his idle chamber of grief. This is also true with us. We cannot do the work God has for us to do if we remain in the idle room of grief. After Joab's visit with David, he came out of his chamber and ". . . sat in the gate . . ." (II Samuel 19:8). David returned to Jerusalem and served as king until his death.

3. *Do not advertise your grief.* What I mean by this is do not look for sympathy from every person you meet; to do so is a symptom of an emotional disturbance. In addition, seeking sympathy will be inclined to cause you to exaggerate your sorrow. Sorrow will heal more quickly if you share it with a friend, then seek God's peace, and let the matter rest.

4. *Do not complain to yourself about your sorrow.* We see most of life through our human minds which entertain, most of the time, human hopes. God looks at life through divine eyes and with divine wisdom. He has intelligently planned the best for His people. Who are we to say that all the sorrow we have been called upon to bear is not the best for our souls? We can complain about our grief and it will fester in our lives and cause us to lose all our noble hopes. God never intended any sorrow to break the spirit and snuff out the torch of life by which we are able to see how to fulfill the purpose and plan of our lives.

An unknown author wrote:

> My life is but the weaving
>   Between my God and me.
> I only choose the colors
>   He weaveth steadily.
> Sometimes he weaveth sorrow
>   And I in foolish pride,
> Forget he sees the upper
>   And I the underside.

Our anxieties about death become more intense because we lack knowledge about this experience. Many people have mistaken ideas about death. Here is a question many people ask me, "Is death painful?" Dr. R. W. Mackenna wrote concerning this question, ". . . I have fought death, and lost the battle, over the beds of young men and women cut down in their prime; and I have watched the old totter down the slope into twilight, and at the end, fall asleep like children, and I can say, with a due sense of the importance of this statement, that my experience has been that, however much men and women may, when in the full vigor of health, fear death, when the hour approaches, they face the end with calmness and a serene mind."

It appears that we leave life, in some sense, as we entered it, with no mental disturbance and physical distress. I have talked with many people who have walked to the door of death and later recovered. Invariably, they have said that death seemed like a welcome experience; they felt that the desire to go on into death would be equally as strong as the desire to move back to life and health.

When the great British surgeon, Dr. John Hunter, faced death, his last words were, "If I had the strength enough to hold a pen, I would write how easy and pleasant a thing it is to die." Mother Nature seems to have been wonderfully kind to have built in a device which causes loss of consciousness to intervene when we reach a certain degree of bodily pain. It would be almost impossible to journey through life without pain, but I believe when we have reached the door of death, our pain and suffering will be over.

Then, people experience intense grief because they look upon death as a lonesome event. It is true, we are helpless in the presence of death. The only thing that we can do is stand by and watch. Death is God's plan and He is present in this experience. Before you release the grip you have on your loved-one's hand, you may be sure that he is in the arms of God. We sometimes forget that each little family belongs to a larger family; that, of course, is God's family and He is the Father. Do not feel for one moment that death is a lonesome valley for the dead. They are never out of sight of the lights that shine from the Father's house. The psalmist said, "Yea, though I walk through the valley of the shadow of death, I will fear no evil: for thou art with me; thy rod and thy staff they comfort me" (Psalm 23:4).

Finally, sorrow sometimes becomes intense because of the unanswered questions about heaven. For example, I have stood beside the grave and heard people say something like this: "If I knew he is in heaven and not in some semi-conscious state, I could stand up and face this better." There are many theories about what happens as soon as one enters the door of death. The belief I find most reasonable and most satisfying is based upon the words of Jesus as He spoke to the dying thief. The penitent thief looked into the forgiving eyes of our Lord and said, ". . . Lord, remember me when thou comest into thy kingdom. And Jesus said unto him, Verily I say unto thee, To-day shalt thou be with me in paradise" (Luke 23:42-43). This is one of the clearest windows through which we can look into the room of death.

Jesus did not say, "When the doors of heaven are opened and the dead shall rise from the grave, you shall have a place with Me." Jesus said, "*To-day* shalt thou be with me in paradise." There can be no misunderstanding about such a short, clear, and concise statement. In other words, Jesus was saying, "As soon as the last breath leaves your mortal body you shall be transported immediately to the Father's house." These words from the dying lips of our Lord give us assurance that we shall enjoy immediate fellowship with Him beyond the grave. Death is not even a comma in the sentence of life. We live forever in His presence and as soon as death comes we shall be with Him.

Grief is an open sore in the heart and mind of a person. If we permit it to become infected, like an infected wound, it will endanger our mental, physical, and spiritual health. How are we to face sorrow? What can God do about it? I am going to offer what I believe are some real truths in helping one deal with the immense and universal problem of grief.

Time will help to heal the hurts of the heart. Time alone will not heal grief completely, but it will help. I have seen a few people who were just as emotional and grief-stricken over the loss of a loved one after ten years as they were the week of the funeral. These are, of course, unusual cases. What I want to get across is the idea that we must cooperate with time. Time, as it passes by, will help us to accept the fact that our loved ones are gone, and it will also enable us to get a true perspective of life. I know a man who almost lost his faith in God and who became bitter because of the death of his mother. Several months after her death he said, "I would not want my mother to come back. I am glad she is at peace with God." When sorrow comes, let time do its work, with your Christian faith working in the process of healing the wound of sorrow.

A surprising amount of comfort comes when you think of what you have gained, instead of what you have lost during grief. The tendency always is to dwell upon our burdens instead of our blessings and upon our defeats rather than our victories. I am sure God would be pleased to have His children look at the ocean of joys upon which we have sailed instead of the storms of grief we have endured.

I am willing to admit that when a loved one departs from the shores of earthly life, the loss is overwhelming; the loss cannot be replaced. The Christian faith makes no claim to erase grief. The saint is as sensitive to the sharp pangs of sorrow as the sinner.

I once had a professor who lost his son during World War II. As were so many others, the young man was in the prime of life. What a tragedy! He stood on the threshold of a life of usefulness and promise. Then, he volunteered to fight in the service of his country. The day his parents received the news that he was dead, an avalanche of sorrow fell upon their hearts. Many friends called that evening, and they continued to call throughout the weeks ahead.

Some friends stood or sat a few minutes in complete silence; they did not know what to say. Others said all they knew to say, "I'm sorry." Some went beyond this, and tried to comfort the distraught parents by saying, "He was a good boy, and he is in heaven. Be thankful that he is in heaven. Be thankful that he will no longer face the hardships of life." Though wounded deeply by grief, the father was already feeling the comfort of God's love and his thoughts dwelt upon his son's rich life.

"I wanted to say," remarked the professor, "that John had never tried to escape the struggles and hardships of life. He stood up to them and faced them with courage. I must admit," he continued, "that I did not find comfort in that approach."

"I did find comfort when a friend came," said my teacher, "and put his arms around my shoulder and spoke gently, 'Thank God, Bill, for the nineteen wonderful years you had with John. Thank God for the joy he brought to your life.'"

When death comes, let us thank God that He has given us such a wonderful relationship with our loved ones. Thank God that they have made us happy, and in some measure, we have brought sunshine to their lives. My professor and friend found comfort as he set his mind not upon his loss, but upon the things he had gained by having a son for nineteen years.

There are many loved ones and friends in my life that I do not want to give up. Yet, I know that someday they will be taken from me, or I shall be taken from them. In spite of this, the joy, peace, and love they have brought will far outweigh the sorrow my heart will know when I bid them farewell. I truly hope that my life will be such that my loved ones and friends can say the same about me. If they can, then I know my life will not have been lived in vain.

God is a traveling companion in sorrow. God made us in such a way that sorrow is our lot: as we have already seen, it is peculiar to man it reveals his kinship to God. Still, there is something of a mystery about the sorrow which is caused by hardship and suffering. I do not know why Socrates lifted the cup of poison to his lips and died while his evil judges remained in office. I cannot explain why Jesus was crucified while the chief priests continued to serve, Pilate held his gubernatorial seat, and Herod continued to pollute a throne with flagrant injustices and ugly sins. I find it hard to understand why God's people, those who had proclaimed Him King, had to walk for three hundred years in the storms of torture and persecutions.

I do know this. Out of trouble, fear, persecution, and death, emerged the Christian church. I cannot explain by logic why we must endure pain, hardship, and sorrow. I do know, however, what Jesus, the brave and courageous soldiers of the early church, and a host of others found to be true, that God stands with His children during the storms of life.

God can really use your sorrow, if you let Him. In a church I once served there was a blacksmith. I enjoyed going to his shop and watching him work. He explained to me how to take a piece of iron and temper it, to heat it, and then cool it. This process of heating and cooling a piece of iron gives it strength and toughness. In some sense, sorrow can temper the soul; however, sorrow does not always strengthen the soul. The result of sorrow depends upon man, not God. This truth is clearly evident in the following lines: "Two men looked through prison bars; one saw mud, and the other saw stars."

It is possible that God is making us stronger men and women as we feel the hard blows of sorrow. I believe Jesus was better prepared to face the cross after meeting temptation and facing opposition and disappointment. All the hard blows helped to prepare Him to face Calvary unafraid.

John Bunyan was locked up in Bedford jail; here, he spent many sunless hours of loneliness and solitude. We would all agree that Bunyan was a greater Bunyan because of this than if he had been free to roam the streets. The prison bars could not confine his soul and his mind.

I like the picture of man as a huge block of marble before a sculptor. In making something noble and worthwhile out of man there is much that needs to be cut away. As God cuts away selfishness, pride, greed, and other deadly evils in our lives, we begin to find our real purpose. As Michelangelo watched the falling pieces of marble fly under the heavy strokes of his mallet he could say, "As the marble wastes, the image grows." As man, with God's help, cuts away the wordly aspects of life, he begins to take on the image of God.

John Homer Miller, a Congregational minister in New England, tells about one of his friends who had to give up what promised to be a great and notable career in the church: at first, he was stunned; his faith was shaky. The question *why* kept coming up in his mind. "Why should this happen to me in the prime of life?" After a few months, his faith righted itself and he was able to see through the gloom. The people who visited him always left a little better than when they came. God did not take away his infirmities, He did something better; He used them not only to make the sickly man stronger, but to make other people better.

"Take care," wrote Scottish Pastor Alexander Maclaren, "that you do not waste your sorrows; that you do not let the precious gifts of disappointments, pain, loss, loneliness, ill health, or similar afflictions that come into your daily life mar you instead of mend you."

Spiritual peace and comfort can be found only in God. David said, "For thou art my lamp, O Lord: and the Lord will lighten my darkness" (II Samuel 22:29). God is the true source of comfort that will bring peace to the sorrowing heart.

When Jesus talked to His disciples about His death, the disciples were confused. Without Christ their future looked hopeless. He assured them that they would not be left alone in a world of tribulations to fight for themselves. "I will not leave you comfortless: I will come to you," said Jesus (John 14:18). This assures us that the broken heart can be comforted. This Comforter is constantly available.

There are many things I do not know about God. His mind will never be completely understood by finite minds. There are some things, however, that I am certain about the nature of God. I know that He loves us; I also know that He understands when our hearts are broken. Then, I know that He can heal a broken heart, because He has healed mine. God made us. He made us to be with Him. His house is the goal of our journey. In Him we find life, purpose, and peace.

E. Stanley Jones tells in his book *The Way* this story about Dr. Lincoln Ferris, whose wife had been infected by a doctor who had just attended a childbirth from a diseased mother. Dr. Ferris spent thirty thousand dollars to bring his wife back to health. In the process, he nearly lost his faith. He asked, "O God, why didn't You stop that doctor at the door?" One day, as he walked along a street, he heard God speak. God said, "Can't you say what Jesus said, '. . . Father, into thy hands I commend my spirit . . .'?" (Luke 23:46). Before he took another step, he uttered those words from the depths of his heart and his despair left and he was happy again. E. Stanley Jones comments, "He entered into life—without a limp."

Surrender your grief to God. In Him you can find peace. Do it now. Say, "O God, into thy hands I commit myself, my sorrow, and my future."

CHAPTER 6

PRAYER: *Man's Search for God*

JESUS MET THE problems of life with electrifying success. The disciples watched Him rebuke the wind and the raging water. At IIis command the storm ceased and there was a great calm. IIe knew the secret of facing disappointment and unrest with poise and cheer. Watching Him, the disciples grew eager to know how to meet the tests of their lives with the same spirit of cheerfulness, for they recognized that in every life there are winds of prejudice, selfishness, and jealousy and in every heart the raging waters of greed, envy, and strife place the soul in jeopardy.

Jesus had the key to situations of earthly trial, sorrow, and temptation; He was able to rescue Himself from the areas that become dangerous for the ordinary man. The disciples found themselves near the edge of spiritual disaster many times, but Jesus was never near the brink of chaos and hopelessness; when He came face to face with temptation, He walked with unswerving confidence to the voice of God. The disciples sought the same calm assurance they saw in their Lord. As did the disciples, man today often thinks how wonderful it would be if he had the power to calm the evil winds that blow in life and still the storms that trouble his soul.

The disciples must have asked themselves, "What is the secret of our Master?" Then, perhaps they remembered something Jesus was doing in which they had not been engaged. Jesus was forever going aside to pray. There were times when He went to the mountains; other times He remained behind and sent the disciples away while He prayed. Still other times He withdrew by Himself and prayed behind closed doors. I can imagine the disciples saying, "Perhaps His secret is prayer."

One day His followers saw Jesus at prayer, and when He had finished one of their number said unto Him, "Lord, teach us to pray" (Luke 11:1). It was at that moment that Jesus taught His disciples to pray the prayer that has been universally acclaimed the greatest ever to fall from the lips of man—the Lord's Prayer.

Through the ages, prayer has not been without its critics. There are those who say, "I do not believe in prayer." Yet for every one person who is skeptical I can find a thousand who live above the shadow of doubt; they know prayer works, because God has answered many of their prayers. Some persons have tried to explain prayer away in terms of psychology. Others have discredited prayer on the basis that it is not reasonable to assume that there is a God who hears every prayer uttered by the lips of man. God is not just a projection of human personality. Prayer is more than simply a figment of man's imagination. What may appear reasonable to the mind of God might look impossible and contradictory to man.

If prayer is not true, this fact would have been discovered by some noble and intelligent man of integrity, and prayer would have been renounced a long time ago. The spiritual world, which has been experienced in the hearts of men across the centuries, is not a baseless product of man's imagination. It is a real world, as real as the world in which we see, touch, hear, smell, and taste. Prayer is just as real as love and beauty.

Someone has asked, "How can we be sure prayer is real?"

My reply is, "How can we be sure anything is real?" Here are some tests that ascertain the reality of a thing. Does it remain the same? Does it have the support of many truthful and dependable people? Does it have its origin outside the mind of man? Prayer can stand these tests. It is always the same; many generations of truthful men have witnessed to its validity. It does not depend upon the mind of man for its existence.

For the Christian, it would be foolish to ask the question, "Do men need to pray?" We might as well ask, "Can man survive without water, food, or air?" A person of average intelligence knows the answer to these questions. If we conclude that the answer to the following questions is in the affirmative, then we know that man cannot live successfully without prayer. Do we need God's forgiveness? Do we need additional strength to face life with cheer and hope? Do we need divine guidance as we journey down life's trail? It was Abraham Lincoln who said, "I have been driven many times to my knees by the overwhelming conviction that I had nowhere else to go. My own wisdom, and that of all about me, seemed insufficient for the day."

Sometimes the burdens of life become so heavy and the problems of life become so complex that the soul has no alternative; it must cry out for help, help that is both outside and greater than mere human strength. There are times in every life when all human advice and resources fail to satisfy the deep and perplexing longings of the soul. Divine counsel is the only answer. This was true with Job. I am convinced that God was "calling the signals" during Job's trying days. Look at the picture: his children were dead; his sheep and oxen were gone; he had lost his wealth and his health, but not his wisdom. His wife advised him to curse God and die. In all his sorrow and misery Job was able to utter his affirmation of faith in God's goodness, "Though he slay me, yet will I trust him" (Job 13:15).

It seems foolish for the average man with average strength

to assume that he is both wise and strong enough to carry on without God's help. Some have lived by this philosophy. There is a story in the New Testament that tells about a man who built his house on the sands. It fell, and the fall was a great one. Jesus, the Son of God, who was aware of His relationship to God, did not live under the illusion that He was self-sufficient. He knew that He must pray not only for the wisdom to know what He ought to do, but also for the strength to be faithful. The fact that Jesus felt the need to pray magnifies in me the great need for the experience of prayer.

Jesus prayed for guidance when He selected His disciples. He prayed before He healed the sick. He prayed for strength when He saw the possibility of the cross, and He prayed while hanging on the cross.

Some time ago a person said to me in a joking way, "I am so busy I do not have time to pray." I said to him, "You had better stop doing so many good things that you neglect your prayer life." The tragedy is that this man's statement is true in many lives. People become so busy doing things that ought to be done that they forget to pray. We would all agree that Jesus led a busy life. People were constantly making demands upon His time and energy. Yet we read frequently in the New Testament that Jesus went into the wilderness or went into the mountains to pray.

It is not necessary to limit one's prayer life to the quiet and guarded periods at the beginning or the end of the day. We certainly should have a quiet time when we can be alone with God, but we ought to pray too as we drive down the road or sit waiting for lunch to be served. Offer a prayer for courage as you put on your shoes each morning, and ask God to give you a clean heart as you wash your face.

Some unknown poet wrote:

> Dear Lord, excuse my heavy boots,
>   My dungarees and cap,
> I'm praying on my way to work,
>   For I'm a working chap.

The bus is just ahead, but, Lord,
I've surely time to pray
For strength to be a better man
Than I was yesterday.

I recall the time several years ago when electric power was made available in my boyhood community. I watched workmen secure the poles in the ground and string the wires. My father had our house wired and, finally, the power was turned on. It was a wonderful experience. Every corner of the room was lighted. One man in our community refused to wire his house for he did not want the unsightly poles across his land. As a result his house stayed dim and dark at night, while other homes were well lighted. Electricity was available to him, but he refused to use it. Prayer is comparable to the situation of the electricity. Man's soul can remain dark if he fails to use the source of spiritual power.

After the power was turned on, all of my family asked, "How did we get along without electricity?" If you make use of God's power plant and light up the dark places in your life, you will ask, "How did we get along without God's help?"

Prayer is more miraculous than zooming satellites, more powerful than nuclear warheads, more exciting than a trip to the moon. All the ships that ever floated, all the armies that ever marched, all the planes that have ever flown cannot equal the power of prayer. It is the most powerful weapon ever to be placed within reach of the human soul. If the impulse of prayer is disciplined, consecrated, and used wisely, it can harness gripping fear, control lustful desire, dissolve malignant hatred, and bleach the checkered and sinful stains of our filthy souls.

What is prayer? Prayer is like a diamond; it has many facets. Prayer is standing in the presence of God. It is lifting the soul above the noise of earth, beyond the clamor of everyday events, to the throne of God. Prayer is man in search of God. At its best, prayer seeks only God and not His outward blessings.

I like to think of prayer as conversation with God, but this idea is more than talking to God about life and then saying, "Amen." You would never think of calling a friend on the telephone and asking a question and immediately putting down the receiver before the friend could answer your inquiry. It follows that when we pray we should not put down the receiver and say, "Good night," until God has had a chance to speak. There should always be a time at the end of every prayer when we could just be still and wait. Before your prayer is ended, always ask God this question, "What do you want to say to me?" I am convinced that God is ready to guide us; He is eager to show us the way. Many times God is waiting until we become still and tune our hearts to the divine frequency.

Some people seem to think that prayer is a time to parade our virtues before God. Therefore, we get God's attention in the same manner as the Pharisee who stood and prayed, saying, ". . . God, I thank thee, that I am not as other men are, extortioners, unjust, adulterers, or even as this publican" (Luke 18:11). The Pharisee was saying, "I have never taken anything from my fellow man unlawfully; I would not be dishonest. I have kept my desires under control; I have lived a pure life." Then he continued, "I fast twice in the week, I give tithes of all that I possess" (Luke 18:12). According to Jesus, this man's prayer was not justified. Prayer is not a time to tell God how good we have been; He knows that already.

Many men pray as if they think prayer is a time to beg, a time to ask God to give them health, happiness, and material blessings. We all sometimes beg God in our prayers for the desires of our hearts. Did it ever occur to you that God knows what is best for us and that the desires of our hearts might be the cause of our spiritual bankruptcy? "We ignorant of ourselves," wrote Shakespeare, "beg often our own harms, which the wise powers deny for our good; so we find profit by losing our prayers."

Someone wrote, "I asked for strength that I might achieve.

I was made weak that I might learn humbly to obey. I asked for health that I might do greater things. I was given infirmity that I might do better things. I asked for riches that I might be happy. I was given poverty that I might be wise. I asked for power that I might have the praise of men. I was given weakness that I might feel the need of God. I asked for all things that I might enjoy life. I was given life that I might enjoy all things."

We may look upon prayer as a chance to inform God how He ought to run His universe. Here, we are doing a dangerous thing. We are substituting our wisdom for God's wisdom. We are placing the finite above the infinite. Some of us are ready to persist in order to obtain our goal. This type of praying is little more than tipping our hats to God.

Prayer at its lowest is seeking to get our own way in life. At its best it is seeking God's will for life. It is the process of reporting for duty. "At their lowest," wrote Harry Emerson Fosdick, "men pray crudely, ignorantly, bitterly: at their best, men pray intelligently, spiritually, and magnanimously." When we pray as God wants us to, we will learn to pray with George Matheson, "It is thee and not thy gifts I crave."

Sometimes I get the idea that people who pray in public, and we preachers do more of this than anyone else, feel that the most important thing about their prayers is the well-chosen words they use. I don't believe that God is interested in the words man uses as much as He is interested in the sincerity and motivating force behind the prayer. I believe God hears the sincere prayer of the man who can neither read nor write as quickly as He hears the prayer of the disciplined monk.

God understands the human heart. Our hearts usually speak more clearly to God than do our tongues. I like to remember the little lad named Johnny whose grandmother came for a visit one winter. Johnny heard his grandmother complaining about the bitter cold, and of her difficulty in keeping warm. When Johnny said his prayer at night, his mother overheard him. He said the usual prayer, but added a little postscript to God. Here is it, "God bless Mommy, Daddy, Sister, and all our friends, and please, dear God, make it hot for Grandma. Amen." God understood what was in that little boy's heart.

Jesus gave us some simple directions for prayer in His Sermon on the Mount. Among other things He said this: ". . . when thou prayest, enter into thy closet, and when thou hast shut thy door, pray to thy Father which is in secret . . ." (Matthew 6:6). In other words, Jesus was saying a man ought to undress his soul before God. We do this only when we are alone. Yet, it is not enough just to be by one's self. Our physical bodies can be in one place and our minds a thousand miles away. Any observing preacher knows this is true. Therefore, Jesus suggested that when we enter our "closet," we must take another step and shut the door, shut out the noise of the world, and let our thoughts concentrate upon God. A man cannot truly pray if he is thinking about the opportunities of tomorrow; neither can a woman pray while she is concerned with planning tomorrow's meals. Jesus knew this; therefore, He suggested that the wheels of business should be stopped and all the distractions of the world be left outside. This type of praying permits us to see ourselves as we really are; we come to recognize in the stillness of a situation such as ours the need for God's forgiveness. It also gives us a clear picture of God. We focus our attention upon Him. We come to know that God's power is more than equal to our needs.

During my childhood we always attended church. We also had a family altar. Many times I have knelt with my family at church or in the living room of our home for prayer. I have heard my father pray hundreds of times, but I do not remember ever hearing my mother pray. I know I have seen her pray; but even if I had never seen her do so, no one would ever be able to convince me that she does not pray often. Her life is the best example that I have ever seen of a life centered in prayer. One could not live as my mother lives without an open line to the throne of God. Mother is one who enters her "closet," closes the door, and prays to the Father who sees and hears in secret. He has done for my mother exactly what Jesus said He would do; He has rewarded her openly.

Jesus made two statements about prayer which people often take out of context. By doing this, they miss the real meaning of prayer; they become confused about prayer and often lose their faith in God.

Jesus said, "Ask, and it shall be given you; seek, and ye shall find; knock, and it shall be opened unto you" (Matthew 7:7). On first glance, one might think that here is the key that opens the door to a full life, satisfying all the wishes of our hearts if we ask, seek, and knock. What did Jesus actually mean? Just a few minutes before He said this, He spoke these words: ". . . seek ye first the kingdom of God, and his righteousness . . ." (Matthew 6:33). All this time, Jesus was talking to the same people. I think the assumption is clear; the man who seeks God's Kingdom first for his life can expect to ask and receive; seek and find; knock and have the door opened. It ought to be said that a man who seeks God's Kingdom first will refuse to ask, seek, or knock in an effort to gain anything selfish.

Most of us emphasize the material side of life too much and too often we neglect the spiritual. Frequently we apply a material interpretation to the teachings of Jesus when we should be searching for the spiritual meaning. It is fallacious to assume that Jesus was talking about diamonds, mink, and fine automobiles when He invited us to ask, seek, and knock, or when He gave us the assurance that we would receive.

His statement tells us of a way of life that man needs. We cannot get along without God; therefore, *we ought to ask Him for help.* To ask is an expression of our dependence upon God. The simple requests that we make are evidence that human strength is not sufficient. To ask is also an expression of our faith in a God who is equal to our requests.

Life is a process of seeking. This process indicates to God

that we are willing to try. The man who sits in an easy chair
and waits for joy to come to him will be disappointed. There
are times when we must seek happiness, peace, and spiritual
assurance. We must often search for ways to solve our problems; God will not do for us the things which we can do for
ourselves.

Jesus' statement illustrates a second undeniable truth: *we
must knock*. There are many doors in life which we cannot
open. Try as we may, the only thing we can do is knock. God
must open the door. The other day a woman called me on
the telephone and told me a very sad story. Her life was miserable; she needed someone to open some doors for her. But
before she could have peace of mind, she had to knock on the
door of forgiveness. She needed to forgive and be forgiven.
Only God could open this door. Then, she needed to walk
through the door of understanding. The woman had no regard for others. She understood her own little problem and
had plenty of self-pity, but she had no sense of understanding regarding the wounds of another person involved. Before
this unhappy individual could enjoy the bright sunshine of
God's love and feel the gentle breeze of peace one knows only
when all his relationships are Christian, she had to ask and
to knock, and God had to open some doors.

Another truth which I see in Jesus' invitation to ask, seek,
and knock is this. Jesus chose this way of revealing that *God
responds to man's actual needs*. By our asking, we are assured
that God will come to our rescue in time of stress. By seeking,
we will surely find all that is necessary to live life as
God wants us to live it. And our knocking opens doors which
could not be opened with mere human strength and wisdom.
On these doors one finds divine locks and only divine keys
can open them.

When I responded to the call to preach, I was totally un-
prepared financially. I knew that a college education and
theological training were necessary, and I knew also that my
family would be able to help me very little, for at that

time, my father's health was poor. He worked only as much as he was able, and we found the family budgeting pretty difficult. My mother had gone to work to help pay the bills. There was not enough money to pay my tuition, therefore I had to do some asking, seeking, and knocking. I feel sure that the day I left to go to college my father emptied his pockets and gave me all the money he had.

I asked God for an opportunity to go to college and against heavy odds I received that opportunity. I sought a job and found one in the school laundry. Later, I was privileged to serve as the pastor of six rural churches. I knocked and God opened doors for me that I never could have opened.

Another statement made by Jesus which is often misinterpreted is this: "If ye shall ask any thing in my name, I will do it" (John 14:14). A casual reader might take this to be a blank check signed by Jesus on the Father's bank. All we are required to do is fill it out. I have heard some people misquote this statement.

Some have asked me, "Didn't Jesus say, 'ask *anything,* and I will do it'?"

My reply is, "No, Jesus didn't say that. He said, 'if ye shall ask any thing *in my name,* I will do it.' " There is a big difference between these two statements. Those three little words, *"in my name,"* make the difference. What, then, did Jesus mean? He certainly did not mean for us to misuse prayer. He expects us to use intelligence and consecration when we pray. What can I ask in the name of Jesus? I could not look God in the face and pray in His name for anything that is of a selfish nature. I could ask, on the other hand, for anything that would help heal the hurts of the world. I could ask for anything that would make me a better person. I could ask Him to heal the wounds of misunderstanding, to cut away the malignant growth of selfishness. I could ask God to give me wisdom, patience, and a spirit akin to the spirit of Jesus. These are the things I could ask, in His name, and I believe He would grant them.

What do I want to accomplish through prayer? Here is an important question regarding prayer that every person ought to consider. In our best moments we would agree that we desire most of all fellowship with God and the wisdom to know His will for our lives. Could we not also agree that all our prayers do not reflect these purposes? Frequently, we insist upon getting our own way in life, yet our way is not always the way of God's will.

I believe our greatest need is to pray for ourselves. By this I do not mean for us to pray selfishly. On the other hand, I do not believe we can properly pray for others until we have prayed for ourselves, and in some measure have asked God to get us straightened out. Here are some rules to remember when we pray.

1. Begin with God. Many people begin prayer by thinking about their wishes, defeats, and troubles. Some begin their prayers in a mood of feeling sorry for themselves. Shut self out and begin with God. If we can learn to forget self and saturate our minds with thoughts about God, prayer will be more meaningful.

2. Thank God for His blessings. This helps us to develop a grateful heart. It takes our minds off our disappointments and failures and places our thoughts on God's unnumbered blessings. He has been better to all of us than we deserve, for we are the recipients of many blessings which we did not seek.

3. Pray that God will forgive our sins. Don't just pray, "God forgive my sins." Ask Him to forgive specific sins. Ask Him to forgive your lack of patience, your unkind words, your deliberate acts of evil. When we go to a friend and ask for help, we don't just say, "Help me." We tell him in some detail what we want him to do for us. You will discover that you feel better after you pray if you recall the names of those you may have offended. We must learn to forgive those who have hurt us, because this is the first step in experiencing God's forgiveness.

4. God's rules for prayer are the same for all; no person has any special privileges in prayer. God expects us to be sincere, humble, and penitent. We must come to Him with a believing heart. He wants us to make our requests known unto Him and then pray that His will may be done. Madame Chiang Kai-shek wrote, "I used to pray that God would do this or that. Now I pray that God will make His will known to me."

5. God wants His children to have the best. Jesus told us that God was like a good father. A good father is one who always tries to give his children the best in life. Our selfishness and lack of wisdom frequently rob us of God's blessings. God is looking out for His children; He strives to keep us from doing things which cause us to hurt ourselves.

6. The door to the Father's house is always ajar. You can go in and out of the Father's house through prayer at any hour of the day or night. I have a large room in the parsonage with a terrace entrance that I use for a study. In this room I have a large desk, a conference-sized table, some easy chairs, and many books. When my son Randall, who is three years old, discovers that I am in the study, he is tempted to come in for a visit. It is difficult to prepare sermons when a little boy is constantly coming and going. My wife and I talked about this problem, and concluded there were two things I could do: I could lock the door and refuse to let Randall come in, or I could leave the door open and be interrupted many times each day. I decided to leave the door unlocked, and my son comes and goes when he wants to. He brings some of his little problems to me, which to him, by the way, are grave problems. He has never found the door locked. I want him always to feel free to come to me any time he wants to talk to me. I believe God wants the same relationship with His children; therefore, He leaves the door open. We can go in and out as we please.

7. God answers all our prayers. I received a letter some weeks ago from a lady who was in the hospital. She was mature in many ways, but she was still an infant in her

prayer life. "I prayed," she wrote, "that God would cure me. I believed that He would. But He has let me down. God did not answer my prayer." I wrote to her, telling her that I do not believe God ever lets us down. He will not desert us. I also told her that God answered her prayer; He did not give her the answer she wanted but, nevertheless, He answered it.

I believe God answers prayer in three ways. First, more often than we deserve, God says *yes* to our prayers: He really does say *yes*. Then, God answers some of our prayers in this fashion, "I cannot say either *yes* or *no*. I will do My part and if you will do yours the prayer will be answered in the affirmative. However, if you fail to do your part, the answer will be in the negative." Consider, for example, the college student who prays, asking God to let him pass an examination. Whether he passes or not will depend upon his effort and his willingness to help himself. What I am trying to say is that many times we can help God to answer our prayers. Often, His answer will depend upon you and me.

Finally, God says *no* to many of our prayers. *No* is just as much an answer to prayer as *yes*. Once a little girl prayed that Santa Claus would bring her a big doll for Christmas. The family was poor in material things and Santa Claus did not bring the doll to her. Some thoughtless person made this comment to the little girl, "God did not answer your prayer."

The girl replied, "Oh yes, He did! God said *NO*." I am convinced that when God says *no*, He does so because our request would either do us harm, or else to answer in the affirmative would mean God would have to go against His own nature. God says *no* out of His unceasing love and great wisdom.

Prayer is God's greatest gift to the human family. Through prayer we can find our way through the troubles of life. We can find the strength for every burden. We can find forgiveness for all our sins. Such power cannot flow through lives that are only half-consecrated. There is an answer to all our problems, and if you have not found the answer to yours, why not pray about it?

CHAPTER 7

HOPE: *The Beginning of Progress*

ONE OF THE saddest lines in all the Bible is the pathetic cry of David: ". . . no man cared for my soul" (Psalm 142:4). David felt that he was alone in the world and no one loved him or cared for him. A great problem that many people have to face in life today is loneliness. One can feel alone in the midst of a thousand people.

I shall never forget the first time I stood in Times Square. It was late at night and thousands of people were tramping up and down the street. The lights were gay and bright, the automobiles and taxis were blowing their horns. In the midst of all this I suddenly felt alone; I suddenly became aware of the fact that I did not know a single person in New York City, and no one knew me. I felt, for a moment, as David did when he said, ". . . no man cared for my soul."

As a minister, I talk with a great many people who look at life through glasses of hopelessness. They are people who have lost the true and noble purpose of life. The future is blurred; they see only disappointment and defeat.

Once a man called me and I detected a note of urgency in his voice. "I need help," he said. He gave me his name and address and asked, "Will you come?" I drove to the address and found him in a hysterical condition. He lived in a sixty-thousand-dollar house. He was one of the top men in his company, being paid more than thirty thousand dollars a year. Because of his immoral life, he had become inefficient, and the company for which he worked discharged him. In his despair, he had turned to drink. He had become so repulsive that his family had left him. "I have no future," he said. "I have come to a dead-end street. The only way out is suicide." We talked for a long time. Among other things, I told him that God never permits His children to get into a situation where the only door out is suicide. I suggested, before I left, that he do four things. First, call upon God. Once when David was facing many troubles, people said about him, ". . . There is no help for him in God . . ." (Psalm 3:2). We never get ourselves in a place where we are beyond the help of God if we call upon Him. David never believed that he was beyond God's help. He said, "But thou, O Lord, art a shield for me; my glory, and the lifter up of mine head. I cried unto the Lord with my voice, and he heard me out of his holy hill . . ." (Psalm 3:3-4).

The second thing I told the wealthy but despondent man was this: "Seek God's forgiveness." I reminded him that God's forgiveness is contingent upon our willingness to forgive those who have sinned against us. Once we meet the requirements of forgiveness, God releases us from the grip of guilt. Jesus said, ". . . forgive, and ye shall be forgiven" (Luke 6:37). In one of David's prayers, he said, "For thou, Lord, art good, and ready to forgive; and plenteous in mercy unto all them that call upon thee" (Psalm 86:5). God never turns His back upon a man who is sincerely seeking forgiveness.

Next, I encouraged that man to ask God to reveal unto him His will. Once, Jesus said, "Ask, and it shall be given you; seek, and ye shall find; knock, and it shall be opened unto you" (Matthew 7:7). I do not know of a more noble prayer than to ask God to reveal His will unto us. The promise is that if we ask, we will receive, and if we seek, we will find.

All along our complex highway systems, I have noticed little information centers. The purpose of these is to help those who travel, and to keep them on the right road. I have driven to New England from Georgia many times. I do not even need a road map to take this trip over the familiar roads. My family and I drove up a few months ago, however, and it had been three years since we had done so, so I asked a tourist service to help me plan the trip. This service routed me over some of the new roads, ones that had been constructed since our last trip. They knew the best roads to travel. Now, life is far more complex than our system of roads, and God is always in the information booth to give us direction when we call upon Him. He knows the best paths to travel through life, and if we follow His direction, we will never come to a dead-end street.

Finally, I advised the discouraged fellow to turn his life over to God. Before I left, he promised to begin by asking God to help him find purpose and meaning in his life. A year later, he had overcome his problem of drinking and had secured another job with another company. Then, two years later, he was transferred to another state and wrote me a letter in which he said two things worth remembering. First, "The road from despair, defeat, and hopelessness, to purpose and meaning, is not an easy road to travel." Then he said, "but if one is willing to try, God is ready to help."

Many people have tried to live without God's help and all have failed. God is not only the source of life, but He is also the strength and purpose of life. Man is fooling himself when he thinks he can get along without God. You can no more build a worthwhile life without God than a fish can swim without water. Tolstoy expressed a universal law when he said, "God is He without whom one cannot live." Without God, life has no real purpose; life becomes happy and meaningful only as we place ourselves in His hands. We have become a restless generation. Instead of finding deep water for smooth sailing in our desire for material comforts, we have drifted into the perilous waters where jagged rocks can easily wreck the ship of life.

In America, we have become rich in the abundance of things and poor in our concern for others. To the rest of the world, we have become a material giant. In our best hours, we must admit that our spiritual lives are anemic compared to the life of our Lord and Master. We have all kinds of gadgets and appliances to help us live more comfortably, but they failed to bring us peace of mind. We are spending more and more money on amusement, and yet we are haunted by a feeling of emptiness. Within the next few decades, we shall undoubtedly conquer the remaining barriers to outer space. This is one of the tragedies of the generation of which you and I are a part: We shall conquer outer space before we master inner space. All our scientific progress and material advances fail to make us better Christians.

Once a man came to Jesus and asked, ". . . what shall I do that I may inherit eternal life?" (Mark 10:17). Jesus encouraged him to live according to the commandments. The man answered, ". . . Master, all these have I observed from my youth" (Mark 10:20). Jesus could sense this man's problem. He was a slave to his possessions. Jesus gave him an invitation to become His disciple, but he refused. He wanted to have assurance of eternal life without the responsibility of a cross. Our way and God's way are frequently poles apart. Abundant living is not the result of living as we want to, but rather it is the fruit of taking up a cross and following the commandments of God. This man let his possessions possess him.

Look with me for a few moments at the disciples after the crucifixion of our Lord. Before this horrible experience, the disciples were ecstatically happy. Their hopes and aspirations were high. Then came the death of our Lord, the experience that shattered their hopes and crushed their dreams. The disciples were thrown into an abyss of utter hopelessness. The atmosphere was one of overwhelming despair. The only future they had was the memory of three wonderful years with Jesus.

As I contemplate this scene, I can hear John speaking to Peter. "It's hard to believe that Jesus is gone. Only a few months ago, we watched Him restore sight to a helpless blind man. And, do you remember the day we met the leper and Jesus touched him and immediately he was made whole? Now, all we have left are our crushed hopes and shattered dreams. What can we do?" Peter places his face in his hands and sits silently for a moment. Then he rubs his eyes and says, "Three years ago, we thought we had found the Messiah. He kindled in us the hope of a new Kingdom. Where is that Kingdom now? I'll tell you where it is. It's out there on Calvary's hill; dead, lifeless, gone. The memories are sweet, but you can't establish a new Kingdom on the victories of the past and the dead hopes of the future."

James interrupts Peter. "Do you remember, Peter, the day we were in the little boat, and in the middle of the night Jesus came walking upon the water? We were all frightened at this strange sight, but He calmed our fears. You stepped out of the little boat and started walking toward Jesus. Then, one day Jesus asked what we thought about Him, and you spoke for all of us when you said, 'Thou art the Christ, the son of the living God.' We loved Him so much, and He made us so happy. We shall never see Him again. No one will ever be as gentle and kind. He loved the outcast, the lonely, and healed the brokenhearted. Now, He is dead."

"Stop," shouts Peter. "I can't stand it. Let us stop talking about Him. I want to try to get Him off my mind. There is only one thing I know to do. I am going to mend my nets, prepare the boats, and go fishing."

When we find ourselves in the room of hopelessness, it can mean two things. First, it can mean defeat; it can be the end of all that is good and worthwhile. Second, it can be the turning point in life; we can look up and see the light of God's love shining through the clouds of hopelessness.

God often calls us to service when we are in despair. Do you remember when Isaiah went to the temple and saw a vision of God? Isaiah saw his sins in the light of God's holiness and cried, ". . . Woe is me! for I am undone; because I am a man of unclean lips . . ." (Isaiah 6:5). It was in this condition that God found Isaiah, and before the vision was over, Isaiah responded to the challenge of God. ". . . Here am I," he said, "send me" (Isaiah 6:8). God lifted Isaiah from the room of despair to a place of hope, faith, and expectation.

I have never seen a person who was sufficiently wise or strong enough to walk from the cradle to the grave without help. It does not matter how much wealth, wisdom, or authority one may have. There are times when these are useless in guiding us safely through the storms of life.

In our family room there hangs a lovely clock. My wife winds it every eight days. As long as she remembers to wind the clock, it keeps perfect time; if it does not get the proper attention, after eight days it will begin to run slow and eventually the clock stops. Life is like that. The wheels of life begin to run slow, and the springs need re-winding with some degree of regularity; our spiritual energy must be renewed and our goals constantly examined.

One question we ought to ask ourselves is this: Why does the future look hopeless? To discover the answer to the question *why* would certainly give us a clue to a solution to our dismay. Some people become despondent because they lack faith in God. Others become sad because they do not get their own way in life. We never stop to think that our way may not be best for us; many never stop to analyze the consequences. We only know that we have a desire, and we want to satisfy that desire.

The miracle of Dunkirk will be remembered as long as men write history. The British Navy, using nearly one thousand ships of all kinds, large and small, rescued over three hundred thirty-five thousand men fighting Nazis soldiers. Almost all their equipment was lost. When Churchill made his report to

Parliament on June 4, 1940, a few days after the evacuation of Dunkirk, he shouted with enthusiasm, "We shall never surrender."

After four years of disaster and disappointment, those fighting against the Nazis rule were still struggling. Churchill addressed Parliament again on June 18, 1940. In that address, he referred to what he called "The Battle of Britain."

"Upon this battle," said Churchill, "depends the survival of Christian civilization. If we do our duty, the life of the world may move forward into broad sunlit uplands. But, if we fail, then the whole world will sink into the abyss of a new dark age. Let us, therefore . . . so bear ourselves that if the British Empire and its Commonwealth last for a thousand years, men will say, 'This was their finest hour.' " This is an expression of determination that suggests victory to those who look at life through glasses clouded with hopelessness. The way we respond to what appears to be a hopeless situation could mean our utter defeat, or it could mean that men will say, "This was their finest hour." Surely, we can say this about Jesus as He hung on the cross and prayed, ". . . Father, forgive them; for they know not what they do ..." (Luke 23:34).

Let me suggest five things to remember when we find ourselves in the dark room of hopelessness. For the sake of clarity, I should say here that when God enters human life, no situation is beyond His power to solve. Therefore, when we place our hand in His, no burden becomes too heavy, no sorrow too great, and no problem beyond a solution.

First, the road to hope opens up when we accept the fact that man is weak. We should not be surprised when we find life so tangled and twisted that human wisdom cannot straighten it out. David pointed out that one of the great things about God is that," ". . . he knoweth our frame; he remembereth that we are dust" (Psalm 103:14). Human weakness, however, is no excuse for immoral living. While God knows that perfection is difficult to attain, most of us could live better lives than we now are living. The person who comes to recognize that he needs the help of God is ready to walk out of the darkness of futility. The psalmist prayed, "Have mercy upon me, O Lord; for I am weak . . ." (Psalm 6:2). No man will lift his voice to God as long as he is foolish enough to believe he can handle life with his own strength.

One day, I met a friend on the street. I was late for an appointment and scarcely had time to greet him. When I asked, "How are you?" he replied, "Not so well." I could tell by his voice that he was dejected. Several days later, I saw him again, and he was on top of the world.

"You remember," he began, "when we met on the street the other day?"

I replied that I did.

"Well," he continued, "I was down, and just about out. My life was getting out of hand. Since then, I have heard God speak to me, and now I have placed my life under new management." The prodigal son did not think about returning to the father's house until he discovered he was weak and his strength was unequal to the demands of life.

Once, while Jesus and His disciples were sailing across the sea, there arose a great storm. Jesus was asleep. The waves were so high it appeared the ship would sink. The disciples knew they were helpless. Their only hope was to cry out for their Lord to save them. Therefore, the disciples came to Jesus, ". . . and awoke him, saying, Lord, save us: we perish" (Matthew 8:25). What did Jesus do when He found His disciples frantically crying out for help? He spoke to them, ". . . Why are ye fearful, O ye of little faith?" (Mathew 8:26). In other words, Jesus was saying, "You do not need to be afraid; I am with you."

My first job in life was working in a little community store near my home. I remember walking home from the little country store after dark; it was only a short distance, yet I was afraid. Many times my father would come to the store about closing-time to walk home with me. I was never afraid as long as he was near.

There is a little chorus which I enjoyed singing as a lad in church school. The words of the song ring out an eternal truth which we need to discover as we journey down the path of life. The song goes something like this:

> Jesus loves me, this I know,
> For the Bible tells me so.
> Little ones to Him belong,
> They are weak, but He is strong.

When our strength seems to falter in the face of some of life's problems, we might do well to remember that we are weak, but He is strong.

When life looks hopeless, remember that we belong to God. In the very first chapter of the Bible, we find these words: "So God created man in his own image, in the image of God created he him; male and female created he them" (Genesis 1:27). We owe our existence to God. He formed us out of the dust of the ground and breathed into our nostrils the breath of life, and we became a living soul. The psalmist said, "The earth is the Lord's, and the fulness thereof; the world, and they that dwell therein" (Psalm 24:1).

I know a mother who has twenty-one children. Now that is a large family. It used to amuse me when I was young to hear her name her children; she could call all the names without a moment's hesitation. She knew and loved them all. It would be hard for me to conceive of a mother's forgetting a child; likewise, as we belong to God, I am confident that He remembers us and is interested in us.

To me, it is a wonderful idea to recognize that I belong to God. If I belong to the Creator of the universe, why should I ever be despondent? I can say to others and believe myself, the following words written by C. D. Martin:

> Be not dismayed whate'er betide,
> God will take care of you.
> Beneath His wings of love abide,
> God will take care of you.

Then, we should remember that God understands us. I believe God knows when we are disappointed. He understands when our hearts are aching with sorrow. The psalmist wrote, "The Lord knoweth the thoughts of man . . ." (Psalm 94:11).

Jesus once healed a sick man, and the scribes looked on and said among themselves, ". . . This man blasphemeth" (Matthew 9:3), and Jesus knew their thoughts. God knows when a sparrow falls, ". . . and not one of them is forgotten before God" (Luke 12:6). The psalmist reminds us of the greatness of God. "He healeth the broken in heart, and bindeth up their wounds. He telleth the number of the stars; he calleth them all by their names. Great is our Lord, and of great power: his understanding is infinite" (Psalm 147:3-5). Jesus tells us that God knows all about us. "But the very hairs on your head are all numbered" (Matthew 10:30).

The psalmist could scarcely fathom the worth of man. He looked all about him and saw the glory of God's world; the moon and stars. Then, he proclaimed, "What is man, that thou art mindful of him?" And, "For thou hast made him a little lower than the angels, and hast crowned him with glory and honour" (Psalm 8:4-5).

Today, we can see a million more stars through our powerful telescopes than the psalmist ever dreamed were in the heavens. Of all the millions of people who have ever lived and died, God understands me and is eager for me to love Him. Augustine said this about God: "He loves us every one as though there were but one of us to love."

When we come to believe that God understands even the secrets of our hearts, it is both a wonderful, and at the same time, a frightening thought. There is comfort in knowing that God knows when I am despondent. On the other hand, it is frustrating to discover that no sin, thought, or deed can be hidden from God.

In days of hopelessness, we should find comfort and courage in the fact that God is our Father. Jesus is the best portrait we have of God, and He taught us that God is like a father.

He told us the story of the man who had two sons. One left home, and the other chose to stay at home. One received from his father all that was coming to him in the way of an inheritance. He foolishly wasted his money. When all his money was gone, he recognized his wretched condition and began to think of home. The prodigal son decided on a course of action.

First, he said, "I will arise . . ." (Luke 15:18). He was wasting his life in the far country. He knew that to sit in the land of utter despair would not help his situation. Therefore, he decided to do something about it. Second, he said to himself, I will ". . . go to my father . . ." (Luke 15:18). This was a wise choice. He could have gone to a friend, but he wanted to see his father; and somehow I believe the prodigal son knew that his father would understand. Third, he knew he had sinned and he wanted to be forgiven. Fourth, the wayward son was willing to serve. He said to himself, "I will say unto my father, '. . . make me as one of thy hired servants' " (Luke 15:19). He did not demand anything from his father; he just wanted to be restored as a servant in the father's house.

The story does not end here. There is a more thrilling chapter. This chapter gives us a clue to the nature of God. The father saw his son down the road and ran to meet him. The father ". . . fell on his neck, and kissed him" (Luke 15:20).

Let me suggest four attributes that a good father will possess. First, he is a friend. While watching television, I heard someone ask a little boy to name his best friend. He replied, "My dad is my best friend." A friend is one for whom we have affection and respect; you can trust a friend. God is our Father; therefore, He is our friend.

Second, a father always seeks the best for his children. My father wanted to be sure that each of his children went to school. When we were ill, he called a doctor. He took us to church, and we sat and worshiped together. He was completely unselfish and he always worked for the best interests of his children. God is like that.

Third, a father is interested in guiding his children. My greatest ambition is to have the wisdom to guide my son down the path of life that will eventually bring him to the Father's house. Nothing else in life is quite as important to me as this. I will do anything within my power to guide my son's footsteps, not so much over the easy road, but in the way which will fortify his soul and develop his life into the likeness of Jesus. Shakespeare wrote, "God shall be my hope, my stay, my guide and lantern to my feet."

Fourth, a devoted father will forgive his children. My son could do a great many things which would cause me great sorrow. There is one thing he can never do, and that is hurt me so deeply that I cannot find it in my heart to forgive him. Forgiveness is the fruit of love. Theodore Speers wrote, "How to forgive is something we have to learn; not as a duty or an obligation, but as an experience akin to the experience of love. It must come into being spontaneously." When you think about this statement in the light of the following words, you can begin to understand something about God's ability to forgive. "For God so loved the world, that he gave his only begotten Son, . . ." (John 3:16).

Author Roy Angell once asked Medical Missionary Sir Wilfred Grenfell to explain what influenced him to give himself so unreservedly to God. After a few moments of reflection, Dr. Grenfell spoke quietly and reverently, "Into the hospital where I was a resident physician, a woman terribly burned was brought one night. We all saw immediately that there was no hope for her. We discovered that her husband had come home drunk and thrown a paraffin lamp over her. We summoned the police, and when they arrived, they brought with them the half-sobered husband. The magistrate leaned over the bed and insisted that the patient tell the police exactly what happened. He tried to impress upon the woman the importance of telling the exact truth, since she had only an hour to live. She turned her face from side to side avoiding looking at her husband, who stood at the foot of the bed, a miserable creature. Finally, her eyes came to rest on his hands, and slowly raised to his face. The look of suffering disappeared from her face and in its place came one of tenderness, love, and all the beautiful things that a woman's face can express. She looked back then to the magistrate and said in a quiet, clear voice, 'Sir, it was just an accident,' and with a shadow of a smile still on her face, she snuggled down in the pillows and died."

Dr. Grenfell said that he went back to his room and sat for a long time in meditation. "Finally," he said, "I spoke out loud, 'This was like God and God is like that. His love sees through our sins.'"

A good father does forgive his children. To know that we can be forgiven of our sins is good news. God is in the forgiving business.

Finally, let us remember that God is greater than any situation in which we find ourselves. When Paul went to Macedonia, he tells us, to use his own words, ". . . without were fightings, within were fears" (II Corinthians 7:5). Paul probably met with opposition within the church as well as attacks from the pagan forces. He was inwardly depressed and outwardly harassed.

Then, Titus, who had been on a mission to the church at Corinth, returned and reported to Paul that the church at Corinth longed to see him and had promised to stand behind him with all the forces at their command. When Paul heard this good news, his outlook was immediately changed. He still had opposition: the struggle had not been lessened, but in all his trouble he said, "Nevertheless God, that comforteth those that are cast down, comforted us . . ." (II Corinthians 7:6).

The same power that was available to Paul is at our fingertips. God can give us the courage to say with Paul during days of hopelessness, ". . . I am exceeding joyful in all our tribulation" (II Corinthians 7:4).

The secret of overcoming the world is to give ourselves

completely and without reservation to the will of God. John, in his first epistle, wrote, "For whatsoever is born of God overcometh the world . . ." (I John 5:4).

Jesus warned His disciples of the suffering that awaited them. This looked like utter defeat. Then, Jesus whispered something that we need to hear over and over again. ". . . be of good cheer; I have overcome the world" (John 16:33). Once, the disciples saw Jesus lose a battle. A man with whom Jesus had been talking turned his back and refused to become a follower. Actually the man who left Jesus was the defeated man. He turned away from all that could be called good and noble and walked toward his possessions. He was a rich man, and Jesus wanted the man to love God more than he loved his wealth.

As that man walked slowly away, Jesus said, "For it is easier for a camel to go through a needle's eye, than for a rich man to enter into the kingdom of God" (Luke 18:25).

For a moment, the disciples were stunned, and they asked, ". . . Who then can be saved?" (Luke 18:26).

Then Jesus said, ". . . The things which are impossible with men are possible with God" (Luke 18:27).

Jesus was saying, "You are weak, but God is strong. You are limited, but God is all-powerful. Your spiritual vision is obscure, but God sees clearly. There are some things in life which you cannot do, but God can accomplish His purpose where you fail." God tends to specialize in the impossible.

Take courage and say with me, "I do not have to sit in this chair of hopelessness; I am weak but God can do for me the things I am unable to do for myself. I belong to God, and He understands me. God is my Father, and He is greater than anything that can happen to me." When we come to know God as our Father, we can take off our glasses of hopelessness and look at life through the eyes of faith.

CHAPTER 8

FAITH: *Light for Life When Things Go Wrong*

I WRITE A column for several newspapers and magazines. As a result of this, many people write and tell me the stories of their confused and twisted lives. Somewhere in their letters most of them manage to ask, "Do you think there is help for me?" My reply is *yes*. I do not believe that any life is beyond God's power to rescue. God can unravel the tangled cords of any life and repair the broken strings of man's heart.

I know a man who has mastered the art of appearing poised, unruffled, and casual. He always looks as if he lives in the imaginary land of Utopia. I asked him one day how he learned to relax and meet the perplexing problems of life with so much confidence. He answered: "Under the cloak of apparent composure there are fears, frustrations, and a constant struggle." I suppose if one could lift up the superficial covering of most lives one would discover confusion and anxiety.

There are times in business, government, and our personal lives when things go wrong. In an essay Emerson wrote: "Every roof is agreeable to the eye until it is lifted: then we find tragedy. . . ." The question that remains unanswered in many hearts is this: "Is there light for living when things go wrong?"

Jesus lived a perfect life, but there were times when things did not go as He wished. By following the example of our Lord we can discover a flicker of light that will help guide us through times of uncertainty.

As Jesus turned toward His hometown, Nazareth, His heart must have been filled with expectation and joy. No doubt He looked forward with gladness to being able to visit with His mother and father. Many questions must have filled His mind as He neared the place of His youth. Will these people believe Me? Will they permit Me to do for their souls what needs to be done? Will they be able to see beyond the boy they once knew and become aware of what God wants them to see in Me?

Jesus did not discover the answers to these burning questions until the Sabbath, when He entered the synagogue and began to teach. He taught the people many truths which would bring joy indescribable to those who lived by them and faithfully followed His example. His message was so inspiring that the people were shocked. They asked: "Is not this the carpenter, the son of Mary, the brother of James, and Joses, and of Juda, and Simon? and are not his sisters here with us? And they were offended at him" (Mark 6:3).

It is almost impossible to imagine the heartache that Jesus felt as He walked into His own home town to find that the people He loved did not understand Him. He wanted to do something for these humble folk and they not only refused to accept His message, they expressed hostility and even contempt for Him. Jesus' morale must have been at a low ebb. He was discouraged. He did not expect such cynicism, to say nothing about the antagonistic insults.

I shall never forget the experience of leaving home to go away to college. It was my first time to be away from those I loved for any extended period. I was eager for knowledge, but sad at the thought of leaving the home in which I had been sheltered, guided, and showered with more love than I deserved.

My first week at school was difficult. I was torn between what I knew I must do and what I wanted to do. My heart told me to go home, but my head reminded me that an education was necessary if I wanted to be of service to others in God's ministry. As the sun sank below the western horizon each evening, my thoughts would run across the miles to the humble dwelling where lived those who loved me most. When Friday came, I decided to hitchhike home. Another student, who owned a car, was going part of the way and he kindly permitted me to ride with him. I arrived home just after midnight. By the time I reached the front door my mother had it open. She may have been a little exasperated at seeing me home, but the joy my heart knew and the welcome I could see written all over my mother's face made it of no import. Needless to say, I received a royal welcome. That first weekend at home was exciting and I enjoyed a hero's welcome from the few people who lived in our community.

How marvelous it would have been if the people of Nazareth had accepted Jesus in this fashion. He held the key to eternal life; He could unlock the doors of despair and release His fellow townspeople from rooms of prejudice, fear, and hate. The people of Nazareth missed the greatest opportunity of their lives. Since that day, kings, presidents, queens, and the great from every land have visited Nazareth; but none could compare with the gentle Saviour whom the people rejected.

Notice what Jesus did when things went wrong. He was discouraged, but not paralyzed. He was disappointed, but not defeated. He was despondent, but not without hope. His dreams were at a low ebb, but not stagnant. His aspirations were blurred, but not blotted.

First, Jesus refused to give up. He did not see in this rejection a hopeless situation; He did not lose His spirit or zeal, but kept on with His ministry. The person who refuses to give up when things go wrong will march across valleys of despair to mountain peaks of sunshine.

Consider Robert Louis Stevenson. He was frail from his infancy to manhood. When he was eight years of age, he almost died of a gastric fever that left him extremely weak for many months. Much of his adult life was spent in search of a climate which would give him some relief from his poor health. Stevenson wrote for many years from his bed of pain, composing lines that have thrilled humanity and encouraged people to pick up their broken dreams and work toward a noble life. Stevenson knew what it meant to have a "broken hope for a pillow at night." After weathering one of the stormy periods of his life he wrote: "There stood at the wheel that unknown steersman whom we call God." As did Jesus, Stevenson refused to give up.

I am a great admirer of Thomas Edison. He is reputed to have said, "When everybody else is quitting on a problem, that is the time when I begin."

In its early stages, the first phonograph invented by Edison was unsatisfactory. The high tones were harsh to the ear and the low tones were muffled. Edison employed a person whose task was to perfect the instrument. The man worked tirelessly for two years, trying everything he could think of that might improve the situation. Finally he became discouraged and went to Edison with the intention of quitting. When he told Edison he wished to resign, in view of the fact that he had spent a large sum of money and had failed to get a single sign of favorable results, the great inventor said: "I believe that for every problem God has given us, He has a solution. We may not find it, but some day someone will. Go back and try a while longer." One factor contributing to Edison's success as an inventor was his unfaltering determination to keep going when things went wrong.

There is not much God can do with a person who is ready to abandon his hopes at the first sign of opposition. On the other hand, there are unlimited possibilities for the person who is willing to take God by the hand and walk confidently when things go wrong.

Second, Jesus did what He could. Even though Jesus was disappointed at His reception in Nazareth, He did everything He could to improve the situation. He went about teaching and ". . . he laid his hands upon a few sick folk, and healed them" (Mark 6:5).

In Florida, where I preached a series of services, I had the wonderful privilege of meeting an admirable lady whose body was withering away, but whose spirit was radiant with qualities buried deep within her soul. She greeted the host pastor and me with a smile such as you see on the face of who who has just received some joyful news. She could not lift her fingers; someone had to take care of her as if she were a little baby. "I have been in this condition for eight years," she said. "When I had the strength, I always went to church and tried to serve my Lord." At our leave-taking, the godly lady said: "I am praying that God will bless all your efforts and that you will have a good meeting." Her wonderful spirit and her sincere prayers inspired me to do everything I could possibly do to preach with divine conviction the good news of our Lord. The invalid could not come to the services; she could not even dial the telephone to encourage others to come, but she did what she could: she prayed.

Jesus was limited in what He could do in Nazareth. The writer of the story tells us that Jesus could do "no mighty work" in His hometown. I have an idea that Jesus wants to do some "mighty work" for us, but, like the people of Nazareth, we stand in His way. Because of our selfishness, stubbornness, and pride we block many blessings that God wants us to have. We are all blessed beyond our deserving and most of us know it.

I know many people who live by the philosophy, "If I can't do a job to perfection, I will not do anything." Some refuse to teach a church-school class or sing in the choir because they feel they might not be able to perform to perfection. This is a coward's philosophy. I have always believed that God chooses imperfect men and women who love Him and who are willing to dedicate themselves to His will to do His work. Emerson wrote: "God will not have His work made manifest by cowards."

No matter how depressing life becomes there is always something one can do about it. God never deserts us. Many people become despondent and look at life through glasses of despair because they fail to do what they can about their own situation. When a man sinks to the valley of refusing to do all he can about his own life, failure is just around the next curve.

When I was in grammar school, I frequently would ask my father to help me with my arithmetic. He was always glad to give me assistance, but he would ask, "Have you tried to work the problems yourself?" If I answered in the affirmative, he would always come to my rescue. God wants us to do all we can do to live the good life and when things go wrong, He is near to supply the strength and courage we need.

In the film story, *Madame Curie,* there is an inspiring scene between Pierre and Madame Curie. They had worked faithfully on a project and after 487 experiments in the laboratory their problem was still unsolved; the answer was not even in sight. Pierre said, "It can't be done; it can't be done! Maybe in a hundred years it can be done, but never in our lifetime."

His wife responded by saying, "If it takes a hundred years, it will be a pity, but I dare not do less than work for it as long as I have life." When things go wrong, we need the spirit of Madame Curie and Jesus. We may not find the answer to our situation, but we must work and do all we can about it as long as God gives us breath.

Finally, Jesus could not do a great work among the villagers of His youth because of their lack of faith. The author of this story reminds us that Jesus ". . . marvelled because of their unbelief . . ." (Mark 6:6).

I know a young man who has a brilliant mind and a won-derful family. He told me once that he believed God had called him to preach. He has declined the summons. He has rebelled against the church and is throwing his life away. Unless he changes, it will not be many years before he will present to God a weary body, a fruitless mind, a withered soul, and a wasted life. If this young man could regain his faith, God could use him in a mighty way. His lack of faith stands in God's way. The youth does not believe that he would be an effective minister. He has lost his faith both in himself and in God.

The absence of faith is an open invitation to fear, anxiety, and worry. Lack of faith will starve the soul and become a great wall which will keep us from walking in God's beautiful garden of confidence and trust. Let me suggest three things about faith that each of us can remember with profit.

1. Faith is the beginning of progress. You will never make a worthy contribution to civilization until you possess faith in God, faith in yourself, and faith in your fellow man. Chris-topher Columbus left the port of Palos to sail west with a bagful of faith. He believed there was a shorter route to the West that would save the ships of the sea both money and time. Orville and Wilbur Wright believed that they could in-vent an aeroplane which would fly through the air. Dr. Jonas E. Salk believed God had placed in this intelligent universe a vaccine to help curb the dreadful disease of polio. Faith is the first step we take as we leave the room of uncertainty to an unknown point on the spiritual compass.

The writer of Hebrews reminds us that faith is necessary if we please God. "But without faith it is impossible to please him: for he that cometh to God must believe that he is, and that he is a rewarder of them that diligently seek him" (Hebrews 11:6). I believe we grow spiritually according to the amount of faith we exercise in our daily lives.

Once as Jesus entered Capernaum a centurion came to Him in behalf of one of his servants. The man wanted Jesus to heal his servant. The centurion expressed a faith in Jesus by coming with the request that Jesus make his servant well. Jesus said to the centurion, ". . . I will come and heal him" (Matthew 8:7). The man replied, ". . . Lord, I am not worthy that thou shouldest come under my roof: but speak the word only, and my servant shall be healed" (Matthew 8:8).

This incident in Capernaum was the greatest expression of faith that Jesus had witnessed. He assured the man that his servant was healed. ". . . Go thy way," said Jesus, "and as thou hast believed, so be it done unto thee . . ." (Matthew 8:13). This is a clear example of how God blesses us according to the measure of our faith.

I like the words of one of Charles Wesley's hymns:

> Father, I stretch my hands to Thee;
>   No other help I know
> If Thou withdraw Thyself from me,
>   Ah: whither shall I go.

2. Live as if you believe in God and your faith will grow. Dr. Wilfred Grenfell encouraged people to "act on what faith you have," and do not fret about your lack of faith. Someone has written:

> Trust Him when dark doubts assail thee,
>   Trust Him when trust is small,
> Trust Him, when simply to trust Him
>   Is the hardest thing of all.

The trouble with many people is that they do not use their faith. We sometimes forget that God has placed within us the capacity for a great faith. Our faith in God begins to develop when we look with observing eyes around us. The orderliness of the universe gives expression to an intelligent Creator. The beauty of nature speaks to us about a God of virtue. The bounty of the earth reminds us that God loves us, provides for us, and cares for us. We discover that faith grows as we cultivate it by daily activity. I often tell people to use what faith they have, and instead of diminishing the supply, they will find that it multiplies.

A father brought his son to Jesus, according to a story in the New Testament, with the faint hope that Jesus would cure him. This man loved his son, and he was anxious for him to live a normal life. The boy was subject to convulsive seizures. The father told Jesus that the boy was possessed with a dumb spirit, "and whenever it seizes him it throws him down, he foams at the mouth, grinds his teeth, and turns rigid" (Mark 9:18, MOFFATT).

Jesus said, "Bring him to me" (Mark 9:19). One of the secrets of life is found in this little phrase, "Bring him to me." The boy had an attack before Jesus, and the father looked into the gentle face of the Galilean and said, "If you can do anything, have pity on us and help us." The father expressed his lack of faith in Jesus by beginning his plea with *if* you can. Before Jesus could help him, he had to turn his doubts into faith.

Jesus said to the father, ". . . If thou canst believe, all things are possible to him who believeth" (Mark 9:22-23). Jesus was simply telling him that He could help his son; but first, he must believe, or else his lack of faith would stand in the way.

The father did not have much faith. He wanted to believe more than anything else, but in all honesty he could not believe. Recently I sat with a father in a hospital waiting room while his son lay in critical condition. The doctors told the father that they did not believe the boy would live. The father said to me, "I will do anything if God will let my little boy live."

The father who stood before Jesus was also willing to do anything. He spoke, with trembling lips, words that came from an honest heart. ". . . I believe; help thou my unbelief" (Mark 9:24). This man was saying to God, "I want to believe that You can help my son. If my faith is not sufficient, make it strong enough so that my son can be healed."

I have often wondered what happened to the faith of this

man so long ago after this wonderful experience. He must have been a man of strong faith the rest of his life, for he used what faith he had and by using it his faith multiplied.

3. Pray that God will make your faith grow. This is what the anxious father did. He cried out, "Help my unbelief." I believe the man was asking Jesus to give him faith equal to the problem he faced. Alfred Tennyson, in writing about faith, called it "a beam in darkness: let it grow."

We pray for everything under the sun: We ask God to help us realize our hopes and dreams; we ask God to make us well when we are sick; we pray that God will come to our rescue when we are in trouble. Why not pray that God will make us strong in faith?

I do not have much confidence in a man's religion if he blames God for everything that happens in his life that he considers bad. I know a man who loses his faith in the goodness of God every time he faces disappointment or any unpleasant experience. This man needs to pray and ask God to enable him to grow a strong faith so that his daily litany is: "I believe in the goodness of God during the long dark nights of sorrow and failure as well as during the bright days of sunshine and victory."

It is impossible to solve a problem by denouncing God and refusing to believe in Him. Thomas à Kempis was writing about faith in God when he wrote: "I find nothing without Thee but unstableness and folly."

When Horace Bushnell was a student at Yale University, he was disturbed about his own relationship to God. His faith seemed to fail. One day in desperation he fell upon his knees and prayed, "O God, I believe there is an eternal difference between right and wrong, and I hereby give myself up to do the right and to refrain from the wrong. I believe that Thou dost exist, and if Thou canst hear my cry reveal Thyself to me. I pledge myself to do Thy will, and I make this pledge fully, freely, and forever." In this prayer Bushnell was saying to God, "Things have been going wrong for me and I would

like to place my life under new management." God took Bushnell by the hand and not only helped him become a great
pioneer in elementary education, but also made out of him
one of the great prophets of the Christian faith.

In the Old Testament there is a thrilling story which I enjoy reading, one that glitters with truth. It is the account of
Joseph's being sold by his brothers. This was a cruel thing to
do. Jacob, the father of Joseph, loved him "more than all his
children"; when his brothers recognized this fact they became jealous. Unless jealousy is mastered and defeated in life
it grows into a monster called hate.

Jacob made a beautiful coat for Joseph. This was evidence
of obvious favoritism; the other children of Jacob did not own
a coat with as many beautiful colors. Joseph was hated by his
brothers because their father expressed more affection for him
than for all the rest. This was the excuse for their hatred. Hate
never has a reason; at best it can only offer a few feeble
excuses.

One day Jacob sent Joseph to the field, where his brothers
cared for the flock. Jacob wanted to know if the boys were
well, and the sheep safe. It seems to me that Joseph's brothers
should have seen, in his coming to see if they were well,
evidence that their father loved them too. However, when
Joseph's brothers saw him coming toward them, they began
to discuss ways to satisfy the evil hate in their hearts. Reuben,
one of the brothers, did not share the illfeeling against Joseph.
One brother suggested that they take Joseph's life, but Reuben pleaded with them not to shed his blood; rather, he suggested that they put Joseph into a nearby pit. Reuben intended to rescue his brother later and take him back to Jacob.
The others agreed upon the plan to put their brother in the
pit. At that moment, however, a caravan of Ishmaelites approached and the brothers decided to sell Joseph. The trans-
action was completed and when the caravan moved on and
finally reached Egypt, Joseph was sold to an Egyptian captain, Potiphar, an officer of Pharaoh. Joseph became such a

faithful and trusted servant that the Egyptian placed him in complete charge of his house.

What did Joseph do when things went wrong? He could have let revenge sour his life. He could have become resentful and let hate grow against his brothers. Surely he thought about his father who loved him; he must have faced the possibility that he would never see his father again. In spite of all this, he did not try to escape his sad plight. He called upon all the courage and strength that was available to him in order to make the best of an unpleasant situation.

I believe the secret of Joseph's attitude is found in the little phrase, ". . . the Lord was with Joseph . . ." (Genesis 39:21). Even when things went wrong, Joseph never lost control of himself. He held his temper; he appeared confident; Joseph knew that no situation is without hope as long as the Lord is near.

Joseph was faithful to the best that he knew during his trying days of uncertainty. He served Potiphar, the Egyptian captain, with unequaled faithfulness. He made every possible attempt to do only that which would bring his master pleasure. He also resisted temptation. When Potiphar's wife made continuing efforts to get Joseph to lie with her, he refused. He did not want to sin against God, or lose favor with those who had confidence in him.

One day, Potiphar's wife found Joseph in the house alone and caught him by the coat sleeve and said, "Lie with me." Joseph left his coat and ran out of the house. In a fit of rage, Potiphar's wife took the coat and clutched it near her breast and screamed. The other servants came rushing into her room and she cried with a liar's tongue, Joseph ". . . came in unto me to lie with me, and I cried out with a loud voice; and . . . when he heard that I lifted up my voice and cried, . . . he left his garment with me, and fled, and got him out" (Genesis 39:14-15). This caused Joseph more trouble. He was cast into prison, but he continued to remain faithful to the best he knew.

While a prisoner, Joseph interpreted Pharaoh's dreams and became known as a very wise and good man. He was appointed to be in charge of Pharaoh's house. It was Joseph's responsibility to gather food during the seven years of plenty and save some for the famine which was to follow.

I once received a letter from a man whose life was so mixed up that he mentioned to me the possibility of suicide. He wrote, "Nothing in my life goes right any more. I have just lost my job and my family is leaving me. Since I am no good to anyone I have thought of taking my life." He was in a pretty bad situation. I wrote to him and told him to hang on to life and do his best to make something worthwhile out of what he had left. "Others," I said, "have been discouraged, and with God's help they have taken their broken dreams and used them as steppingstones back to a life of usefulness."

Joseph must have been despondent, but he never surrendered himself to his self-pity. As a good soldier he marched forward with undiminished hope during life's most difficult battles. Joseph learned that God can use all of life if man is willing to make room for God in his life. Listen to the thrilling words of Joseph as he looked back on his life. ". . . For God hath caused me to be fruitful in the land of my affliction" (Genesis 41:52).

Just because things appear to go wrong does not necessarily mean that life is hopeless. God often takes a life that has lost its lustre and looks defeated and molds out of it a noble life which sparkles with eternal truth. Joseph was sold as a slave, unloved and unwanted by his own brothers, and cast into prison because of the evil tongue of Potiphar's wife. Yet he remained faithful to God and God used him to save the starving thousands during the famine.

John was cast on the Isle of Patmos as an exile. While he was without earthly companions, he was conscious of the presence of God. Here he saw the throne of heaven. He wrote about that noble company of saints, ". . . These are they which came out of great tribulation, and have washed their

robes, and made them white in the blood of the Lamb. Therefore are they before the throne of God, and serve him day
and night in his temple: and he that sitteth on the throne
shall dwell among them. They shall hunger no more, neither
thirst any more; neither shall the sun light on them, nor any
heat. For the Lamb which is in the midst of the throne shall
feed them, and shall lead them unto living fountains of
waters: and God shall wipe away all tears from their eyes"
(Revelation 7:14-17).

Paul was cast into prison, but he continued to witness for
Christ. From behind prison bars he wrote: "For to me to live
is Christ, and to die is gain" (Philippians 1:21).

George Washington Carver fought against terrific odds to
make something worthwhile out of his life. Born of slave parents, his life was a constant struggle. He worked his way
through college by cooking, washing dishes and working as
a janitor. He became a great botanist, and the products he
developed from the peanut and sweet potatoe at Tuskegee
Institute made him world famous. Doctor Carver's philosophy
was this: "Let down your buckets where you are." He encouraged people to make the best of whatever life gave them.

Once Carver was offered a salary of $175,000 a year to work
with Thomas A. Edison in his laboratory in New Jersey. This
might have been a great temptation to many, but not to
George Washington Carver. He declined Mr. Edison's offer.
This is the reason he gave for refusing to leave Tuskegee:
"I felt that God was not through with me yet in Tuskegee;
there was still plenty of work to do for Him here."

We may not be able to change our situation in life, but I
am convinced that God can use us where we are if we will
only dedicate ourselves to Him. God can take our feeble efforts, our failures, and even our afflictions and make them
count for good if we are dedicated to His will. Then we can
say with the psalmist: "For this God is our God for ever and
ever: he will be our guide even unto death" (Psalm 48:14).